HEROIC CHILDREN

Heroic Children

Untold Stories of the Unconquerable

by
Hanoch Teller

NYC

New York City Publishing Company
a division of M.E.T. llc

ISBN 978-1-881939-23-8

Registered in Library of Congress
Library of Congress control number: 2015941011

15   14   13   12   11   10   9   8   7   6   5   4   3   2   1

Comprehending the Incomprehensible
CD LECTURE SERIES

A riveting and enlightening history of the Holocaust by one of Yad Vashem's most celebrated docents. For over two decades Hanoch Teller has been guiding youth and adults through the darkest period in history making his tour of Yad Vashem an unforgettable life milestone.

This eleven-part lecture series takes the listener descending from the halls of Yad Vashem into the bowels of the Holocaust, from seething Germany in the thirties to the apathetic America of the forties; from the murder apparatus in Poland to the rescue efforts in Switzerland. For one who wishes to learn and understand what really occurred there is nothing as compelling, lucid, concise, and insightful.

Each of the lectures has been recorded in a studio at the highest fidelity. Thirteen hours of captivating listening encompass the historical events and personal accounts of survivors before and during the war years, providing an in-depth analysis of the political, social, religious, and moral issues affecting perpetrators and victims, collaborators and resisters, apologists and rescue workers.

Available at www.hanochteller.com

Distributed by

Feldheim Publishers   LEHMANN   קולמוס
www.feldheim.com   Hebrew Booksellers   Book Distribution
                www.lehmanns.co.uk/home.html   0722-44-1660

עוז והדר לבושה, ותשחק ליום אחרון

Heroic Children is dedicated in loving memory
To our unforgettable
Mother, Grandmother, and Great-Grandmother

Mrs. Gizella (Genendl) Berkowitz a"h

Whose abiding attributes, bravery, contentment, diligence, devotion,
enthusiasm, frugality, gentleness, humility, intelligence, love, modesty,
perseverance, quiet demeanor, righteousness, simplicity, sincerity,
tenacity, uniqueness, work ethic and wisdom,
continue to inspire, motivate and energize our lives, as we endeavor to
walk in her balanced path of דרך הממוצע

אשר היא דרך הישרה, והיא דרך החכמים, והיא דרך ה'
(רמב"ם הל' דעות א')

You may be gone from our sight,
but you are never gone from our hearts.
It takes someone really brave to be a mother,
someone strong to raise a child,
and someone special to love someone more than herself.

הגיד לך אדם מה טוב, ומה ה' דורש ממך
כי אם עשות משפט ואהבת חסד, והצנע לכת עם אלוקיך (מיכה ו' ח')

Gates of memories will never close…
How much I miss you no one knows…
Days will pass away into years;
and we will think about those memories with silent tears.

.ת.נ.צ.ב.ה

באהבה רבה ואהבת עולם

Avrohom Pinchos & Mindy Berkowitz
Children & Grandchildren

Also by
Hanoch Teller

Once Upon a Soul ⊙ Soul Survivors ⊙ 'Souled!' ⊙ The Steipler Gaon
Sunset ⊙ Courtrooms of the Mind ⊙ Above the Bottom Line
Pichifkes ⊙ The Bostoner ⊙ "Hey, Taxi!"
Bridges of Steel, Ladders of Gold ⊙ The Best of StoryLines
Give Peace a Stance ⊙ It's a Matter of Principal
A Midrash and a Maaseh ⊙ Welcome to the Real World
13 Years ⊙ And from Jerusalem, HIS Word
It's a Small Word, After All
The MINI A Midrash and a Maaseh
In an Unrelated Story…
Builders ⊙ Too Beautiful
For the Love of Torah
О Том, Что На Душе
Героизм Нашей Души

ועמך כולם…
בצדק תשפט
Érase Una Vez
Desde Jerusalem…

Do You Believe in Miracles? (DVD)
The Righteous Live On (CD series)
Comprehending the Incomprehensible (CD series)
Building Bene Brak (CD series)
Reb Elimelech and the Chassidic Legacy of Brotherhood
(Documentary)

Contents

Author's Note   *x*

Foreword   *xi*

Preface   *xix*

Introduction   *xxi*

Comprehension   29

Disharmony   57

Youthful Spirit   105

Resistance   159

Moral Spark   193

Parental Devotion   229

Nonexistence   269

Honor Thy Father   287

Sheer Will   311

Glossary   335

Bibliography   339

Acknowledgments   341

Index   345

Author's Note

In colloquial parlance, when referring to the era from Hitler's rise to power through World War II, the terms "German" and "Nazi" are used interchangeably; in fact, they are essentially synonymous. However, there is a distinction that this type of usage obfuscates.

The word "Nazi" is shorthand for *"Nationaisozialistische Deutsche Arbeiterpartei"* (the National Socialist German Workers' Party); it is based on the German pronunciation of the first two syllables of "National." Unless referring directly to this party or its ideology, however, "Nazi" is not the correct or appropriate terminology. The perpetrators of the Holocaust were the Germans and their willing collaborators throughout Europe; fixing the blame upon an ideology absolves the murderers. Furthermore, they are labeled as "the Germans" by their Jewish victims (irrespective of countries of origin) as well as in all archived documents: letters, diaries, testimonies and so on. Many never even heard the term "Nazi" during the war years. Accordingly, and to uphold the authentic historiography of this volume, "Nazi" is employed only when referring to a specific ideology (even though this did present a stylistic hurdle).

As a rule, Anglicized spellings were employed for city-names and locations, i.e., Vilna over Vilnius or Wilna, Dvinsk over Daugavpils or Dwinsk. But where there were no such adaptations, original names and native spellings were retained.

The one-of-a-kind map that graces the end-leaves of *Heroic Children* was designed expressly to illustrate its never-before-told stories. The task of identifying tiny, obscure Jewish hamlets—enclaves that the Germans, even with their maniacal determination (and their 35 million collaborators in Poland alone) nearly overlooked—proved to be a sizable challenge to four cartographers using the most sophisticated and powerful geographic-location software. And yet, after considerable effort (and expense), all of the locations referred to in this book have been pinpointed on the map and color-coded according to each story. After much deliberation, we elected to create a map with contemporary (rather than World-War-II-era) borders, to give today's readers a clearer understanding of where the events actually took place.

Foreword

Ma'asim Tovim Foundation

Allow me to begin with the lyrics of this soul-wrenching Abie Rotenberg song:

I met a man last Sunday; he was on his way back home,
From a wedding in Chicago, and was traveling alone.
He said he came from Vilna, a survivor I could tell.
And I helped him with his suitcase—he could not walk very well.

A stewardess gave us coffee, as we settled on the plane.
I asked him why he bothers—at his age, there'd be no blame.
"No simcha is a burden, although I miss my dear late wife,"
And then he shared with me the story that changed my view of life.

I remember liberation, joy and fear, both intertwined.
Where to go; what to do; and how to leave the pain behind?
My heart said, "Go to Vilna", dare I pray yet once again,
For the chance to find a loved one, or perhaps a childhood friend.

It took many months to get there, from late spring to the fall,
And as I, so came many others, close to four hundred in all.
And slowly there was healing, darkened souls now mixed with light,
When someone proudly cried out, 'Simchas Torah is tonight!'

We ran as one towards the shul, our spirits in a trance.
We tore apart the barricade, in defiance we would dance.
But the scene before our eyes shook us to the core:
Scraps of siddur, bullet holes, and bloodstains on the floor.

Turning to the eastern wall, we looked on in despair
There'd be no scrolls to dance with, the Holy Ark was bare.
Then we heard two children crying, a boy and girl who no one knew.
We realized no children were among us, but those two.

We danced round and round in circles, as if the world had done no wrong.
From evening until morning, filling up the shul with song.
Though we had no sifrei torah, to gather in our arms.
In their place, we held those children—the Jewish people live on!

We danced round and round in circles, as if the world had done no wrong.
From evening until morning, filling up the shul with song.
Though we had no sifrei torah to clutch and hold up high.
In their place, we held those children—Am Yisrael Chai!

Who was heroic? Was it the two children who instilled a spark into 400 beaten souls, or perhaps the dancers who elevated themselves back to life and living—or conceivably both? "Religious" is the person who understands the suffering of others. No one cares how much you know, until they know how much you care…

Out of the Depths, Have I Cried unto Thee, O G-d!

Rabbi Michoel Dov Weissmandel *zt"l* wrote his introduction to his monumental, personal narrative, *Min Ha'meitzar*, several days before his anguished heart could beat no longer, and he returned his tortured soul to its Maker. Among other thoughts, he writes:

> Thirteen years have passed since the culmination of the Great Sacrifice, the brutal slaughter by the monstrous nation, of the holy and the pure, six times the multitudes that crossed the Red Sea during the Exodus— and the silence is deafening. A stillness has descended upon the world, and there is no awakening. The ways of the wicked are flourishing, to silence the whole world regarding the murders they committed. Forgetfulness, which is getting stronger and deeper with the passage of each day—but not just simple forgetfulness, but rather devious and artfully deceptive forgetfulness, brought about by reparation payments. Thus, I would not be surprised, that as we get older, our children and grand-children will deny the Holocaust in our faces: "Perhaps a thousand Jews were killed during the war as a result of some accident—and this silly old man is confusing a thousand with hundreds of thousands. He is confusing adults with children, and accidents with deliberate pre-planned genocide."

What an amazing prophecy in 1957! Today, we are witnessing Holocaust deniers of all stripes: from individual anti-Semites to white supremacists, to rouge leaders of nations—but Rabbi Weissmandel predicted these falsifications and perfidies, almost 60 years ago!

The rabbi was a hero many times over. Not just for his superhuman efforts to delay the transports and deportations and rescue the Slovakian Jews. Not just for the numerous correspondences he dispatched to many world leaders, exposing the atrocities being committed. Not just for unmasking the apathy of the established Jewish organizations who were interested in protecting their positions, rather than saving lives.* But more so, for the fact that despite losing his wife and children to Auschwitz, and despite the fact that he was so dis-traught that he would pound the walls and cry bitterly on what had befallen him and his people—nevertheless, he pulled himself together to establish the Yeshiva Farm Settlement, where he taught Torah to the next generation, to assure the continuity of *Klal Yisroel*. Not only did he provide for his students' spiritual needs, but he also established a farming community, so the students, upon marriage, can have an income to sustain themselves and their families.

The Yeshiva and Settlement were founded on two guiding principles: 1) to marry off the *bachurim* at the earliest opportunity and provide them with a *parnasah* for self-sustenance; and 2) an unbending and unyielding commit-ment to truth. If any settler would be caught lying 3 times, he would have to leave the Settlement, without any recourse or appeal. Two principles, and one solid leader—creating many new leaders. A Rebbe shepherds followers, but a leader creates other leaders. Rabbi Weissmandel was a heroic leader. His chil-dren who perished in Auschwitz were heroes of one kind: *kedoshim*, martyrs who sanctified His name. His disciples in Yeshiva Farm Settlement were he-roes of a different kind: they helped build the next generation of *Klal Yisroel*.

Courage is Taking a Stand, when Nobody Else will Stand with You

During the Holocaust years, as incredible and frightening as it may seem, the entrenched Jewish establishment, exemplified by the American Jewish Committee, proclaimed: "Future efforts should be directed towards sending Jewish refugees to other countries, instead of bringing them here to the U.S." It was in this time frame that Gilbert and Eleanor Kraus, a stylish Jewish couple living comfortably in Philadelphia, decided to do the extraordinary, and make a difference.

They sailed across the Atlantic, and made their way into Nazi-controlled

---

* In his famous letter of 5/15/44, he chastised these organizations: "...how do you keep silent in the face of this great murder? Silent while thousands upon thousands, reaching now to six million Jews, were murdered—and silent now while tens of thou-sands are still waiting to be murdered? Their destroyed hearts cry out to you for help, as they bewail your cruelty. Brutal you are, and murderers too you are, because of the cold-bloodedness of the silence in which you watch..."

Austria. Their mission: to rescue 50 Jewish children from Vienna, and bring them to safety in the U.S.A. This was a formidable task, given the fact that American immigration laws and quotas severely limited the number of foreigners allowed into the country. Many Jewish organizations were also opposed, due to their fear that attempts to bring Jews into the U.S. would fan the underlying flames of anti-Semitism, quite prevalent at that time.

Nevertheless, the Krauses were unrelenting and persistent. Strong people stand up for themselves, but stronger people stand up for others. Mr. Kraus persuaded the U.S. ambassador to Austria to set aside some unused immigration visas, rather than let them expire. Parents who, during ordinary times, would never separate themselves from their children, eagerly grasped the glimmer of hope represented by the Krauses' "life boat." Each parent pleaded, "Yes, please, take my child! Take my child to a safe shore."

The Krauses made sure that upon arrival to the U.S., all the children found warm homes with relatives, or foster families. Many of the children saved by the Krauses ultimately reunited with their parents, because, as a by-product of the Krauses' heroic act, parents found it easier to obtain visas, after their children were already in the United States.

Fifty heroic children, who went on to establish families and build new homes, is a miniscule number, compared to the 1.5 million children tortured, gassed and murdered by Hitler's extermination machine, in his deranged pursuit of the Final Solution. But each life saved, carried with it a powerful message: A testimony to the possibility of ordinary people doing extraordinary things. Our Sages declare (Tractate Sanhedrin 37a): "He who saves one life— is as if he saved an entire world," because every person is a world unto himself.

Albert Einstein writes: "The world is a dangerous place, not just because of those who do evil, but because of those who look on, and do nothing." Courage is not the absence of fear—it is the resistance to fear. Among the many heroes in this book, we also need to honor the Krauses, two brave souls who rose above the general apathy, to make a difference in the lives of 50 children. Let their remarkable accomplishment serve as an example for us to emulate.

The Impact of Six Million Paper Clips

In 1998, something amazing happened in the town of Whitwell, a small rural community of fewer than 2,000 people, nestled in the mountains of Tennessee.

Whitwell Middle School principal Linda Hooper asked the associate principal to begin a Holocaust education class that would be the basis for teaching tolerance and diversity in a voluntary after-school program. When the students struggled to grasp the concept, the enormity, and the number of the six million Jews who died during the Holocaust, they decided to collect six million paper clips—one for each soul who perished.

Why paper clips? The students' research found the mandatory Yellow Star that Jews were required to wear on their clothing, and that Norwegians wore paper clips as a silent protest and symbol of resistance against Nazi occupation during World War II. It was this simple idea that eventually, and quite unintentionally, turned into a worldwide phenomenon, drawing international media attention and letters of support from literally every continent.

The "Paper Clips Project" extended over several years, and in 2001 the school dedicated a Children's Holocaust Memorial, which includes an authentic World War II German railcar/boxcar actually used to carry prisoners to concentration camps, filled with a portion of the more than 30 million paper clips they eventually collected. At first, the students brought paper clips from home, or asked family and friends to contribute. Then the idea began to spread. They set up a web page asking for help, and for people to share their thoughts and feelings about the Holocaust. A few weeks later the first letter arrived, then more, and by the end of that school year the class had 700,000 paper clips. Within a couple years not only had they reached their goal of six million, they had passed it. Along the way, incredible, compelling stories were coming in with the clips, from all over the world.

The school did their best to absorb the numbers, and realized how successful the memorial became at illustrating the gravity of the horrible events. Imagining each clip as a human life was astounding and shocking, in the reality they brought to light. The weight of the suffering of the people carried to their untimely deaths—in this very car—was crushing.

The project and the museum demonstrate how a committed group of children and educators could provide hope and inspiration to countless others around the globe. Kudos to the educators of Whitwell! They understood that injustice anywhere, is a threat to justice everywhere. A plaque at the entrance to the boxcar museum, summons: "As you reflect on the horror of this tragedy, we ask you to affirm the enduring spirit of those who survived. With the dedication and vigilance of each person who visits this memorial, an atrocity like this will never occur again."

From all the research I have done, it appears that none of these children at the Whitwell, Tennessee school were Jewish. Yet they were instrumental in putting together a hallowed place to commemorate the six million and other victims of the Holocaust, and perpetuate their memory. Aren't these children heroes? I think they deserve to be inscribed among the heroic of the nations of the world. In the boxcar, there is a quotation from Eli Wiesel: "Take sides! Neutrality helps the oppressor, never the victim. Silence encourages the tormentor, never the tormented."

Revenge for the Blood of a Small Child, Satan has not yet Created

This Foreword would not be complete if we didn't allocated some space to the heroic children of the Kovno Ghetto, as detailed in the responsa *seforim* of Rabbi Ephraim Oshry, entitled *Mima'amakim*, Questions and Responses from the Deepness of the Depth.

The *sefer* contains a question from a young boy who asked whether he is permitted to put on *tefillin* even though he is not yet 13 years of age. His concern was the Nazis' *Kinderaktion*, which they carried out every few weeks, where they would gather hundreds of children and transport them to death. The young lad's soul was yearning to put on *tefillin* while he was still able, because he was uncertain if he will survive to reach the age of 13. Rabbi Oshry permitted him to do so, and just in time, because the lad's premonition turned out to be accurate, for a short time later his life was snuffed out via a barbaric *Kinder Aktion*—may G-d avenge his death.

After one of those *Kinderaktions*, came a group of parents to ask whether they need to say *kaddish* after the young children who perished. The reasoning behind the question was that the *kaddish* prayer is primarily recited as a plea for mercy so that the departed soul may avoid punishment. Accordingly, youngsters who have not even reached the mature age of punishment (age 13), and thus are pure and holy, should not need the *kaddish* prayer...

Then we find the heart-breaking question of the lad who related that his friend, who is a greater scholar than him, was captured by the Germans and marked for transfer to the killing fields. This young lad volunteered to exchange places with his friend, the greater scholar, citing that the SS Guard agreed for a bribe to do so, as long as the total quantity of victims remained unchanged. The young volunteer asked Rabbi Oshry whether he is permitted to offer himself, to go through with such an exchange...

Among other questions appearing in *Mima'amakim* are parents asking whether to save children's lives, can they transfer their offspring to nuns and priests in convents, as a chance for survival, even though there is a strong likelihood that the child will grow up estranged from the religion of his ancestors.

These were the heroic children of the Kovno Ghetto, and they definitely deserve prominent and honorable mention amongst all the heroic children of Israel. Merciful G-d, act for the sake of nursing infants who did not sin; act for the sake of the weaned babies who have done no wrong; act for the sake of innocent school children. Act for Your sake, if not for ours, *ve'ho'shi'einu*—and save us from such catastrophes!

Lest We Forget What Our Eyes Have Seen...
Teach Them to your Children...

The Torah instructs us: "Remember what Amalek did unto you, on the way when you came forth from Egypt. ...and it shall be, that when Hashem, your G-d, gives you rest from all your enemies all around...thou shalt blot out the remembrance of Amalek... Thou shalt not forget!" The question is almost self-evident: If the Torah instructs us to "Remember," then why is there a need for the duplication of "Thou shalt not forget?" If we are instructed to remember, then of course we are forbidden to forget. Why does the Torah say it twice?

Answers Rabbi Oshry: The Torah represents timeless teaching to the Jewish people. The Torah understands that we will remember what the Nazis did to us. Of course, we remember the *Kristallnacht*, the concentration camps, the forced labor camps, the deportations, the cattle cars, the mass murders, the animalistic brutalities, the savage slaughter, the crematoriums, and the barbaric blood-thirstiness. Of course, we remember. It is perfectly natural to remember these unparalleled atrocities. Nevertheless, the Torah's concern is, "... when Hashem will give you rest from all your enemies all around"—when you will settle in your new world, when all the survivors will rebuild their lives, establish new families, create businesses and new sources of livelihood—what then? When you will see blessings in your new achievements; when you will find contentment in your new homes after escaping the horrors of the past; when you will accept German reparations to build the new land; when you will drive the Volkswagens to save on your fuel costs—what then? The Torah knows that there will be a tendency to forget the previous pains and to cross out all the dreadfulness of the past. People will clamor to forget the awfulness and gruesomeness of their prior history. They will rationalize: "What purpose is there to dwell on the past? It's a brand new world! Today our former tormentors are our new allies. The Nazi hands drenched in the blood of our people, have been cleansed. They are wearing new uniforms! Perhaps it is time to move on…?" Comes the timeless Torah and declares: " …And it shall come to pass that when Hashem, your G-d, gives you rest from all your enemies all around…"—even then—"Thou shalt not forget!"

"Beware and guard yourself carefully, lest you forget the things your eyes have seen, and lest they stray from your heart, all the days of your life, and you are to make them known to your children, and to your children's children…" From their endurance, their sacrifice—our grateful current and future generations thrive, and we shall always remember. Let their death not be in vain. As it is so eloquently inscribed in the Holocaust Museum in Washington, "Thou shalt not be a victim. Thou shalt not be a perpetrator. Above all, thou shalt not be a bystander."

To Forget the Dead, would be Akin to Killing them a Second Time

We express our gratitude to the prolific and master author and storyteller, Rabbi Hanoch Teller, for keeping the flame of remembrance alive, with yet another beautiful historical book, loaded with years of research on the *Heroic Children* of the Holocaust; and for including our *Keren Ma'asim Tovim* as a spiritual partner in this holy endeavor of "Thou shalt not forget." May the blessing of the *Chasam Sofer* be bestowed upon him and his beautiful multi-branched family: "May their well never dry, may their tree never lose its energy and vigor, and may all the fruits of the tree blossom and bloom to perfection" —and so shall be His will!

Completed on the 37th day of the Omer, *ge'vu'rah she'be'yesod*, the strength of our foundation.

Avrohom Pinchos Berkowitz
for Ma'Asim Tovim Foundation
37th day of the Omer, 5775

Preface

"Within each child there burned a moral spark that could vanquish the darkness at the core of human nature."
Betty Jean Lifton, Ph.D.
(*The King of Children: The Life and Death of Janusz Korczak*
St. Martin's Griffin edition, 1995)

As night falls, in all corners of the world, in all households where there are parents and children, the tender music is the same. Listen carefully — can you hear it? The timeless sound of a lullaby. The soothing voices of Mother and Father, promising their babies that they are safe and protected, that all is right with their world.

This has been the message of every lullaby, in every language and culture, since the days of antiquity. The word itself, some believe, derives from *"layla,"* the Hebrew word for "night." Enveloped within a parent's solid embrace, "lulled" by a familiar bedtime song, children are reassured that no harm will ever come to them.

But what happens when, in one dark, helpless moment in human history, this sacred promise from parent to child cannot be kept?

This was the fate of the 1.5 million unsuspecting Jewish children under the age of twelve throughout Europe who were extinguished in the flames of the Holocaust. The extraordinary stories that follow are the testimonies of nine who miraculously survived, overcoming beginnings so traumatic that their entire world seemed to have spun off of its axis. They chronicle a time and place in which morality, justice, decency and law were eclipsed by evil.

The graphic accounts of degradation and horror, while incomprehensible to good people of all stripes, are all true; every minute detail has been methodically researched and corroborated. Before Germany could be stopped, six million—according to recent research, closer to seven million—Jewish victims were murdered by the Nazis and their collaborators throughout Europe; countless more, maimed and displaced. Centuries of vibrant Jewish life, in Eastern Europe in particular, came to an abrupt, torturous end.

Yet while *Heroic Children* is a study of horror, it is also a study of hope.

It is about the life and times of those heroic children ... and it is also about you and me. About each of us, trying to make our way in an increasingly complex world.

Few of us will ever face struggles as monumental as what these nine youngsters endured under the reign of Hitler. But this doesn't change the fact that today (or tomorrow) you may find yourself overwhelmed by serious challenges, devastating setbacks, or periods of profound despair. It is my hope that the experiences of these children will serve as inspiration; for if they, of such tender years, were able to heal and flourish in the wake of unimaginable adversity, then surely you will be able to confront head-on whatever obstacles may appear, and summon the strength to triumph.

Introduction

There are few eyewitness accounts of the Holocaust from the vantage point of Jewish children, because so few were able to survive. Wrenched from their parents, they were simply too tender in years to fend for themselves and too small to be considered useful for slave labor. Those who did not perish from hunger, exposure or disease, were routinely murdered brutally—as they were considered the biological future of the Jewish people—immediately after falling into the hands of their captors.

Unlike those who were older when Hitler and the National Socialists came to power, those who were children during the Holocaust possessed, tragically, few happy or even benign memories of early "normalcy." The youngest survivors emerged with little vocabulary for the typical games of childhood, for the comforting rhythms of family life or friendship, for the rituals of school or synagogue. These boys and girls would first acquire this vocabulary—the universal language of childhood—after the war, in a new tongue, in countries and cultures that were foreign to them.

Many shouldered the terrible burden of being the only surviving members of their families. Before they could bear witness to genocide—as they have so courageously in this book—they had to develop the life-skills to put the past behind them, and set their eyes to the future. Indeed, the individuals profiled in *Heroic Children* transcended the trauma of their formative years with remarkable grace and success.

All of them went on to build rich, productive lives*—personally, professionally, communally, Jewishly.

More than seven decades after the destruction of European Jewry, we stand poised at another key juncture in human history. The majority of the older survivors have either passed on, or are in the grip of very old age. Soon, only the voices of the child-survivors will remain to be heard.

And not for very long.

In the late 1990s, inspired by Rabbi Moshe Chaim Hier of The Simon Wiesenthal Center in Los Angeles, I embarked upon a mission to seek out those remaining voices around the world, and to codify what they revealed. As a student and teacher of the Holocaust and as a long-time docent at Jerusalem's Yad Vashem (Israel's National Holocaust museum/memorial), I assumed that my extensive background would prepare me for what I would hear. I was mistaken.

The youngest survivors are all grey-haired now, but when they shared their riveting sagas with me, time hurtled backward and I could see the frightened child behind their eyes. All of their accounts— permanently embedded in their memories and in their psyches—were astonishingly graphic and horrifically detailed, portraying torture (both physical and mental), starvation, displacement, separation, isolation, deprivation, exposure to the elements, absence of sanitation or medical care, inhumane living conditions, forced labor and systematic extermination.

The reality that the Germans and their ardent supporters throughout Europe actively targeted even the youngest Jewish child, the most guileless innocent, drives home the full extent of the racist evil that engulfed the region—the full extent of the War Against the Jews.**

♦ **Michael Thaler**, M.D., a retired medical researcher of world renown (who now teaches Jewish history at UC Santa Cruz and UC Berkeley) chronicled a series of harrowing escapes orchestrated by his father, including a run from Ukrainians that catapulted the young boy into an open mass grave of Jews who had been massacred weeks earlier.

♦ Violinist **Cecilia Boruchowitz** (Gradis) (today of Johannesburg)

---

* In fact, according to follow-up studies, the vast majority of Holocaust survivors of all ages went on to lead very successful lives. See William B. Helmreich, *Against All Odds: Holocaust Survivors and the Successful Lives They Made in America*, Simon and Schuster, 1996.
** Title of Lucy Dawidowicz's history of the Holocaust and an approach to understanding the Nazi agenda in World War II as developed in this book.

was a celebrated child prodigy in Dvinsk. But the Nazi scourge pulled her from the concert stage to form a suicide pact with her sister Nadia as they ran for their lives—and, eventually, back onto the stage, performing in the lion's den before appreciative German audiences who would have murdered her on the spot had they discovered she was Jewish.

+ In a memoir dictated to his wife Lynn, *Walking to Vildieri*—completed only five hours before his death at age 65—Long Island manufacturer **Albert Sharon** (Szajdholc) outlined his teenaged imprisonment and daring acts of defiance and treason, and his family's desperate flight from the Germans—a heart-thumping journey from Brussels over the Pyrenees to a host of towns and villages throughout France and Italy.

+ Chicago jeweler **Israel Starck** (Storch), of Munkacs, Czechoslovakia (Hungary since 1938), endured the horrors of the notorious extermination camp Auschwitz-Birkenau and slave labor camps Mauthausen (where he last saw his father), Melk and Ebensee, surviving thanks to a few well-placed miracles… and the pact he made with his teen comrades, that they would do everything to help each other to survive.

+ In Zürich, community leader **Gutta Sternbuch** (Eisenzweig) recounted heroic efforts to feed, protect and nurture the doomed orphans of the Warsaw Ghetto as a protégé of the legendary educator Janusz Korczak, though she herself was only a very young woman.

+ Rabbi/Professor **Isser Fisher** of Flatbush, Brooklyn shared a six-year-old's view of the squalid ghettos of Vilna and Radin, and of being buried (with his mother, sister and a teenaged friend) in a hole in the ground, under a tree in a forest—harbored there (for years!) and fed by an alcoholic landowner whose behavior ranged from saintly to sadistic.

+ In Mexico City, **Dolly Bestandig** (Hirsch), also a longtime Jewish educator, told of being a baby in Auschwitz, hidden through a cold winter by her mother, in a dumpster outside her barracks, underneath the garbage—one of a long string of horrors she was too young to recall firsthand, but reported to her by the uncles who raised her after her mother died several years after liberation.

+ In a Brooklyn apartment filled with holy books, **Esther Biegelman** (Springer) described how, at age five, she kept her baby brother quiet and confined to a filthy, splintery wooden plank in their father's bunk in the concentration camp Bergen-Belsen, lest they aggravate the other adult prisoners… over the course of two-and-a-half years.

✦ On a 70-mile death march from Warsaw into Germany, in the sweltering summer heat, **Shlomo Zalman Teichman** another youth from the celebrated Jewish enclave of Munkacs—today "Sol," a Los Angeles business magnate—saved the life of his younger brother, carrying the boy on his back the entire distance.

WE ARE EMPOWERED by their stories, and from them, we learn:

~ That even the youngest child in the worst of circumstances **can cultivate the courage, tenacity and determination of a hero**, when nurtured from infancy by loving parents, grandparents, clergy and teachers who honor ethical behavior and moral responsibility. These personal connections are the bedrock of faith and conscience that strengthens us to soar above the depths of our environment.

~ The **powerful bonds of family and friendship can galvanize** even the youngest child to overcome more than he or she ever could alone. That loyalty, camaraderie, fellowship and love are practically biological imperatives, enabling the human race to survive.

~ That the **humane, selfless actions of a righteous few**—courageous individuals of any faith, culture or socioeconomic class who dare to buck the tide—can make a life-saving difference in the world.

~ That **baseless hatred and racist evil can metastasize**, destroying the very fabric of society, when democratic ideals are not safeguarded, and when so-called decent citizens choose to look the other way.

~ That we must view everyday challenges (and even the more serious setbacks) of our own lives with a **healthy dose of perspective**, a jolt of humility, and a profound sense of gratitude.

My own challenge in faithfully bringing these epic stories to light, was to do so without any overlay of cynicism or undue editorializing. At certain junctures, however, I could not avoid calling the reader's attention to the perpetrators' grotesque, fanatical commitment to pursue "The Final Solution of the Jewish Question" regardless of cost, risk or expediency. I grappled, too, with how to effectively transmit the necessary historical/geopolitical context for the entire collection. The key events described by most of the protagonists occurred largely during the years 1940–45; there are, thus, overlapping events and even (in some instances) overlapping locations. How to do justice to each individual story without inserting excessive, repetitive background information? I hope that the broad, basic time line of events, the annotated map, the deliberate order in which the stories appear, and the glossary of terms that follows the text, enable the reader to develop a strong sense of time and place that will provide a framework for these testimonies.

First, however, a few important points must be highlighted.

It is commonly believed that Adolf Hitler and the Nazi Party scapegoated the Jews in order to gain power. History has borne out just the opposite: they amassed power, in large measure, in order to annihilate the Jewish people. Indeed, even when defeat was inevitable—with Germany losing on two fronts, and troops and trains desperately needed for the retreat—nothing, on orders from the very top, could be diverted from the murder machine.

"The Final Solution" evolved in stages. The original policy of the German government was to force the Jews out of Germany, subsequently Austria, and then all the other countries that were occupied, to create a *Judenrein* (free of Jews) environment. In Germany, where it all began, Jews were stripped of their citizenship, eliminated from schools, from public office, from the various professions, and from intellectual, artistic and social life. They were deprived of their assets and sources of livelihood, of freedom of movement and communication, and would soon be forced to wear yellow badges. Outside of Germany and Austria, however, the circumstances of the Jews under German dominion deteriorated with stunning speed. Subjugation, oppression and (by 1941) expulsion to killing fields were often immediate.

Those whose fate was not instant extermination were shunted into ghettos without sanitation, food or protection from the elements, and were subjected to rampant disease, slave labor, brutality and humiliation. At a later stage, the ghetto inhabitants would be deported to the extermination camps.

The term "ghetto" today is associated with a neighborhood (usually urban and lower-income) in which members of a particular cultural, ethnic, racial or religious group live in high concentration, typically by choice; this definition is light-years away from the reality of the ghastly forced ghettos in which Jews were imprisoned during World War II.

Most people know about the concentrations camps and gas chambers

that were the fate of Jews under German rule, but not of the subterfuge that got them there. The Nazis preyed upon the Jews' innocence,
decency and wishful thinking, employing sophisticated methods of
deception, fraud, and manipulation of language to ensure the victims'
ignorance of what lay in store. Even amongst themselves, the Germans
carefully engaged in verbal camouflage, referring to their killing centers
simply as "the east," and to extermination by gassing as "the showers" or
Sonderbehandlung ("special treatment").

Where ghettoization was implemented, panicked Jewish citizens—
jobless, victims of severe discrimination, suffering food shortages, fearing assault and arrest, seeing their synagogues burned and their rabbis
beaten and humiliated—were ordered to report immediately (to ensure the hurried abandonment of moveable property) to ghettos, so
that they would be concentrated while their tormentors contemplated
the next blow.

It did not take long. Once the murder apparatus was operational,
the liquidation process began with continual deportation to extermination centers. The train ride itself was designed to be lethal and, like
all aspects of German–Jewish subjugation, exquisitely tortuous.

In some instances, like the Warsaw Ghetto, where the Germans
knew that many Jews were still in hiding, other techniques had to
be employed. Accordingly, the ghetto inhabitants were buoyed by
German reassurances of "relocation" and "resettlement" to points "east,"
where they were promised shelter, food, work, schools, and reunions
with relatives. Their fears of the unknown were greatly reduced by the
receipt of picturesque postcards bearing upbeat messages from recently deported loved ones—messages these doomed individuals were
forced to pen shortly before being herded into gas chambers.

For those desperate souls already crowded inside Europe's ghettos,
the myth of "resettlement" created wild surges of hope. After all, who
could conceive of anything worse than the squalid circumstances
in which they were already imprisoned, some for years? Grinding
starvation, horrendous overcrowding, unrelenting cold (all blankets,
coats, sweaters, furs, even towels, were confiscated), the stench of
human waste and rotting corpses in the streets as epidemics decimated
the weakened population, mass public shootings to punish minor
infractions—these were the daily realities of life in the ghetto. Even

if they could manage an escape over its high, heavily-guarded walls, the ghetto-dwellers knew such acts were fruitless—in fact, suicidal; their "good neighbors" would lose not a moment in delivering them back into the hands of the Germans. Hundreds of ghetto inhabitants would pay the ultimate price as a collective punishment for a single soul desperate to escape. Better to opt for deportation to a place far from the unbearable death-trap, to pick crops at harvest-time...

When the Jews were transported to extermination camps, the packed cattle cars pulled up to what appeared to be a regular train station, with schedules posted. (The depot in Treblinka, for example, was nothing more than a façade, shades of a Hollywood movie set, complete with a large, faux clock and a "barber shop" that was perennially closed.) After their long journeys, these battered Jews would arrive to promises of hot coffee and cake, clean clothes and work-assignments—after they took showers for "disinfection." Those who appeared ill, the old or the very young, were taken (as a matter of policy in Treblinka) directly to the "infirmary," a place where every patient was immediately executed, usually by being thrown alive into a pit with raging flames.

Those not selected for the flames were forced to disrobe, fold their clothing and tie their shoes together. They were brutally forced out of the changing-room to what the camp wardens referred to as "the Road to Heaven." There the naked skeletons were driven with whips into—the final deception—gas chambers disguised as showers. As the bodies were crammed and crushed inside and the doors bolted shut, the gas pellets released their deadly fumes. *"Ivan, turn on the water!"*—this was the code-phrase that signaled the last breath of countless Jews.

Who could conceive of such an unspeakable horror? Not innocent, tyrranized people, fully depleted after everything they had already endured. The very monstrosity of the crime made it, in a word, unbelievable.

And so they went. For the most part, quietly. Hopefully.

Hitler coined the expression the Big Lie for a falsehood so colossal that no one would believe that someone "could have the impudence to distort the truth so infamously." The Germans understood how to employ this concept with chilling efficiency. Hence, it was the Jews who became war profiteers while the German folk fell defending their Fatherland in WWI. The Jews (comprising only .8 percent of the population!) controlled Germany's commerce, industry, and food supply, their treasonous acts a vicious stab in the back (*Dolchstoss*) from which the country could not recover.

Big lies also obscure big truths: that, per capita, more Jews fought and died for Germany during World War I than any other group of that country's citizens. That the Jews were staunchly loyal members of German society, contributing mightily to the country's economic, cultural, and scientific achievements.

Anti-Semitism had been deeply entrenched in Europe for hundreds of years, and when it exploded during the Holocaust, there was virtually no protest from citizens, churches or governments, whether free or under German dominion (except for the Danes, led by King Christian X, who succeeded in rescuing the majority of Denmark's Jews by smuggling them into neutral Sweden, and to a lesser extent, the Bulgarians.)

Nazism's Big Lie has tentacles that reach into the future. Holocaust denial is on the rise across the globe, and sickeningly prevalent on hatesites that abound on the Internet. The gas chambers are declared a fabrication by Ph.D.-credentialed professors on college campuses. The genocidal murder of six million Jews is considered a greatly exaggerated headcount of accidental victims of war. On the rise, too, is anti-Jewish violence, especially in Europe.*

Combating lies and distortions with truth will be the duty of generations going forward. Few of us will be victims of outright evil, and even fewer will be perpetrators. But frequently, in ways large and small, we all find ourselves to be bystanders. Even one raised voice can make a difference when silence rules in the face of cruelty and injustice—whether it occurs on the playground, in the academic or professional arenas, or on the world stage.

That voice could be yours.

The nine children portrayed in this book, through their unforgettable stories, will lead readers to the beating heart of the Holocaust. Their spirits are beacons of light in the darkest days and nights of modern human history.

It is my fervent hope and conviction that good people the world over will be inspired by that light, and will harness it to illuminate a just and safe path for all humanity.

---

* Stephen Roth Institute for the Study of Contemporary Anti-Semitism and Racism, 2006 and 2007 Reports, Tel Aviv University.

Comprehension

Michael

This is a story of comprehension.
It is the tale of one small boy's harrowing journey to freedom … a journey mapped out by a father who had keenly grasped the full extent of the Nazi evil.

In the years before the full blackness descended, young Michael Thaler spent his early childhood blissfully ensconced in a darkened theater, cocooned in a world of make-believe. His father, Meyer, was a bookkeeper for the movie house in their shtetl of Brzeżany, Poland. Too young for school, Michael would accompany his father to work nearly every day.

The boy was still so little that he was nearly swallowed up by the seats, and many of the films, epics of love and war, were beyond his understanding. None of this mattered to Michael Thaler. For him, the greatest pleasure was to be at the side of "Tato," a gregarious, intelligent fellow who was admired by Jews and non-Jews alike.

Brzeżany was a town of 12,000 citizens, of whom approximately 10,000 were Jews. It neighbored the city of Lvov, a noted center of Torah learning, and was located in a region of Poland that contained more than 300,000 Jewish souls before the war.

Compared with the other Jews of that time and place, the Thalers would have been considered progressive and secularized, even avant-garde. Michael's mother, Fanny, was a "liberated" woman. She wore lipstick—hardly the standard among the extremely pious Jewish women of her day—read the works of the German poet Schiller, and played the violin.

Meyer Thaler was an ardent Zionist who was passionately involved in communal affairs. His dedication and energy were barely hampered by a major spinal deformity, scoliosis, which was the result of a childhood illness.

For the Thalers and their Jewish neighbors—bearded and non-bearded, observant and secular—living in eastern Poland had its pros and cons in the "relative" scheme of the Holocaust. The obvious advantage was that they were spared the initial brunt of the Nazi agenda, as their region fell first under Russian, rather than German, occupation in the fall of 1939. But by the summer of 1941 when the Germans controlled all of Poland, their proximity to the Ukraine worked to the Jews' distinct detriment. The Ukrainian neighbors managed to exceed the Germans in their barbaric and determined efforts to solve the "Jewish question."

It was there, in a picturesque town near the Ukrainian border, in a region distinguished by its fierce anti-Semitism even compared to the rest of Europe, that Michael Thaler had been born in 1934.

From the time the Russians occupied Brzeżany in 1939, they kept a tight seal against information from the outside world. Still, Meyer Thaler's job at the theater provided the family with an unusual degree of exposure to international events and divergent political ideas.

Young Michael would sit raptly, watching the same movies over and over until he practically had them memorized. The manager of the theater did not object to the little boy's presence; in fact, he hardly noticed him. A member of the Communist party, he rarely let his work get in the way of playing chess with his esteemed employee, "Comrade" Thaler. He also devoted a good portion of his day to imbibing vodka.

THE DAY that would change the Thalers' lives forever—June 29, 1941, one week after the launch of Operation Barbarossa*—started out much like any other. Meyer was deeply engrossed in a chess match with his boss; Fanny was going about her daily business of errands,

---

* Code name for the German invasion of the Soviet Union.

community work and intellectual pursuits; and Michael sat inside the theater, watching a film for the umpteenth time.

Suddenly, in the midst of the screening, the boy developed—for the very first time in his young life—an excruciating headache. He begged Tato to take him home. Meyer tried to cajole his son into waiting, since he was loath to abandon a winning game, but the boy refused. Michael was an only child, and a master at getting his doting father's attention.

Resigned to his parental responsibility, Meyer took Michael by the hand and exited the theater. They were not more than 200 meters past the movie house when a German fighter plane roared and screeched through the sky just overhead, emptying its war materiel onto the street below. A bomb instantly flattened the theater, killing everyone inside.

More than 200 schoolchildren died in the theater that afternoon.

Germany's surprise attack against its former Soviet ally revealed the depth of the Nazi commitment to their "War Against the Jews." Opening up this front would ultimately bring about the fall of Germany, but it would also result in the almost total annihilation of Russian Jewry.

Aerial aggression was focused on Jewish targets; therefore, major buildings, auditoriums, city halls, churches, government offices and even military installations escaped relatively unscathed. It was on unassuming streets of Jewish neighborhoods that so many were killed and maimed. Alas, many non-Jewish locals had to pay the price for their proximity to Jewish neighborhoods ... like the moviegoers of Brzeżany.

Most of the town's residents, including the Thalers, sought safety from the saturation bombings by fleeing to the nearby woods, located in an area of Poland that had become part of the Ukraine when the Russians took over in 1939. When the air raids subsided and the civilians began to return to their homes, Michael Thaler learned a new word, a word all too well known to his elders, but not part of a seven-year-old's standard vocabulary.

The word was "pogrom."

Seeking revenge for all of the Ukrainian political prisoners who were executed prior to the retreat of the Soviet troops, the local peasants, armed with crude weapons, swarmed through the Jewish district and began to massacre the innocent residents. That the Jews had nothing to do with the political executions was irrelevant to the Ukrainians' bloodthirsty agenda. In a chilling harbinger of what lay ahead, their lust for slaughter could not be sated. Jews were trampled, beaten to death, tortured, and buried alive. By the end of the day, upwards of 200 Jewish citizens of Brzeżany had been murdered in retaliation for a crime that they did not commit.

Meyer Thaler had an uncanny nose for danger. He understood to an extraordinary degree, even more so than his intelligent wife, that whatever civil rights he had acquired as a Polish citizen were null and void after the German invasion.

From that day forward, Meyer Thaler adopted a policy of action based upon the *true intent* of the Germans. He reasoned that what the Nazis intended was never good for the Jews, and the safest policy was to do precisely *the opposite* of what they instructed—especially if they purported to be acting in the Jews' best interest. This strategy proved to be not only remarkably insightful … but ultimately, lifesaving.

In the wake of the pogrom, Meyer Thaler was nowhere to be found. His wife and son instinctively trusted that he had found a way to circumvent the perils that lurked on every corner, but they did not know his whereabouts. Fanny and Michael, neither of whom looked particularly Jewish, spent a day searching the town for him. When they returned to their street, they saw, to their horror, that their house was being ransacked and looted by a mob of Ukrainian peasants, under the supervision of a German officer.

The Thalers had had the foresight to conceal many of their possessions inside their cellar prior to retreating to the woods. But nothing was safe from the marauders, who broke through the brick wall behind which the belongings were hidden.

Amidst the trove was Meyer's suit, which was promptly inspected for legal tender. The results were disappointing, but the despoilers did discover his worker's permit—an official document with a hammer-and-sickle insignia that labeled its owner as a card-carrying Communist. The incriminating paper was handed over to the German policeman overseeing the pillage, who demanded loudly, "Who knows this man?"

Fanny Thaler had the presence of mind to feign ignorance as to the identity of her husband, but was unable to contain her fury at being robbed, and decided to take matters into her own hands. Unlike her husband, she still had not fully grasped that lawlessness was now the law, and that as a Jew, she was completely disenfranchised from the larger culture in which she had once been a full-fledged participant.

Fanny grabbed her son and headed down the block in search of help. She hadn't taken more than a few steps when she came face-to-face with a German officer on patrol, and alerted him to the grand larceny taking place under his nose. She did not let on that the pillagers were inside her home, confining her complaint to the crime being committed. The officer replied that he did not handle these matters and they should be directed to headquarters.

He might have replied that robbing a non-German house was not an especially heinous crime, and emptying a Jewish one was a matter of policy. Oddly, the officer did no such thing. Instead, he escorted Fanny to army headquarters and corroborated her complaint to the commander in charge. Remarkably, the commander dropped what he was doing and raced over to the house with Fanny.

What would happen next would be one of the war's more implausible moments, considering standard operating procedure for German occupation. The German commander blew his whistle and unholstered his pistol, indicating the end to the festivities. The junior officer continued to search for the missing Communist, and the frustrated looters departed practically empty-handed.

Fanny was so pleased with the resolution of the situation that she rewarded the commander in charge with a bolt of leather that had been hidden in her cellar. Justice had prevailed, perhaps for the last time in Jewish Brzeżany.

But where was Meyer Thaler?

DIRECTLY behind the front-line troops and the *Ordnungspolizei* (order police, in charge of annexing territories and hunting Jews) followed the SS (the most powerful terror force in Nazi Germany, overseers of the concentration and extermination camps), who employed unbridled terrorism in the persecution of perceived enemies, indicating the priority the Germans placed upon the eradication of Jews. The method the SS used to repress and subjugate their victims was perfected to a science, and they were always on the lookout for additional ways to humiliate and torture.

What they would now do in the Lvov region had already been perpetrated numerous times throughout western Poland. Eventually, nearly all communities that maintained a Jewish population would fall victim to their plan.

The formula was as follows: gather up the Jews throughout the area, herd them into the one spot that had received the heaviest aerial damage, and create an island of despair—better known as a ghetto. Shelter was at a premium amidst the rubble and ruin.

Life, if one could call it that, in the ghetto defied adaptation. Even if one could adjust to the unbearably cramped quarters and the absence of sanitation and heat, hunger and disease never abated. Death was frequent and continual. The very notion of improvement or repair was *verboten*.

The lives of the Jews were governed by the SS via the *Judenrat*, the "Jewish Council" that executed the Nazi will. Traditionally, although not exclusively, the most influential Jews were appointed to the *Judenrat*, and Michael's uncle, one of the wealthiest men in the area, was named as its head.

The duties of the *Judenrat* were dreadful. They had to confiscate the Jews' valuables and present them to the Nazis. They usually determined who was to live where in the ghetto, who was to work, and who would fulfill the quota of those to be "transferred," never to return. But these were details. The Germans made all of the significant decisions and it was up to the *Judenrat* to see that they were implemented.

The *Judenrat* also had to ensure that the German fanatical attachment to detail was fulfilled. The most minute deviation spelled instant death. For example, the *Judenrat* was to enforce the wearing of the armband* that branded a Jew as such. It had to be put on in such a way that it was perfectly visible from both the front and back. If it was even a centimeter off of the prescribed position, the offender would pay with his or her life.

The German authorities in the ghettos, subsequently the SS, made it patently clear to Jew and non-Jew alike that its will must be meticulously obeyed, and that any tampering with its policy of subjugating and isolating the Jew would be dealt with capitally. The German modus

---

* Depending on the region, Jews were forced to wear either a yellow star over their heart or an armband with a yellow star visible from both the front and back.

operandi forced the Jews to conclude that any attempt to disguise their religion would be fatal, that escape from the ghetto was futile, and that resistance was doomed. The only hope for survival, it seemed, lay in strictly abiding by the Nazi dictates. Starvation, disease, beatings, absence of shelter and fear of the approaching winter, created among the prisoners a mounting sense of demoralization, hopelessness and panic. The Germans used this to their cunning advantage.

The SS offered this reasoning to members of the *Judenrat:* "You know not to expect any aid or sympathy from the Poles or the Ukrainians, but the Reich needs workers, so we will look out for you."

In a world that had gone mad, there was a modicum of logic to this way of thinking. It dovetailed with the tragic cycle of Jewish history, in which persecution followed persecution, but ultimately, the beleaguered nation always persevered. And the logic was further enhanced by the inability of Jewish innocents to fathom the ever-worsening array of atrocities that lay ahead. The result was the oft-heard refrain of delusion: "As long as we are an asset to the German war effort," one Jew tried to assure another, "our suffering may continue, but our safety is guaranteed."

Little wonder, then, that when all the males between the ages of 16 and 65 were ordered to register with the German authorities and list their professions, they willingly complied. They naively believed that employment would mean stepped-up food rations for themselves and their families.

There was one person who did not buy this rationale.

MEYER THALER had himself admitted to the hospital in Brzeżany in order to avoid the compulsory registration process. The real motive behind the registration was to establish who was a white-collar worker versus who was a manual laborer. Thaler, the bookkeeper, had a hunch that educated men like himself, who were not skilled with their hands, were totally expendable to the German war machine.

He was a man of logic and probabilities. While most under German subjugation fell victim to the mindset that their oppressors were foisting upon them, Thaler refused to succumb. Nor would he allow wishful thinking to influence his behavior. This was not a simple approach to maintain when the Holocaust Kingdom was built upon the incomprehensible slaughter of innocents. One constantly found oneself asking, "What is rationality? What is logic?"

These were questions that could not be answered then, and cannot be answered now. But Meyer Thaler was right to concoct an illness that would land him in the hospital during that pivotal juncture. After the registration was completed, doctors and lawyers, accountants and teachers, journalists and violinists, were loaded onto trucks. The unsuspecting passengers—men who had assumed that their professional stature would assure them of employment in an assortment of fields—were delivered to a killing field.

The following day, reports of a mass shooting in a nearby village filtered back to the ghetto. At first the unsuspecting widows and orphans did not connect the killings with the truckloads of men who had departed amidst assurances and embraces. But when they saw local peasants wearing the attire of those who had departed, the horrifying truth was fully grasped. Acute mourning erupted and wailing echoed throughout the night.

Even after the dawn rose, young Michael Thaler had the sense that the ghetto was engulfed in consummate darkness. He could not imagine a sorrow more intense.

In one fell swoop, the Germans had guillotined the community's leadership by annihilating its intellectuals and professionals. Those who remained were so shattered that resistance was never viewed as an option. One European country after another was steamrolled by what was perceived as the invincible German army; there wasn't a military power on the continent that offered genuine resistance to the Nazi juggernaut. How then could starving, defenseless ghetto inhabitants—under the heavy boot of trigger-happy, torture-intoxicated SS monsters—ever even consider resistance?

Still, the Nazis took no chances. Any material that could be used as a weapon was removed, and any individuals with the ingenuity or influence to fight back were eliminated. The slightest hint of insurrection was punished by the slaying of at least 200 innocent ghetto inhabitants.

No one could imagine a more miserable or dangerous place to live … but life on the outside was no safer. Any Jew found outside would be murdered, and any gentile who harbored him would share the same fate. There was no shortage of informers eager to collect the price placed on every Jewish head.

After the mass execution of the ghetto elite, Meyer Thaler, using the sophisticated analysis that was his hallmark, entered the ghetto. Being caught on the outside—and the odds of this happening were overwhelming—meant instant death; living on the inside meant living within arm's reach of the SS.

He had ascertained that the peril was the greatest where Jews were concentrated and isolated, yet he violated his own tenet of survival for the sake of an even higher goal. He was consumed by one thought above all others: to find a safe haven for Michael, his only child. The solution to this thorny problem could only be contrived in the temporary safety of the ghetto.

MEYER THALER stared at his young son. He and Fanny had nurtured such great dreams for him. Now he was a hungry, filthy child of the ghetto whose very survival was in doubt.

Restlessly, the father pondered his decision. But not for long.

There was no other choice.

Earlier that year and before the establishment of the ghetto, Meyer, concerned for his family's safety, had moved them from Brzeżany's Jewish district to a neighborhood on the outskirts of town, near the old Jewish cemetery about four kilometers away. There they had established a warm rapport with their elderly Catholic neighbors, the Holowinskis, a childless couple who had always shown great enthusiasm for the Thaler's engaging little boy.

Risking his life, Meyer stealthily ducked outside the ghetto in the dark of night. He made his way back to his home on the outskirts of town. There he had deliberately stashed all the family's items of value, before being confined to the ghetto. He had known that in the ghetto all goods would be confiscated. Now he would utilize these possessions to save his son's life. He filled a few boxes with valuables and set aside some furniture, and then sneaked over to his Catholic neighbors.

Meyer's proposition to the Holowinskis was stunning in its directness and pragmatism. "I have been forced to enter a Nazi penal colony from which I will probably never emerge alive," he said slowly. "I beg you to take our Michael, so that he will have a chance to live. If what I fear comes to pass, when the war is over and the Germans have been defeated, you are free to raise him in any way you wish." He then presented them with what remained of his possessions, explaining, "The contents of these boxes will help finance Michael's rearing."

From the expressions on his neighbors' faces, Meyer Thaler understood he had gambled wisely once again. Within days, the Holowinskis lovingly accepted eight-year-old Michael Thaler into their home and their hearts. They had sorely missed having a boy of their own, and despite the enormous risks involved, viewed him as the answer to a lifetime of prayers.

Although the Holowinskis' modest home was relatively secluded, informers were everywhere, and everyone was suspect. The sudden appearance of a child under the roof of an aged couple, the sound of his sweet voice or anxious sobs wafting through the windows, would be the kiss of death for Michael and his kind-hearted hosts.

Despite his tender years, the boy was already wise enough to understand the inviolable rules of his sanctuary. He could not go near a window or step outside. He also had to remain perfectly silent. Essentially, he had to become completely invisible.

The stress of the situation was overwhelming to the young boy, causing him to frequently wet his bed—something that he had not done since infancy. He was desperately homesick for his parents. Deep in his heart, he knew that there was little chance he would ever see them again.

But like his perceptive father, the boy was stunningly adaptable. Michael soon adjusted to his new reality, and began shifting his allegiance to his surrogate parents. And a fundamental part of his metamorphosis was to embrace not only the Holowinskis, but also their religious fervor.

The Holowinskis were deeply devout. The walls of their home were covered with Christian ornamental art, and the Virgin Mary and her son on the cross gazed down upon Michael from every nook and mantle. The boy learned to read his very first words from Christian Bible texts, the only literature on the premises.

Trapped inside the house, the boy had nothing to do but read Christian scripture and memorize the details of the saints' lives—a far cry from a dimly recalled, exuberant childhood spent in a darkened movie theater. It was a far cry, too, from the sights and sounds and smells of the ghetto on the other side of town, where prayers were murmured in Hebrew with life-and-death urgency, and parents sang plaintive Yiddish lullabies to children who were too hungry to sleep.

Michael Thaler spent a good portion of his day on his knees, praying for his own safety, and that his parents—who were still Jews—would be forgiven.

THE FRIGID WINTER of 1941–42 created even harsher conditions inside the Brzeżany ghetto. And there was more: the Nazi obsession that every Jew be accounted for had reached a fever pitch. Not one Jew was to escape the Final Solution, and they had concluded that some of Brzeżany Jewry was still at large.

With typical German efficiency, the Nazis began to scour the suburbs and the countryside, conscripting the eager natives in their searches. Meyer Thaler was convinced that while remaining in the ghetto spelled doom, the upsurge in house-to-house searches meant his son and the Holowinskis were in immediate mortal danger.

Yet he feared that if he went to the boy and was caught, he could be sealing everyone's fate. Fugitives and host families who were discovered were publicly hanged or machine-gunned, and this was happening on a weekly basis. In response to these terrifying spectacles, many hidden Jews were returning to the ghetto voluntarily, or being expelled by their protectors.

Meyer concluded that a Jewish child was now safer in the ghetto than in a region subject to constant searches and scrutiny. It was time for Michael to rejoin his true family and his true people. Ever so quietly Meyer left the ghetto and arrived at the Holowinskis' again, after nightfall. The pious boy's prayers were answered. Miraculously, his father had come back!

The trip back to the ghetto through deep accumulations of snow was enthralling for Michael, who had been deprived of the pleasures of the outdoors for months. And that was not all.

Inside the ghetto walls Michael was permitted to raise his voice, and he did not have to fear being seen. There were playmates his age, and matters to discuss other than the coming of the Kingdom on Earth.

Ah, the irony. Amidst the rubble, starvation, disease, extreme cold, and under the easily provoked muzzles of the SS guns, Michael lived in relative freedom.

The children of the ghetto were frequently left to their own devices and had a wonderful time frolicking atop the ruins and running in circles around walls that were on the verge of collapse. Indeed, one day a sizeable stone dislodged from a wall and fell onto Michael's nose, leaving its mark forever.

The children's expertise in making their way through the crumbling ghetto was harnessed for the benefit of its desperate residents. The most agile youngsters were sent on missions that involved crawling through sewers, tunneling beneath buildings, and wedging their shrunken bodies between breaches in fences to retrieve food or to locate items that could be bartered.

Meanwhile, the adults were engaged in the clandestine activity of "bunker" construction—ghetto terminology for creating a hiding place thoroughly concealed from prying eyes.

The bunkers were designed to shield inhabitants from detection during a roundup, known as an *"Aktion."* They were usually underground, but could also be located behind a false closet or chimney, or any other ingenious contrivance that would disguise its whereabouts.

The Germans spearheaded *Aktions* on a regular (but unpredictable) basis, with the goal of fulfilling a specific killing quota—usually about 1,000 souls. Those collected during an aktion never returned; hence, everyone huddled in the bunkers were keenly aware that the slightest cough, movement, or child's yelp could expose their cover and sacrifice the lives of all those hiding.

The bunkers afforded a modicum of safety when a quota had to be filled, or a police detail (made up of either the SS or Ukrainian collaborators) was on the prowl. Once the intruders were spotted within the ghetto confines, the streets were immediately deserted. There was always the looming fear that the Jewish police, who worked as stooges for the Nazis and were privy to the bunkers' whereabouts, would reveal their location.

The bloodthirsty Ukrainians, employed by the SS to police the ghetto, were free to lay their hands on any Jews they could grab. The captured prey were always roughed up and then hauled off to the local jail, the first stop in a graduated *Aktion*. The lockup had a capacity of 200, and once it was filled the prisoners were marched to the old Jewish cemetery near the Holowinski home, where they were shot.

To avoid capture, Jews huddled in the bunkers for interminable periods. The conditions were so appalling that not even a candle could remain lit, for lack of oxygen. It was not unheard of that mothers would suffocate their babies to prevent them from crying. Young Michael Thaler witnessed these and other unspeakable atrocities, and his gruesome education expanded.

As a result of the *Aktions* and the horrific conditions, the population of the ghetto withered at a constant rate. But the attrition did not increase the breathing room for the cramped survivors. Directly after every mass killing, the SS reduced the area in which Jews were permitted to live, shrinking the ghetto space.

The rampant disease, starvation, sub-zero temperatures that numbed the body, ongoing torture and murder, and a perpetual state of abject terror definitely had an effect on Michael. His initial delight at having been "freed" from the Holowinski home was long gone.

BY THIS TIME, Meyer Thaler was not the only one who had caught on to the Nazis' ominous intentions. Gruesome eyewitness reports had been confirmed regarding the purpose of the various transports that had departed from the ghettos. The news was relayed by children who had managed to climb out of the miniscule windows of the trains bound for extermination camps. By now it was clear to even the youngest passenger that no one was being relocated for the purpose of employment—not when travel conditions were deliberately designed to kill as many as possible en route.

Prior to these reports, the ghetto inhabitants had voluntarily, often eagerly, lined up for "relocation." They were starving and could not imagine anything worse than what they were currently suffering. The Germans fostered these hopes by saying, "You are parasites—here is a chance for you to finally work!"

The children of the ghetto prepared themselves for the inevitable. Inside their threadbare socks, they stowed fragments of hacksaw blades. This way, if they were locked inside a boxcar they could try to slice their way out of the tiny, mesh window-screens. Then they would jump from the moving train, risking a fate as dire as the one at the journey's end.

Inside the ghetto's walls, Michael Thaler and his comrades honed their escape skills by leaping from the rubble of second-story buildings.

ON ONE OCCASION, when the *Judenrat* was unable to fulfill some German demand, the SS apprehended Michael and his parents in the middle of the night. It was standard Nazi policy to gather Council members' relatives—which the Thalers were—to apply pressure that would ensure the fulfillment of German orders.

The terrified relations, cowering as they faced Nazi rifles, had no illusions regarding their future. There was a formula which the Nazis meticulously maintained that spelled death in a few quick steps. The men were either executed immediately or taken to forced labor camps; women and children were thrown into jail, and when all the cells were full to capacity, they were taken to the Jewish cemetery to be shot.

Meyer's mind raced as he again plotted how to save his son. Behind a desk in the *Judenrat* office, he spotted a trashcan and realized that the narrow window of opportunity would get no wider. Furiously, he stuffed Michael inside the receptacle and told him to stay put until everything was quiet. "Maybe they'll forget about you."

Meyer's plan was never to simply abandon Michael there and hope for the best, though this would have been preferable to everyone else's likely fate. He intended to alert one of his many contacts among the Jewish policemen that they should look the other way when the group—or the garbage—was cleared out.

But young Michael Thaler, buried beneath the garbage, had his own ideas. As decent and kind as the Holowinskis had been to him, the wrenching trauma of separation from his own mother and father had left deep scars upon the boy. He had no illusions about the drama unfolding that night; he understood that all those who milled about the *Judenrat* office could be slaughtered by daybreak. Yet whatever the dark future held, he was determined to remain with his parents, and to share their destiny. Stubbornly, he popped his head out of the can, and then hoisted his entire body.

Meyer Thaler made no attempt to disguise his agitation as his son staggered from the trash to stand by his side in the crowded office.

One look at his father's angry face, and the boy was filled with shame. Wartime had transformed their lives into utter chaos, but one thing had not changed: His father knew what was best for him, and Michael Thaler was expected to show absolute obedience.

Alas, this was impossible. Underneath his bravado was a frightened child who had wept soundlessly in his bed night after night, praying continuously to the Saints for nothing other than to be reunited with his Tato and Mama.

The fifty Jews detained in the *Judenrat* office would be held there overnight, it was announced, with their executions postponed until morning. Everyone's name had been recorded and Jewish policemen were assigned to guard the group. The slightest discrepancy would prove fatal for the Jewish policemen and, conceivably, others.

Meyer was well known to many in Brzeżany, including, as it happened, his jailer. He asked permission to take his young son to the bathroom. The two were granted clearance and hurried down the long staircase of the building not far from the ghetto entrance. Alone in the pitch-dark, Meyer ordered his son to return immediately to the Holowinskis. He was confident that the absence of a child would not be noticed. Struggling with his own emotions, the father evaded his son's eyes and immediately went back upstairs.

Standing alone and shivering in the blackness, Michael was unable to comply. Like a moth careening toward its own destruction, Michael trudged back up the stairs toward his source of light.

When the boy reappeared in the *Judenrat* office, Meyer's brief hopes were dashed. Michael had again proven that he would not save himself. *He's only a child*, Meyer tried to remind himself. *For Heaven's sake, only a child*. But in the Holocaust Kingdom, childhood was a luxury no Jew could afford.

Meyer Thaler's restless, nimble mind raced, desperately searching for a way to save his son. Fanny looked at him with pleading eyes. What could be more dreadful than to know that your innocent child has been sentenced to death—and that you are powerless to save him?

THE GREY DAWN began seeping through the barred windows of the *Judenrat* office indicating that the endless night was nearly over. It was then that a tall man with bushy eyebrows and legitimate access to

the Judenrat appeared. Meyer's message, sent via one of the Jewish policemen, had been delivered.

"Tunis," whose pre-war Zionist activities had kept him in constant
contact with Meyer Thaler, was considered a managerial asset to the
Germans. For this reason he was one of the few Jews allowed a modicum of liberty; he even possessed a pass allowing movement outside the
walls of the ghetto.

Wordlessly, Tunis took Michael by the hand and led him out of the
building. They made their way out of the ghetto and into the town,
arriving at an imposing courthouse where the man was employed.
Silently, he brought the boy into what appeared to be a basement
dungeon.

Tunis pushed a filing cabinet away from the wall, revealing a cavity
large enough for a boy to crawl through. He helped Michael through
the hole and before he sealed it (by replacing the cabinet) he tersely
instructed the boy, "Stay put!"

Locked inside a dank, subterranean vault, Michael wondered, what
other choice did he have?

He soon discovered that he was not alone, as countless rats called
the cellar home. Scores of them squeaked and scurried across his face.

In the darkness and the isolation, with the rats driving him to the
brink of lunacy, Michael became disoriented and lost all track of time.
Had he been there a day, a week?

He could not stay in this dark, infested den even a moment longer!

Michael pushed against the heavy obstruction until it crashed to the
stone floor with a thunderclap. His heart stopped beating and for one
long moment even the rats stopped scampering. But as loud as the noise
was, no one else seemed to have heard it, or at least cared enough to ex-
plore. When he was finally able to resume breathing, Michael continued
his foray into the adjacent, cavernous room.

He noticed some light filtering through a barred window, and
crawled in that direction. Slowly and steadily, Michael continued to
grope along until he was high enough to peer through the slight opening to see the jail right across the plaza from the courthouse.

The lockup had apparently reached its capacity that morning. As
Michael watched, the Nazis proceeded with their trusted method of

dealing with Jewish overcrowding. The prisoners were brutally shoved outside, and the women separated from the men.

Michael searched frantically for his mother, who wore a red kerchief … but to his ever-mounting frustration and panic, so did every third woman in the courtyard that morning!

And what of the gray-bearded men who were unable to run as fast as the Nazis demanded? They paid for their lack of agility with a bullet to the head.

The group was marched to the cemetery and a few hours later Michael could hear the reverberations of distant gunfire. Afterwards there was an eerie calm and Michael's heart sank. His parents were probably on their way to Heaven, reasoned the desperately confused, newly minted Catholic boy—or wherever it was that Jews went...

LATE THAT SAME AFTERNOON, Tunis reappeared to fulfill his pledge to Meyer, by escorting Michael back to the ghetto. It was crucial to get Michael to a safe place, away from the *Judenrat* building or anywhere else he might be seen that day. But Tunis carried no "pass" for the child's return. As they neared "home," he instructed Michael to run toward the nearest point of entry, known only to Jewish children—and to rats.

Michael knew every twist and turn of the ghetto, and instinctively made his way back to where he had lived with his parents. He could think of no other place to go, no other place that he cared to be.

He opened the door, expecting only emptiness and squalor. But there, to his amazement, stood his mother. Had there ever been a more beautiful ghost? And Tato, she said, was also alive. He, along with the other men from that group, had been taken to the Kamionka slave labor camp, a notorious house of death.

Work at Kamionka centered around excavating a quarry under conditions that precluded survival. What worse place could there be—even in the Holocaust Kingdom—for a handicapped individual like Meyer Thaler?

Even in the abyss, Meyer's winning personality worked to his advantage. He persuaded the overseers to put him in charge of soup delivery to the workers in the quarry. This would save him from heavy labor and its natural outcome. It also afforded him the opportunity to quietly make an arrangement with a Ukrainian driver who transported the rocks out of the quarry.

The bookkeeper was able to leverage some "accounts payable" and make it worth the driver's while to deliver messages to his family in the Brzeżany ghetto. Meyer's most urgent communication was that he needed a pair of shoes, without which he would be unable to survive the remainder of the winter. As always, he understood the Nazi scheme, and realized that long-term survival was not an option in Kamionka. Escape was inconceivable without a pair of shoes.

To fulfill Meyer's instructions, Fanny, with the aid of her son, executed an ambitious plan fraught with danger. It was nothing less than a major engineering feat, one that involved escaping the ghetto, arriving undetected to the Holowinski's property (where the Thaler's possessions were stored), and smuggling the shoes into Kamionka.

And it was a plan blessed with miracles—because, astoundingly, it worked.

BY THE SUMMER OF 1943, survival in the ghetto was as perilous as in the slave camp. The initial Jewish population of over 10,000 souls had dwindled to a mere 2,500. *Aktion* followed *Aktion*, and the extermination of the last Jews of Brzeżany was no longer unthinkable. It was inevitable.

Fanny had received word that all of the Jews of the nearby town of Zborow, where her sister lived, had been liquidated. It was clear to her that the fall of Brzeżany was more imminent than she had dared imagine. To remain in the ghetto meant certain death; to attempt escape meant slightly less certain death. If Meyer was going to try and run away, she and Michael might as well try, too.

But what did "escape" mean in the absence of a secure destination? Fanny's only hope lay in the Holowinskis. Even if the Polish couple turned her away, she believed they would do anything to help Michael.

There was no luxury of waiting for the "right" moment. Whatever chance existed now, might not tomorrow.

In the dead of night, mother and son ran for their lives. Despite the boy's frequent exits and re-entries in the past, this maneuver was anything but routine—any error could be lethal.

Stealthily, Michael led his mother out of the ghetto. In many ways, he, like most children of war, hardly resembled a nine-year-old. But on this night, he childishly clutched under his arm his prized possession—his beloved stamp and postcard album.

It was an act that might have cost him his life.

For just as Michael crept outside the ghetto's walls, he encountered a gang of Polish teenagers eager to perform their civic duty. They surrounded the boy, grabbing at his collection. But it was practically the only remnant of the previous life that Michael remembered, and he refused to part with it. The thugs drew closer, cursing and menacing him.

Scrawny little Michael Thaler was hardly a match for the hulking youths. Violence, fatal violence, was in the air. Suddenly, Fanny Thaler emerged from the darkness. Under five feet tall and at far less than her pre-ghetto weight, she lunged like a lioness protecting her young, clawing at the assailants and gouging their eyes. Realistically, she could never have overpowered them. But remarkably, she frightened them enough to cause them to scatter.

Deeply shaken, Fanny hauled Michael back through the trapdoor in the wall, and they made their way back to their home in the ghetto. The mission had to be aborted.

Mother and son were petrified that the youths would not allow themselves to be out-maneuvered a second time and would be waiting in ambush. This fear, along with danger lurking throughout the route, foiled the next night's attempt at escape.

Finally, on the third night, the flight to freedom had a successful launch. From his father's careful instructions, Michael remembered the least-likely-to-be-detected route to the Holowinskis, one that involved crawling through fields, racing down alleyways, and jumping off roofs. Eventually they arrived at the home of the elderly couple.

Michael softly tapped on the windowpane and waited. When Mrs. Holowinski saw who it was, she was plunged into a terrible dilemma. The punishment for harboring a Jew was known to all, and the neighbors would not hesitate to inform on her and her husband. But the couple had grown to love the little boy whose face was pressed up against the glass, and they had wept bitterly the day that he left. He had filled their quiet house with a joy they had never known before.

The Holowinskis were also deeply touched that he had embraced the Catholic faith they held so dear.

Outside, shivering in the cold, was a boy they cherished, a source of pride and a redeemed soul. The choice was not an easy one. Then they saw that he was not alone, making the decision all that more difficult.

How could they accept Michael and send his mother to her death? Mrs. Holowinski had no time to weigh the issue as she stared at the two fugitives huddled on her doorstep. Her temporary solution was to send them to the barn. "Go, hide in the hayloft," she said in a hushed voice, "and do not stir!"

Fanny nodded and gazed at her with overwhelming gratitude. "Go now!" declared Mrs. Holowinski with great solemnity. "I have no idea that you exist!"

For two full days, mother and son lay motionless under the hay. On the third day, the ladder to the hayloft shook as if it were tapping out a secret code. Michael slithered to the edge of the loft and peeked down to the floor below. There, at the foot of the ladder, was a pail of milk and some bread that he quickly brought up to the hiding place.

On their fourth morning in the loft they were awakened at dawn by horrific screams and an incessant barrage of rifle-fire emanating from the nearby Jewish cemetery. Michael attempted to count the gunshots. They numbered over 2,000 before he finally gave up, hours later.

These were the final, agonizing sounds of the Jews of Brzeżany. They had been forced to undress—women, men and children together, standing naked and utterly defenseless. The dead and living fell together, on top of each other. Ghastly moans could be heard all day long.

The Nazis used machine guns to mow down those prisoners who tried to flee by climbing over the cemetery's walls. By midday the hill leading down from the cemetery was covered with naked corpses. The hundreds of bodies littering the hillside were but a small percentage of those who never made it out of the range of the guns.

Looking through the cracks of the hayloft, he could see nearby Polish and Ukrainian families assembled on their rooftops, holding up their young to get a better view of the massacre. The locals were indulging in the most gruesome sort of carnival to celebrate the barbarism, gleefully showing their children the Jews' naked, bloodied corpses. The

lack of shame, not to mention reprehension, at the commission of genocide upon innocent neighbors, coupled with the oddness of what the locals sought to show their children, proved yet again that the Ukrainians
eagerly condoned and applauded every atrocity the Nazis perpetrated
against the Jews.

The once-vibrant Jewish life of Brzeżany and its surrounding towns
had been extinguished, and the efficient murderers were ready to continue the extermination in other locations. But first, they had to make
sure that the numbers fully tallied. Based on their torture and interrogations they had determined that not all of the Jews were accounted for.

The SS made a stab at locating all of the hidden bunkers inside the
Brzeżany ghetto. But when they realized how labor-intensive it was,
they simply set the major buildings ablaze in the hope of smoking out
any remaining victims. Ultimately, this became standard procedure.

THAT NIGHT, Fanny and Michael were jolted from their fitful sleep
by the sound of coughing in the barn below them. Their blood ran
cold. Most likely it was a suspicious neighbor launching a Jew-hunt on
the premises. Or perhaps one of the Jews had managed to escape the
slaughter and had found shelter in the barn, exposing their hideaway.

Either way, the ultimate outcome would be the same for the hidden
duo in the hayloft: they would be discovered, and either killed on the
spot together with their hosts, or forced to flee the Holowinskis and
face the mortal dangers of the open road.

Mother and son were careful not to make a sound as they contemplated their final moments. In their ravaged state, they could not even
think of overpowering anyone, and to jump from the loft would have
been suicidal. But to remain in the line of sight, near the ladder, could
also be fatal.

Their only choice was to crawl in reverse, farther back in the loft.
They moved as quickly as they could, trying desperately not to make
a sound, but even the crackling of the straw sounded like church bells
pealing and was deafening to their ears.

All night they lay camouflaged beneath the hay, barely breathing.
They could hear the sounds of the intruder tossing and turning on the
dirt floor below.

Their very worst fears were realized in the morning when the intruder began to ascend the ladder. Frozen in terror, Fanny and Michael knew they were finished and the bile rose to their throats.

It never occurred to them that the intruder could be ... Meyer Thaler!

EARLIER THAT DAY, as the streets of his town ran with blood, Meyer Thaler had escaped from Kamionka and headed back to Brzeżany. His return trip was facilitated by the same Ukrainian truck driver who had served earlier as his courier.

Their first stop was the driver's home. Once there, the man told Meyer that he was going into town, and ordered him to hide under the bed, assuring him that he would return with the latest news of the ghetto. But first, the driver explained, he planned to stop in at the local tavern and spend the money that he had earned by transporting Meyer out of the camp.

The driver was true to his word and approached the ghetto for an update. He was not prepared for what he saw and heard. Witnessing the unrelenting violence being perpetrated against the last remaining members of the ghetto—elderly and babies alike—made the driver's notion of getting drunk no longer merely appealing, but mandatory.

He learned, too, that Meyer's brother-in-law, the richest Jew in town and head of the *Judenrat*, had led the condemned column to the cemetery. It was a classic hallmark of the Nazis to force the head of the community to walk at the front of the extermination march.

The shaken driver spent much of the evening in the tavern, attempting to forget what he had witnessed. Ironically, his boisterous drinking companions were the very perpetrators of the horrors. Alcohol was a staple in the SS—used first to fuel the officers who were engaged every day in murdering defenseless men, women and children, and afterwards, to celebrate their job well done. When the truck driver finally shuffled home, he told Meyer Thaler in a thick, slurring voice to run for his life, for there wasn't a single Jew left in the entire area.

And what of Meyer's wife and young son? The driver had asked several of the bystanders about the whereabouts of Fanny and Michael Thaler. Neither of them, he told Meyer, had been observed in the procession of the doomed. This information was enough to give him hope.

Meyer knew that if by some miracle his family had survived, there was only one place they might be. He made his way to the Holowinskis' home under the cover of night. Not wishing to wake or frighten the elderly couple, he slipped into the barn and slept on the floor directly beneath the hayloft.

IT WAS IN this barn that the family remained hidden for the next three weeks, surviving on the meager rations that their benefactors were able to spare. That they were finally reunited was a source of great comfort and hope to the Thalers. But all of them, including Michael, understood that the danger encircling them drew ever closer.

And then came that day, when shots and screams echoed throughout the nearby tracts of farming land. The Holowinskis rushed into the barn. "The Germans have surrounded our neighborhood," the ashen matron cried. "They are doing house-to-house searches!" The elderly couple was certain that an informer had betrayed them.

The Thalers ran out through the barn's back door and hid under a thicket of bushes that bordered the Holowinskis' property. As darkness fell, they tried to move further from the area that was saturated with Gestapo activity. Every avenue of escape was being systematically sealed. They were trapped in a dragnet, and if they didn't cover ground faster they would never make it through the night.

The only route still open was through the back of the Holowinskis' vegetable garden, and then up the hillside in the direction of the Jewish cemetery. All of the roads and paved areas were already closed. The darkness worked to their advantage—until Michael fell victim to a barbed-wire fence that surrounded the property.

Extricating the boy was a painstaking operation that made them all sitting ducks. Using force only impaled him more tightly on the barbs, with even greater reason to cry out in pain. Steadily prying Michael loose from the sharp daggers in the pitch-darkness, when every second felt like an eternity, was exquisite torture for them all.

Eventually, Meyer and Fanny managed to free their son, and the threesome dashed to the cemetery. Even before entering, they were nearly overcome by the fetid stench. Other potential dangers also lurked over the cemetery wall, as they would be trespassing into territory that ferocious dogs had staked out as their own. The plentiful flesh and bones amidst the gravestones did not diminish the hounds' hostility to intruders.

Choked by the unbearable odor, the Thalers nevertheless forced themselves to forge on and away from their pursuers, and they scaled the wall of the cemetery. What lay on the other side was the most macabre scene, defying all description. Once again, the darkness was a blessing.

Only a few weeks had passed since the massacre. Neighborhood youth had rummaged among the corpses looking for items of value, and the shallow mass grave was a feeding ground for carnivorous wildlife from the nearby woods. Alas, even in the dark, the sight was as grisly as it was ghostly.

Michael fell into the ghastly mush of decomposing corpses. Unable to get a foothold, he began to descend into a whirlpool of putrid, maggot-filled quicksand.

Together, Fanny and Meyer grabbed their son before he was inexorably swallowed, desperately struggling to position themselves lest they meet the same grotesque fate.

It was as though they had stumbled into Hell.

Through the graveyard, down the hill so recently strewn with corpses, and across the dark fields of the countryside they trudged, racing against time, exhaustion and terror. When they reached the forest beyond the fields, they were greeted by a cacophonous chorus.

The wrenching wails of Jewish babies rent the night. Some families had managed to escape to the woods, but they could not feed their children or alleviate their fears.

Although the Thalers had now put a reasonable distance between themselves and the Gestapo, their situation had not vastly improved. Aside from the obvious perils of exposure and starvation, they were also fair game for the predatory shepherd boys who zealously combed the woods, hoping to earn the price placed upon every Jewish head.

The Thalers had survived until that point because of a healthy dose of luck, a few well-placed miracles, and one additional factor: the bold and clear-headed strategic thinking of Meyer Thaler.

It was readily apparent to Meyer that the forest was a death trap and that the family would probably not survive the night under the stars.

The stench emanating from Michael would attract the creatures of the forest, which would finish him off even before the Gestapo.

And then the rain came. The unrelenting downpour made the need for shelter even more urgent.

Meyer's mind raced until one desperate possibility finally occurred to him. His father had been a tanner and had had dealings with many of the farmers in the area. It was time to call in a favor, a huge favor, and at the same time deplete the last of the valuables that they possessed.

WITH TREMENDOUS TREPIDATION, but prodded by survival instincts of the highest order, the family approached a farmer who lived on the edge of the forest. Meyer's father's connections, two generations of goodwill, plus Fanny's diamond ring earned the Thalers a one-week stay in the rear section of the farmer's barn. The shed was partitioned between the various animals that it housed. In the front were the horses, cows and pigs and in the back was the poultry division.

The Thalers were quartered with the chickens, and they would receive their "feed" (a small amount of gruel) each morning when the farmer came to tend to his animals. One morning, as Michael was looking forward to his daily ration, he heard vehicles outside. Through the cracks in the barn wall he was able to see that the building was being surrounded by German troops.

Michael heard a Nazi officer ask the farmer if there were any Jews inside. He had no idea if the Germans had been tipped off to look specifically for them, or if they were just methodically doing their primary duty.

It hardly mattered, for the soldiers had entered the barn hell-bent on their mission. All of the white-knuckled close calls that the family had endured paled before this final attempt to cheat the inevitable. Michael began praying fervently, calling up all his Catholic and Jewish devotions.

But as they entered the barn, the Nazis' search for the Jewish enemies of the state appeared to be put on hold. The Thalers could hear them become very animated, and even start to cheer. There, before their very eyes, stood a lavish feast on four legs. The farmer was harboring an unbranded calf—a punishable offense, since the occupying forces had mandated that all livestock be registered (and thus available for seizure). But this was one misdemeanor that the troops would deal with themselves without involving headquarters.

The hunt for Jews would resume later; for now, there was a tender young animal to be roasted over the fire, upon whose flesh the indulgent soldiers would gorge.

The sacrificial calf provided a stay of the Thaler family execution, but it was necessary to act immediately, for the stay would only be brief. At nightfall they crept from the barn, heading to ... heading to the only choice they had. Clandestinely and meticulously they retraced the exact route that they had taken one week earlier.

They returned to the Holowinskis in the hours before dawn. It was pitch-black inside the barn as they made their way back to their familiar hiding place up in the loft.

But in the morning would they be greeted with consternation and brusquely sent away? Over and over, they had endangered the lives of these simple folk.

Based upon the histrionics of Mrs. Holowinski when she discovered them the next morning, the Thalers knew that they had reached the end of the road. They had no more money or possessions to pay for their keep, and winter was coming. They would not survive outdoors. After four years of fire, their resolve was ash. There was a modicum of solace that their end would come in this familiar place.

The old woman ran for her husband and he joined her in the barn. They crossed themselves, dropped to their knees, railed and wailed. The prayers were unending and Meyer and Fanny hadn't a clue what service was being offered—even their "Catholic" son was at a loss. The consensus was that it was a devotion associated with the Last Rights for non-believers.

There was something bizarre about this religious send-off the Holowinskis were orchestrating for them. True, the old couple had ordered them out and they had nonetheless returned, but it still would have been far more elegant to collaborate with the Nazis—or at least protect their own interests—without invoking all of this religious mumbo-jumbo.

Upon reflection, the end of the road suddenly did not look so bleak. The emotional upheavals of the last few days had taken their toll, and the family was finally ready to succumb. They had pitched a valiant battle, but had depleted their will to fight on in the process.

Just as Meyer was preparing his parting speech, the Polish couple offered a brief translation and synopsis of their prayers.

They were passionately thanking God for saving the Thalers, as they had been unable to sleep at night for having cast out the family to face a gruesome death. The two were certain that they would burn in Hell for their evil deed and never be allowed to repent. And since all the Jews that they had ever known had been murdered, it was clearly a miracle and the Thalers had risen from the dead.

The Holowinskis were consumed by contrition and solemnly swore to shelter the Thalers from then on. They remained true to their word until the arrival of the Red Army in July, 1944.

AS SOON AS the area was liberated from the Nazis, the few Jews who had managed to escape emerged from hiding. Once again, Meyer Thaler's insight into events proved lifesaving. He would not allow his family out into the open until the Russians were in control for a full two weeks. He reasoned that the battlefront might shift, and the Germans could launch a successful counter-offensive.

Tragically, this is precisely what happened. In nearby Tarnopol, nearly a thousand Jews emerged from hiding to hail their liberators, and when the area was recaptured by the Nazis, they were all murdered.

When Brzeżany came under Russian control for the second time, Meyer resumed his two-week, wait-and-see policy. After fourteen days it was very clear that the Germans had truly retreated and were running for their lives away from the Russians.

Once again, Meyer wisely understood the new reality that was unfolding. The family was finally safe, but they were not free. The head of the Thaler household knew what had to be done next. It was time to resume their trek—this time away from the Iron Curtain.

EPILOGUE

The Thalers moved to Western Poland in 1945, when Brzeżany became part of the Soviet Union. They emigrated from Poland later that year, ending up in an Austrian DP camp. The Holowinskis also moved to Western Poland, where they died in the 1960's. The Thaler family finally left Europe in March, 1948, settling in Toronto, Canada. Michael received a world-class education in Toronto, earning an M.D. degree in 1958. He moved to the United States for postdoctoral training and launched a distinguished career in academic medicine.

Until his retirement in 1998, Michael was a Professor of Pediatrics and Chief of the Division of Pediatric Gastroenterology and Nutrition at the University of California in San Francisco, where he still resides with his wife, their two children and two grandchildren. Currently, Michael is a Visiting Professor of History and Jewish Studies at the University of California in Santa Cruz, California. He is also active in Jewish affairs, having served as president of the Holocaust Center of Northern California for 12 years.

Meyer Thaler died of a heart attack in 1974; his wife Fanny passed away in 1999, just ten days before her 92nd birthday.

Disharmony

Cecelia

This is a story of utter, crashing disharmony.
Every individual engulfed by the Holocaust was wrenched from free-
dom to servitude, from sustenance to starvation, from the cradle of
family to horrifying isolation. But for some, this polarity was so pro-
nounced that it resounds deafeningly throughout the tale. The din is
the clash between high culture and the basest inhumanity, between
the exquisite, quavering notes of a violin concerto, and the sobs of two
terrified sisters—homeless and hunted, in the belly of the Nazi beast.

Even at the age of six, Cecilia Gradis displayed the mark of virtuosity
as she brought her delicate instrument to her chin, and the bow to the
strings. Little Cecilia's musicianship went beyond technical skill and
stylistic flair. When the petite child played—brown eyes closed, dark
hair gleaming—her violin became an extension of her very soul, luring
her audience into believing that they had been admitted to heaven. She
played with a passion and complexity beyond her tender years, creating
instrumentation so breathtaking that hills and mesas of music arose
from an ocean of silence.

The Gradis' prominent apartment resounded with music and culture. It occupied the entire second floor of a handsome building in the
thriving, cosmopolitan city of Daugavpils. "Dvinsk," as it was far better
known in Yiddish, was the Latvian center of commerce and Jewish life,

with Jews comprising nearly half the city's 100,000 inhabitants. Shraga Feivish Gradis (known to his neighbors as "Pavel"), a prosperous textile merchant who hailed originally from Moscow, was determined that his wife Rochel and their three accomplished daughters (Liza and Nadia, both teenagers, and Cecilia, the precocious "baby") would have the best that life had to offer.

The girls attended private schools and were given individual lessons according to their talents. The parents' greatest joy was to sit in their salon enjoying pastries prepared by Nadia (who was gifted in the domestic arts and in business), as Lisa sat at a fine Blutner piano, beautifully accompanying Cecilia's dazzling strings. The family's beloved housekeeper Fedora, who had served them faithfully for years, would stand by, beaming and applauding.

All three girls were lovely and bright and artistic, but Cecilia was the definition of a prodigy. When she was just eight, the little girl—to the delight of Shraga Feivish and Rochel—was accepted to the prestigious Music Conservatory in Dvinsk. She became the prized pupil of an esteemed master-teacher, Professor Paul Kruminsh.

The child possessed yet another distinction within the Conservatory's student body. The year was 1936, and she had been the only Jew even to be auditioned, let alone accepted. By the time Cecilia was twelve, Professor Kruminsh understood that for all his musicianship, he and Cecilia's principal tutor, Professor Adolph Metz, had nothing left to teach their brilliant young protégé. She had outgrown everything that the Dvinsk Conservatory had to offer.

From the professor's perspective, there was only one logical next step for a student with the promise of Cecilia Gradis: the world-renowned National Conservatory in Riga, under the direction of the leading maestro of the Baltic States.

When Kruminsh broached the subject with Cecilia, she declared the notion absurd. A Jewish girl, little more than a child, admitted to this world-class institution, at a time when Jews were being spat upon in the streets?

She conveyed her skepticism to her father, but found no ally in Shraga Feivish Gradis. His own passion for classical music was the main reason his daughters had been introduced to lessons at such an early age. The man was practically delirious that one of his own children might study at the National Conservatory under the revered maestro, a star of unequalled brilliance. And surely then Cecilia's own star would rise, reflecting some of that brilliance…

For Jewish parents in those dark years, optimism did not come easily. World War I had dealt a body-blow to Europe and a virtual knockout to its Jewish inhabitants. Everyone had suffered, but the Jews had suffered the most, as victims of pillage and plunder by all of the warring parties. How were they to know that the future had something far more gruesome in store?

But for one delicious moment, Shraga Feivish and Rochel Gradis could hope and dream. Though their daughter was the youngest applicant to the Conservatory that year, her audition was flawless and she was admitted with ease. She became one of only two Jewish students in the entire school.

Housing was not a problem, as Cecilia's beloved "aunt and uncle," Shmuel and Ida Weinberg (actually her father's cousins), lived in Riga. Boarding with them was a pleasure, and in tandem with her musical studies, they enrolled her in Latvia's finest educational institution for girls. Every morning she would immerse herself in the academic disciplines at the highest levels, and in the afternoons, she attended the Conservatory.

For Cecilia Gradis, the next five years were filled with great literature and performance, culture and musicology, language and science, etiquette and refinement. She was being groomed for an exceptional life.

But there are some lives for which there can be no preparation.

ON JUNE 22, 1941, Germany invaded Russia. The conquest of neighboring Latvia was an integral part of the battle plan. It had taken the Germans less than a day to conquer all of Lithuania, and Latvia could not expect a better fate.

Only a few hours into the onslaught, German paratroopers and saboteurs had infiltrated Riga and were poised in attics and on rooftops, ready to shoot down anyone who stood in their way. Simultaneously, dozens of Junker and Heinkel fighter-bombers roared over the streets and squares of the city. They dropped bombs from both high altitudes and close range; they strafed the boulevards and buildings, indiscriminately killing civilians.

They also dropped tens of thousands of leaflets denouncing Jews, sternly warning the locals not to assist "the enemy" in evacuation.

From the outbreak of the fighting, 17-year-old Cecilia Gradis was desperate to return to her parents. The Weinbergs pleaded with her to stay but their appeal fell on deaf ears. Violin in hand, Cecilia boarded a train bound for Dvinsk. She had no inkling at the time that this was the very last train before commercial rail travel to the region would be suspended under the German occupation.

At home, Cecilia was greeted with mixed emotions by her parents and Nadia. (Liza had already married and was living with her husband, an attorney, in Kovno.) "My child, what are you doing here?" her father demanded. "You have yet to finish your exams!"

"For God's sake, Shraga," Rochel interjected, "there's a war going on! You see how many refugees have fled to here from Lithuania—obviously Latvia is next."

Shraga Feivish conceded that Cecilia should stay, but nevertheless he chose not to dwell on his pragmatic wife's predictions, just for that one night. He set aside all thoughts of the gathering storm, and quietly exulted in the return of his daughter and in the heartbreakingly beautiful, plaintive wail of her instrument.

The very next morning, the Germans marched into Dvinsk. As always, their first order of business was the systematic elimination of the Jews.

Dvinsk in July of 1941 had the feel of a furnace. For one, it was the hottest summer in the region's recorded history and a blistering sun beat down upon the city.

Compounding the heat and the horror of the occupation were ubiquitous fires—lingering reminders of the Russian Army, which had torched numerous neighborhoods during its hasty retreat. The homes of many Jewish families were left burning, or as smoldering heaps of ash.

LIKE IN RIGA, VILNA, KOVNO and in so many of the Baltic cities, Nazi oppression of the Jews began with the edicts of isolation. The Jews had to be gathered and accounted for in preparation for their imminent extermination. The decrees of isolation were eagerly enforced by the locals, who lacked none of the cruelty or zeal of the invaders.

The Latvians knew who the Jews were and where they lived, and they provided this information with diabolical efficiency. By mid-July they would be tagged in front and back with the emblem of the yellow star, ensuring that the defenseless Jews could neither hide nor escape.

The world closed in.

Large posters in German, Russian and Latvian were plastered throughout town, ordering all Jewish men up to age sixty to report to the central marketplace, a large open square where farmers from the surrounding villages once came to sell their fresh wares. Failure to appear would result in execution.

Leaving the terrified women and children huddled in whichever apartments remained habitable, the Jewish men, some cowering, others hopeful about the German promises not to harm those who worked, were rounded up and delivered to the marketplace, one by one. Among them were Shraga Feivish Gradis and his brother, Max.

First the prisoners were forced to labor in the scorching streets, clearing the rubble from the shelling and burying the corpses that littered the square. Hours later they were herded to a massive warehouse that served as a jail. Every window was sealed and the heat inside was unbearable. Crowded inside this filthy, decrepit building, which the Germans themselves had declared unsuitable even for horses, the prisoners were systematically tortured and humiliated.

The drunken German and Latvian guards called it "sport." To the Jews it meant merciless beatings and degradation—they were forced to hop like frogs and to make bizarre grimaces and gestures. The beards of the religious ones were ripped out by the roots.

In their final moments, just before they were shot, the prisoners were commanded to shout *"Heil Hitler!"* and to sing the Nazi anthem *Horst Wessel Lied* and extol *Deutschland, Deutschland, über alles.*

During the chaotic transfer of one labor battalion from the market-square to cellblock, several of its members managed, miraculously, to escape. Shraga Feivish Gradis and his brother were among them. Home they fled, to wives and children who sobbed with relief, having feared the worst. Breathlessly, the two men began to report the horrors they had witnessed, grateful that their own homes remained intact.

But the reunion was cut short by a fierce pounding on the door. Six Latvian brutes wearing Nazi armbands invaded the house and ordered everyone to leave "without taking a thing." Despite the intense heat, through force of habit Cecilia's mother innocently reached for her coat. "*I told you not to touch a thing!*" snapped one of the thugs, brutally slapping her repeatedly with an open hand while her horrified family watched in stunned silence, helpless to intervene.

Rochel Gradis reeled with pain, but inwardly she clung to a small sense of triumph, for she had managed to foil the intruders in another way: just one day earlier, she had given all of the family's valuables to the gentile neighbors downstairs for safekeeping. Educated, wealthy and kind, the Shevelkovs had been happy to perform this surreptitious deed.

THAT NIGHT, like every other Jewish family in Dvinsk, the Gradises were herded inside the synagogue of the spiritual giant of Dvinsk, Rabbi Meir Simcha HaCohen, who had been known as the *Ohr Somayach*. At the turn of the century, the *Ohr Somayach* and the *Rogachover Gaon*, Rabbi Yosef Rosen, had transformed Dvinsk into one of the world's greatest Torah centers, famous among scholarly Jews all over the world.

Echoing the moniker of the esteemed rabbi, this shul had long been a repository of "joy" and "light," a second home to many of these families. The rhythm and fabric of their lives had reverberated within its dignified, albeit humble, walls. There they had consecrated their marriages, named their babies, celebrated the festivals and ushered in the holy Sabbath.

But on this day, the appalling scene defied description. Wailing babies clung to their desperate mothers, children were struck dumb with terror, and the old people trembled and sagged. In this moment, all that had come before—all of life—receded, as if it had been only a dream.

And then came the next blood-curdling order.

All of the remaining males, including the little boys, were swiftly and brutally separated from the women. The armed guards made it clear that any protest would be dealt with severely and immediately. Thus the women had no choice but to watch in terrified silence as their sons and husbands were led mutely away.

They were not given even a minute to say good-bye. But as Shraga Feivish Gradis was pushed with the others towards the exit, he pressed a handkerchief into his daughter's hand. Inside its folds he had camou-flaged his ornate gold timepiece.

"Why, Papa?" Cecilia whispered. "Why are you giving me your watch?"

For Shraga Feivish this was the final round. He had already experienced enough to crush any illusion that there would be another escape from his bloodthirsty captors. "Give it to Mama," he said hoarsely. "I won't be needing a watch anymore..."

Those were his final words to his family.

That night, Shraga Feivish Gradis and all the others—sons and fathers, husbands and brothers, grandfathers and grandsons—met their deaths in a nearby forest. The Jewish women and girls of Dvinsk, like all women of their day—whether resourceful or retiring, independent spirits or homebodies—had relied upon these men as their protectors. As they watched them file out of the shul, broken and haggard, a new level of terror rose in their throats. Commensurately, the next level of horror began.

USING FOUL LANGUAGE that was designed to humiliate—language that few, if any, of these genteel, pious females had ever heard before—the Germans bellowed at their prisoners to extend their hands so that rings, watches and bracelets could be confiscated. Earrings and necklaces were torn off, as insults and vulgar curses were hurled without respite. Cecilia Gradis and her sister Nadia could do nothing but cling to their mother, all of their senses assaulted and debased by the mayhem.

Every moment of this awful night was devoted to the fulfillment of Nazi racist ideology. After the women were stripped of every item of value, they were forced to watch as the soldiers wrenched the Torah scrolls from the Ark, shredding and trampling them in a gruesome dance. Hour after hour, the women prayed silently for their captors to tire, for there to be a break in the thunderous shouting, the random beatings, the leering and grabbing and foul vilification. But none came. The soldiers' venomous hatred and rage was only stoked by the helplessness and fear of their captives.

As dawn seeped through the synagogue's smashed windows, orders came for work parties to be formed. There was no shortage of volunteers, as no one wished to spend another minute inside the dese-crated building.

Cecilia and Nadia were separated from their mother. Throughout the sweltering day, their group was forced to scrub the streets, which were covered in blood and debris.

Towards evening, the sisters returned with their fellow workers to the synagogue.

As before, the sanctuary was crowded with frightened women and girls. For Cecilia and Nadia Gradis, it took a moment for a horrifying realization to sink in: they knew no one else in this room. Their mother was gone, and so were all the women and girls who had surrounded them throughout their young lives: their schoolmates, neighbors and teachers, and the rebbetzins, seamstresses and shopkeepers of Dvinsk. This was a new roundup of women, obviously taken from the Jewish neighborhoods of surrounding towns.

The Gradis sisters felt utterly alone and struggled against their mounting panic. Though the younger of the two, Cecilia had seen more of the world and was bolder. Peering out of the windows, she saw that night had not yet fallen. "Nadia, look, look up at the sky!" she pleaded, unleashing the imagery of her creative soul. "The sky is yet blue and there is still so much time for us to live. We're too young to die now! There are free people in other parts of the world, places the Nazis have not conquered. *We must get out of here!*"

"Stop your nonsense, child," uttered Nadia in a robotic voice. "What will be, will be."

Cecilia Gradis had been raised to heed her elders, but in this sense-less, random new world, different rules would have to apply. She re-fused to spend another torturous night of degradation. The young girl left her sister's side and marched up to the Latvian collaborators who were standing guard. In perfect Latvian that had been refined through her education—devoid of the heavy Yiddish accent that immediately gave away the ancestry of most Dvinsker Jews—she asked them if she and her sister could leave.

It was an absurd request, and each guard conveyed as much by his incredulity and contempt. But Cecilia remained undaunted. She knew that there was nothing to lose.

Then to the sisters' amazement, one guard tersely barked at them to go. Others within earshot jumped at the opportunity, but only the Gradis sisters were freed.

Perhaps it was a twinge of conscience on the part of this guard, or perhaps he simply understood what the two girls had not yet processed—that without a home to return to, or parents to look after them, their chances of survival were as slim outside as inside the airless holding pen, the once-elegant synagogue of the *Ohr Somayach*.

The two stepped outside and immediately unpinned the yellow stars from each other's clothing. This act alone was a capital crime in Nazi-occupied Europe, but so was their very existence! They had already vaulted for freedom and there was no turning back. Feverishly, they began to formulate a plan to survive.

But who could help them? The daily lives of Shraga Feivish Gradis and his family, like the generations before them, had been circumscribed by their religion. They had always relied upon their fellow Jews in times of crisis, but now there were no Jews left to turn to. It was only Cecilia who had ventured out into the greater world, its doors opened by her music.

Professor Paul Kruminsh!

In the past, even with the clouds of anti-Semitism already gathering, her beloved teacher had supported her. Cecilia instinctively trusted that he would not betray her now. Besides, she had no other alternative.

With hearts beating like a drum and eyes glued to the ground, the sisters surreptitiously made their way to the professor's nearby home. When Kruminsh opened the door, not a word was said. By not turning them away, Kruminsh understood that he was risking his own life, and his family's.

The girls were directed into the farthest room and instructed not to make a sound. They crawled under low beds and remained there, motionless.

For the next few weeks they stayed with Kruminsh, but this dangerous arrangement could not last. Reluctantly, the sisters made their way to the Dvinsk ghetto, where nearly all the remaining Jews of the city and its surroundings were being warehoused. The contemptuous laughter of the townspeople rang in their ears as they neared its walls.

The ghetto was a former stable and had not been cleaned since the horses were supplanted by the frightened Jews, who now slept huddled on the filthy straw.

Each day, workers were taken out of the ghetto to perform menial labor throughout the city. Nadia and Cecilia worked in an apartment where a group of German soldiers were housed. They washed the men's clothes, scrubbed their floors and their toilets. A soldier mentioned to Cecilia that she and her sister were the fifth "cleaning service" who had been assigned to them.

"Where are the other women?" Cecilia asked.

"*Kaput!*" said the soldier, cryptically. Cecilia understood that the other workers had been killed. She cried inside, at first refusing to return to the ghetto. But there was no other option.

Meanwhile, Kruminsh was carefully reaching out to a select group of friends. Among them was a young clerk in the passport office, a former student of his who had been working overtime since the fires had destroyed the identity papers of so many citizens. He was easily able to produce realistic-looking documents attesting that these girls' identities were Lydia Kruminsh (Cecilia) and Irini Liepens (Nadia), the nieces of Paul Kruminsh.

The plan was to send the girls, with papers in hand, to a close friend of the professor's, a chemist in nearby Kraslova. The man had already contributed to their cause, in a manner that was unthinkable except in those unthinkable times. Via Kruminsh, the chemist had sent the girls a weapon from his professional arsenal: two cyanide tablets.

Who would believe that two girls in the bloom of youth would consider this deadly substance a Godsend and a panacea? From the day Kruminsh solemnly furnished them, the pills would always remain in reach. It comforted Cecilia and Nadia to know that they had the means to escape torture and prevent their betrayal of those who had so selflessly helped them; the pills would enable them to take risks that they otherwise would have been afraid to attempt. The pills had come with very explicit instructions: if the girls were ever captured and interrogated, they must immediately take their "medicine" lest they reveal who had harbored them.

But just as everything was ready for the move to Kraslova, Kruminsh learned that the girls' papers were invalid. A newly issued law required the subject's photograph to be affixed to all documents, and that the documents be signed by the bearer in person at the passport office.

The professor brought home a camera with a tripod and photographed the girls himself. He also saw to it that each paper was notarized by two witnesses who could testify to the identity of the bearer. Kruminsh served as the first witness, and, marshaling his connections, arranged for none other than a policeman, Leon Pawlowich, to be the second. Paul Kruminsh, *maestro extraordinaire*, did not want a single false note.

Therefore, he jeopardized his own safety by accompanying his "nieces" to the passport office—the final leg of this operation—where they needed to sign their papers.

The passport office was located inside the police station. Its walls were plastered with newsprint collages of the infamous anti-Semitic Nazi newspaper *Der Stürmer's* choicest caricatures, depicting Jews as hook-nosed devils and parasites.

Cecilia and Nadia managed to appear natural and composed, but soon after their arrival, clerks began emerging from their offices to stare at the girls, point fingers, and converse in hushed tones. Something was clearly amiss. Kruminsh wandered into a back room to see if he could figure out what it was.

The tension rose to a horrible crescendo when he shuffled back into the waiting room, looking paler than they had ever seen him. Not daring to even make eye contact with Cecilia or Nadia, Kruminsh walked unsteadily toward the exit. As he passed them, he muttered in a barely audible tone, "Girls, girls, it's no good..."

And then Professor Kruminsh disappeared into the street. The girls later found out that he was briefly taken into custody that same day and questioned about the role he had played in procuring their false papers.

Someone had recognized Cecilia Gradis as the little Jewish violinist who had performed onstage. The sisters were summarily arrested and placed in separate jail cells.

FOR THE NEXT ten days and nights, they heard the ceaseless screams and wails of prisoners being beaten and molested. The sounds of torture were unrelenting and unbearable: the snap of whips, the slap of rubber hoses and the thud of blunt objects, intermingled with pleas for mercy and loud prayers for Divine intervention. Several times a day, the girls were interrogated, and each time, they stuck to their story: they were not Jewish and this was all a terrible mistake. And each day, they feared the brutal punishment that loomed ever closer.

Enduring day after day in the torturous prison traumatized Cecilia so profoundly that she began to give up her will to live. A deep despair settled upon her and she started to mourn her own death. She prayed to God that she be spared the agony of those in the neighboring cells. The cyanide pill was tucked inside her clothing. But she had not yet summoned up the courage to take it. Soon ... soon ...

On the eleventh day of captivity, when a German officer entered her cell, Cecilia had no doubt about why he had come. His appearance would have instilled panic in even the most self-assured adult: he was tall and wore a long black leather coat, gleaming boots, and was covered in intimidating SS insignia and medals.

"Have you come to kill me?" Cecilia blurted out.

The man's expression was flat and unreadable. "On the contrary—I am the bearer of good news," he responded in perfect Latvian. "It appears that you are going to be released."

Cecilia could barely breathe. Was this some kind of cruel Nazi joke? She had no idea if she could trust this officer, who continued, "of course, I am unable to release you personally as this is a police matter."

"Where will they take me?" Cecilia pressed.

"If you are a Latvian—and by the sound of it, you are—you will be released," he declared. "But if you are really a Jew, you will be sent to the ghetto."

"And what about my sister?"

"The same applies to her."

Cecilia's mind raced. She was convinced that Professor Kruminsh, whose contacts were well placed in all strata of society, was quietly behind this extraordinary turn of events. Later that same day she and Nadia were transferred to the police station and interrogated over and over. The sisters' responses were identical and never wavered.

They were released to the custody of their "uncle," Paul Kruminsh, and everything that had been confiscated upon their arrest was returned to them.

The professor knew that it was only a matter of time before the truth about the Gradis sisters would be discovered. During their imprisonment, he had sought a more out-of-the-way refuge. Overnight, the girls were moved to a little village where they were sheltered by peasants who had no idea that they were Jews.

The girls were sent to work in a flourmill, and one afternoon, a Latvian peasant woman came to accompany them to a new lodging. Their route led through a thick forest. At one point along the way, the woman paused before a parcel of land that was bare of trees or any other foliage. "Look here, girls!" she exclaimed, pointing to the barren expanse. "This here is a lucky spot."

Cecilia and Nadia stared uncomprehendingly, until the woman began to elaborate with glee: *"Right over there it happened—that's where they shot the Jews! Hundreds, maybe thousands, who could count? Women and children, mostly ... heaved right into the pit and buried alive, most of them."*

Both girls immediately felt like they might faint. Sharp cramps nearly overtook them. Their guide spared no detail describing the orgy of slaughter, certain that these good Christian daughters would take pride in her revelations.

"Goodness, you girls missed quite a scene!" she chortled. "The ground shook for three full days and you could hear their moaning for tens of kilometers in every direction. What a ruckus!"

Cecilia and Nadia Gradis wanted to tear their clothes in an act of mourning, to scream and to weep, to throw their bodies on top of the churned brown earth. Instead, they forced themselves to giggle.

THE DAYS IN HIDING turned into months. The oppressive summer turned into fall, and then a bitterly cold winter. Cecilia and Nadia traveled from hovel to hovel, sleeping on floors or under beds. Some of their benefactors were friends of Kruminsh returning a favor; others were destitute peasants in desperate need of the few coins the sisters could spare for lodging.

One exceptionally brutal winter day, their hostess received a warning that the Germans were going to inspect the area that evening. Without a flicker of remorse, she demanded that the girls leave her house immediately and never return.

Once again the sisters found themselves outdoors without a course of action. Their despair jagged through them like a thunderbolt. Shivering in the plummeting afternoon temperatures, they realized that this time, the elements were also their enemy. Without a roof over their heads they would not survive the night.

There was little hope and nothing to lose. Fitfully they began to debate plans of last resort. And then they remembered Fedora.

The idea of seeking shelter from a woman who had served as their family's maid and nanny for years was theoretically reasonable. Fedora was a jovial woman who had ample reason to show appreciation to a family that had always treated her with generosity and respect. But then, so did countless other Latvians who had been aided by Jewish physicians, professionals and employers. This did not prevent them from leaping to collaborate with the Nazis.

Fedora lived in Dvinsk, a distance that was manageable on foot for an individual with a full stomach, warm clothing, sturdy shoes, and hours of daylight ahead. The Gradis sisters had none of those advantages, and the winter days were short; yet their journey was remarkably without incident.

At the entrance to the city, however, their hopes plummeted. The bridge leading into Dvinsk was heavily guarded. It was of strategic military importance, and Cecilia and Nadia watched in horror as every vehicle and pedestrian underwent meticulous scrutiny.

The sisters had nowhere to go back to, and no way to go forward.

The air was cold and sharp, and the moon settling over Dvinsk was nearly full. Tiny needles of frost pricked the girls' nostrils and lungs as they lowered their weary, defeated bodies onto an embankment covered with a thick blanket of hardened snow. A pristine layer of powder had fallen in the last hour and glittered in the moonlight. Snowflakes pirouetted and their breath hung in the wind. Up ahead, the icy river, the soaring bridge, even the soldiers, all appeared frozen in a dreamlike tableau.

For a fleeting moment, in all this aching beauty, their suffering receded. A curious feeling of calm warmed the two sisters. They gave each other a long, knowing look. It was over. It was better it should end this way. Here. Now.

Slowly and deliberately, Cecilia and Nadia removed the cyanide tablets from the hiding places inside their garments. Together, they began to recite the *Shema*, the classic prayer affirming the oneness of the Almighty. Lying together on a thick bed of snow, they were prepared to die.

Suddenly, the night was pierced by a screech of tires and thunderous shouts.

The startled sisters observed that a military truck approaching the bridge had skidded across the ice and had become wedged in a snow-drift, nearly tipping over.

Apparently, the truck was laden with "precious cargo": a large crew of Russian POWs. All of the soldiers manning the checkpoint sprinted toward the vehicle to extricate it from the snow.

Cecilia and Nadia Gradis instantly understood that the God whom they had praised moments earlier had other plans for them. They crammed the cyanide back inside their clothing and hurried, unnoticed, across the bridge and into Dvinsk.

With the miracle of their safe passage and the bittersweet feeling of "home," the sisters were bolstered by a renewed sense of hope. By the time they located their former nanny's house, the streets had been dark for hours. Fedora opened the door, and her jaw dropped.

"I … I … j-just c-cannot …" she stammered. But the girls would not budge from the doorway.

"You must understand," Fedora said gently, "my daughter-in-law lives nearby and she hates me. If she discovers you are here, she will have us all killed instantly."

"But we will be *so* quiet," Cecilia pleaded. "No one will know … We won't eat a thing, we'll stay under your bed and not stir!"

Fedora did not dare continue the conversation in full view of the neighbors. Reluctantly, she allowed the girls inside and quickly latched the door.

For that one night they had found shelter. In the world of the fugitives that they had become—in which all were united in their pursuit—one night, even one minute, could mean the difference between life and death.

ON THE FOLLOWING DAY, Cecilia's faithful patron, Professor Kruminsh, acting from then on through connections in the underground, located another refuge, this time in the nearby village of Kalkuni.

Their host this time was a black-marketeer who traded in the most lucrative and sought-after commodity of the times: food. Meat, especially, was difficult for ordinary citizens to obtain, as it was earmarked for the military's consumption. And so, hidden inside the house, along with the Gradis sisters, were containers of meat and sacks of potatoes, smuggled in at great risk and sold at great profit.

One day, Cecilia was alone in the house when their host unexpectedly came home. Wordlessly he stripped off his shirt. She was paralyzed with fear as he came near. Miraculously, the next moment, his wife entered the house, along with Nadia. Once again, Cecilia was convinced, God had interceded in her favor.

Then one quiet evening the girls heard footsteps and voices outside. They immediately dove behind a threadbare curtain. Moments later, storm troopers broke into the house. An informer (a woman who had begged the host for a little meat, and had been refused) had revealed the man's black market activities.

Working on this disgruntled lady's tip, the SS was dispatched to arrest the culprit and confiscate his goods. The SS men strode through the apartment in their heavy boots, bellowing curses and using their weapons to poke and overturn furniture. Behind the curtain, their frail bodies pressed to the wall, Cecilia and Nadia stared at each other in horror. They had little doubt that the men were about to uncover far more contraband than they had ever imagined. Once again the cyanide tablets emerged; and in a silent but furious pantomime the two sisters debated when to perform their final act on earth.

They could hear the SS troopers drawing closer to the corner of the room where they crouched, and they held their breaths. Every strained nerve ending felt like it was on fire. Was this the moment?

Crash!

One of the men tripped over a crate that stood near the curtain. His body was splayed just inches from Cecilia, separated by only a filmy screen. Suddenly, his rants turned to triumphant laughter. The crate contained the cache of meat they had been searching for. The Nazis grabbed their find, hoisted it into the air and departed.

Once again, a miracle had saved them. But there was not a moment for rejoicing. Their lives were still in danger, and they did not dare remain in a hiding place where the owner was a wanted criminal.

The sisters' wanderings continued, from stranger to stranger. In these times, who could be trusted? Good and evil were indistinguishable. An angel could be found in the unexpected form of a black-marketeer, and a sympathetic cleric could be the devil in disguise.

PROFESSOR KRUMINSH was himself under the scrutiny of the authorities and had lost most of his influence, but he remained steadfast in his devotion to his former protégé and her sister. Their chances of survival if they remained in Latvia were nil, Kruminsh concluded, so he sought a way to smuggle them out of the country.

The key to the girls' escape would be Leon Pawlowich, the policeman who had co-notarized their false identity papers. He had since been stripped of his badge and demoted to a train conductor. In his routine runs between Latvia and Poland, this courageous civil servant covertly aided the Polish underground.

Pawlowich was a crucial contact, for the girls' false papers were long gone, and the journey was extremely risky and subject to frequent identity inspections. Pawlowich secured two train tickets and arranged that his connections in Vilna, Lithuania, would find yet another safe house for the two sisters.

After all they had endured, Cecilia and Nadia were unsentimental about leaving the land of their birth. There was but one piece of unfinished business.

They hadn't forgotten that the Gradis family's valuables had been given to kindly neighbors for safekeeping. The sisters prayed that these fine people, the Shevelkovs, had been able to hold these goods over the half-year that had passed. They had no other possessions in the world, and desperately needed whatever they could lay their hands on in order to survive in a foreign land where they did not know a soul.

Quietly they returned to their former building. The Shevelkovs received them with open arms. It was all there. Jewelry—piles of it—and silver and furs, and even their warm winter clothing.

The sisters were overwhelmed with intense and disparate emotions. They felt a frisson of hope, because they now had desirable commodities to trade and sell, and tremendous gratitude to the good people who had kept their word—a rarity in the society that had crumbled around them. Yet they also felt terrible heartache as they remembered, like it was yesterday, the day their mother had handed over these treasured objects. And every item held a memory and told a story—of a happy, loving Jewish family that was no more.

The neighbors gave the girls a small suitcase for their wares. They pledged to offer prayers for them in church. "You have nothing to fear, for the Lord will watch over you," they blessed the Gradis sisters. "You will both survive the war."

Filled with equal measures of optimism and fear, Cecilia and Nadia boarded the train to Vilna, and mercifully, their journey was without incident. Carefully they followed the directions they had been given to the suburb of Antokol. But when they arrived at nightfall on the door-step of their contact, Maria Strensasna (a nurse with whom Pawlowich, the trainman, had arranged for them to stay), the news was grim. The nurse solemnly informed the girls that they could not stay with her, or even enter her home.

"There has been a wave of arrests of Polish underground members. Why, it's even possible that whoever offered you assistance is already in jail—or worse!" she declared. "There is no doubt that the Nazis will look here, too, and when they find you, it will be a disaster for everyone!"

It was practically a death sentence, transmitted with clarity and con-viction. Utter despair filled Cecilia and Nadia. They had come so far—for *this?* Moving from place to place had become commonplace to the sisters Gradis. But in this unfamiliar terrain, they were profoundly lost.

"Listen, girls, one thing," the nurse said carefully. "Do you have, per-haps, 'anything' with you?"

"Money?" Cecilia asked, and Maria nodded.

"No money," said Nadia. "Jewelry."

"How much?" pressed Maria.

"*A lot,*" they replied.

"I see. Well, then, perhaps some ... *arrangements* ... might be made," Maria said, cryptically. "Now go—far away—and do not come back un-til tomorrow, after dark."

And with that, Maria Strensasna hastily sealed and bolted the door.

ONCE AGAIN the girls had to become invisible for an entire day, and wait for the unknown. They trudged for several miles until they came upon an old Polish cemetery. There they sat down to ponder their appallingly uncertain future. *Who was this mystery woman Maria? What were her true intentions? Where would they sleep? Where would their next meal come from?*

Their only consolation was that having no answers was no longer an unfamiliar phenomenon.

After darkness fell the next day, the girls retraced their steps to Maria's house with the aid of some markers they had left along the way. The nurse cracked open the door and gave them their instructions. "I have found you a place," she rasped. "But it will cost you *every* piece of your jewelry."

What other option did they have?

The girls were directed to the home of a Polish woman named Halina. Their first order of the day was to pay for the lodging. In advance.

Wordlessly the girls poured out the contents of a bag that was buried inside their suitcase. Ornamental bracelets and rings of precious gems, diamond-studded brooches and antique lockets, gold and silver chains and pearl necklaces spilled out onto Halina's battered kitchen table. The woman's eyes spread wide as saucers.

These were the heirloom treasures of the Gradis sisters' grandmothers, and of their mothers and grandmothers before them—a steep rent for such pathetic lodgings. Images of the pious women who had worn these jewels flashed before Cecilia and Nadia. It broke their hearts to give the last vestiges of their family legacy to a stranger. But what was the price of a life—of two lives? Surely it was above rubies.

Halina could easily have confiscated the loot and reported the two Jewish girls to the police for a handsome reward. This was a common procedure. But to her credit, she was true to her word, and for the next month, the sisters remained in her home, frequently venturing outside despite the heavy German military presence everywhere. Once again, however, things would abruptly change. In the lives of the Gradis sisters, the only constants were change and fear.

With no explanation, Halina told them that they were about to be transferred. Some poor peasants in a nearby village just across the Polish border had agreed to take the girls, in exchange for a portion of the funds that Halina had collected from them. Minutes later, they were on their way, escorted by a lumbering old Polish woman. She brought them to a dilapidated old barn. Inside, a few emaciated goats, chickens, pigs and a limping cow wandered aimlessly in their droppings. Nearly overcome by the indescribable stench, Cecilia and Nadia naively waited to be led to an adjacent home.

But this wretched barn *was* now "home"—to them and to this destitute family of Polish peasants—the grandmother, her son and young grandson. And the floor of filthy, dung-filled straw was where they would rest their weary heads.

Sleep, at least, rescued Nadia and Cecilia from the awful reality of their living conditions. Meals were a different matter.

Despite their gnawing hunger, the well-bred sisters could not bring themselves to partake of the communal bowl of gruel that was their daily repast. That the slop was rancid was bad enough. To share a single wooden spoon with the others as they boisterously cussed and chewed and drooled and spat, plunging grimy fingers into the encrusted bowl and then licking them as they did, was also significantly bad enough. But watching the communal bowl become the final terminal for the triumvirate—the child's cascading mucus, the father's fingers that commuted between his nose and mouth, and the grandmother's half-chewed bites that slid out perpetually—was a tad too much for two young ladies raised in a home in which manners were paramount.

Their sole nourishment became the milk supplied by their bovine roommate and a few hunks of tough, tasteless black bread baked by the grandmother.

Despite these wretched conditions, the glittering bequest the sisters had made to Halina had proven worthwhile. Just as Professor Kruminsh had done before her, Halina—though for a fee—continued to surreptitiously pull the strings, deftly arranging for safe passage whenever danger drew near or circumstances appeared too risky. Soon, again, it was time to move on.

THIS TIME they were brought to the basement hovel of an indigent, elderly Polish woman. Philomena suffered from cancer of the throat and she could barely speak. But she was a kind soul who shared what little she had with the girls, including her bed. In Philomena's kindly presence, for the first time since leaving home, Nadia and Cecilia felt a measure of love and security.

With winter upon them, the basement was dank and cold and reeked of mildew, and the bed sheets were moist. Mere scraps of food were divided three ways. But the crowded sleeping arrangements proved fortuitous, because huddled together, they all found a measure of warmth.

And yet it was there that for the first time, Nadia's frayed temper truly erupted. As the Christmas season arrived, Philomena carefully arranged tufts of evergreen around the table, as was the Polish custom. Cecilia was eager to show her appreciation. "This is so wonderful!" she burbled. "Just like our mother used to do."

Philomena's expression abruptly grew stern. "All this time I have never asked about your mother!" she whispered tersely. "Why on earth did you have to bring up the subject?"

Philomena had quietly assumed the girls' mother had never decorated a Christmas table. The basement's harmonious living situation had been shakily built on a conspiracy of silence. And Cecilia had now broken it.

"Silly girl—you and your big mouth!" Nadia raged at her frightened sister. "This good lady is so ill, and now you have upset her! Shame on you!"

"Dunce!" she continued to fume, "as if she isn't sick enough, now you have to add to her problems by giving her heartache! She was willing to play along all this time; play dumb, for what you don't know can't hurt you. But no-o-o-o, Cecilia with her slack lips was not willing to let well enough alone. It's a wonder I'm still alive with a nincompoop sister like you!"

Cecilia's first impulse was to snap back at Nadia, but she was at a loss for words. For a few tense moments the three of them stood, just staring at each other in edgy silence. Finally Philomena pulled Cecilia close and embraced her, and it appeared the transgression was forgotten.

Soon after that, the girls received word that Halina wanted to see them. She had some confidential information, she declared, and it was no longer safe to stay with Philomena. Cecilia pleaded with Halina to allow them to stay where they were, but the woman would not relent.

"There is only one safe place left for you," she said emphatically. "The Vilna ghetto."

The stunned sisters recoiled. A ghetto, a "safe" place?

Yes, insisted Halina. And to prove her point, she had craftily arranged for two Jews to slip outside the ghetto's walls to affirm her assertion.

The two agents could not have exited safely without the behind-the-scenes machinations of Jacob Gens, the head of the Vilna ghetto's *Judenrat*. Gens, whose wife was Christian, had not tried to escape the fate of his fellow Jews, unlike many in the same circumstances. By entering the ghetto together with his co-religionists, he had earned their respect and trust.

Gens' methodology was (and remains) the subject of debate, but most believe that he was not a traitor to his people. Inside the ghetto, his natural leadership abilities thrust him into a prominent role. He had a wide array of responsibilities under the rubric of Jewish administration, and sought even more. On July 12, 1942, the Germans dissolved the *Judenrat* (the ghetto's Jewish council), and Gens was dubbed the "ghetto representative."

Gens' emissaries, a man and a woman, had removed their yellow stars and snuck all the way to Halina's house to persuade Cecilia and Nadia to smuggle themselves into the ghetto. Getting *in* at this stage, they explained, was almost as difficult as getting out. The couple had risked their lives to come—as well as the lives of many others who could be forced to pay the collective price for even one person's escape.

The duo explained to Cecilia and Nadia that without documents they would eventually be caught. "Life is not safe in the ghetto," they admitted. "But it isn't safe on the outside either … and at least in the ghetto you will be among your own people, and not so alone."

This reasoning was very compelling to Cecilia, who craved to be with her people. It was agony for her to have to pretend all the time and worry about every word she uttered. One day of *not* pretending—even under the most awful conditions—would be a welcome relief for her.

Characteristically, her sister's reaction was different. Nadia had blond hair, blue eyes and Aryan features and thus believed she might, in fact, be considerably safer outside the ghetto. But Cecilia's mind was made up. She told her sister that she was leaving for the ghetto—even if this meant going by herself. Eventually Nadia consented to join her.

WAS THIS DESPERATE DECISION really the right one for the sisters Gradis? The choice between living as undocumented fugitives versus living in the belly of the Nazi beast was a conundrum that would plague them day and night.

Especially at night, when visions of a densely wooded area on the highway to Grodno haunted their dreams.

Ponar.

Some eight kilometers south of Vilna was the Ponar forest, which had long been a favorite spot for holidays and recreation. But the ugly winds of war would forever alter the character of this once-pastoral retreat. The Soviets had dug massive cavities in the earth to store enormous fuel tanks. The pits were extremely deep and wide, with high embankments formed by the extracted earth.

The Nazis used these former petroleum repositories as mass graves for tens of thousands of Jews from the Vilna ghetto.

Smuggling people into the ghetto violated German orders and was punishable by death. Furthermore, by this juncture of the war, the Vilna ghetto was to have been purged of all children as well as non-Vilna residents. Gens risked his life to bring the girls inside, mostly because he was desperate for a source of news about how the Jews were faring in Latvia.

He, like every other Jew of his day, had no way of knowing that the blanket of doom covered all of Europe. The terrible end result for all of them would be the same; the only variables were its speed and efficiency.

In order to get inside the ghetto, the girls were instructed to join a labor detachment that routinely worked on the outside. They were to re-fasten the yellow stars onto their clothing, meld with the group, and then, prior to entry, undergo a careful inspection by the German, Lithuanian and Jewish police. The scrutiny was primarily a body search, for it was strictly forbidden to bring anything into the ghetto. The stringency of this edict was later impressed upon the sisters, when they were forced to watch the public hanging of a woman who had attempted to smuggle a few peas into the ghetto. Her dangling corpse was left on display for five full days.

The girls made it through inspection and were directed to Jacob Gens. The man was very cordial, and curious about what they had to say. In turn, he advised them about whom to avoid in the ghetto and what to say to prevent divulging information.

When Gens heard that Cecilia played the violin, he arranged for her to receive an instrument so that she could join the ghetto's orchestra. The Ghetto Symphony embodied the strength and nobility of the Jewish spirit behind the ghetto's high walls. Virtually every evening, the starving and the filthy, the tormented and the weary, both performed in and attended these musicales. The music was of a professional caliber, and it allowed the attendees to forget themselves and enjoy a few moments free from shouts, threats and beatings.

The symphony orchestra performed as if—in the truest sense—there would be no tomorrow. No one knew who would be shipped to Ponar in the middle of the night. But while the orchestra performed, the future was on hold, and for a few brief moments, the present felt pleasant and harmonious.

CECILIA WAS ASSIGNED a job in a German clinic not far from the ghetto. The bare-bones facility provided care to German nationals who did not require intensive monitoring or hospitalization. Through her work, she met a Lithuanian man named Rutkauskus, a friend of the doctor who managed the clinic. The doctor was aware that Rutkauskus, a kind-hearted passport official in Rudamina, a town near Vilna, could arrange passports for Jews. (It would later be documented that he had saved at least 170 Jewish lives.)

One day Rutkauskus secretly informed Cecilia that the ghetto would soon be liquidated, but he could get her false papers that would allow her to live on the outside. Cecilia shared with Rutkauskus that she had a sister, and he agreed to secure papers for her as well.

When Cecilia told Nadia about Rutkauskus' kind offer, she became enraged. "What possessed you to speak to this man? You and your big mouth all over again! How do you know that he is not a Gestapo agent or some other kind of collaborator who is setting up a trap?"

Nadia was the classic older sibling, more careful than her impetuous younger sister. Cecilia at times viewed her as dour and pessimistic. Under the tense circumstances and close quarters in which they found themselves, the sisters often got on each other's nerves. But each knew that without the attributes of the other—Nadia's caution and Cecilia's courage—they would never have come this far.

Cecilia tried to convince her sister to accept Rutkauskus' offer, but

Nadia remained unmoved, and aghast at her sister's naiveté. In mufled, yet audible whispers, the two girls argued late into the night.

Their bitter debate was overheard by an older woman who had fled to Vilna from Warsaw with her two daughters earlier in the war, and who understood that their days in the ghetto were numbered. She stared at Cecilia and Nadia with naked envy. "The Lord is surely looking out for you. What luck you have, to travel from another country and still survive!"

Her face was contorted with a mother's fear. "Please, I beg you, my girls are just about your age," she murmured. "Can't you ask this man if he could get them papers as well?"

Suddenly Nadia realized that this desperate woman was right: she and her sister *were* lucky. Nadia's perspective shifted instantly. God had been with them so many times before, and He would be with them again.

To be eligible for Rutkauskus' offer, they would first have to extricate themselves from the suffocating trap of the ghetto. This was negotiated with the help of a Jewish partisan who knew his way over every roof in the vicinity. Cecilia and Nadia, together with the Warsaw woman's two daughters, succeeded in escaping to the home of Rutkauskus.

The passport official was a good man, but like so many others at that time and under those circumstances, he was an alcoholic. Because of his inebriation, he could never deliver at night what he had promised during the day. In fact, it took him several days just to figure out exactly who these four girls were before he could arrange for their papers.

Rutkauskus' wife was aware of what was being plotted, which could have doomed the plan, but Cecilia understood that her silence was assured. The Rutkauskuses had a little girl who was the apple of their eye. Cecilia had no doubt that she was a recently adopted Jewish child, as she would constantly parrot the most unlikely thing for a natural offspring to say: "This is *my* Mommy, this is *my* Mommy!"

Cecilia and Nadia had good reason to wonder if they would *ever* secure documentation, until Rutkauskus' sobriety finally lasted long enough for him to find a man who was able to produce what was needed. This was the first step in an intricate plan that would place the girls so deep inside the lion's den that their safety would be better assured than it had ever been before.

Cecilia and Nadia Gradis became "Walentina and Helena Paw-lowska." The other sisters, née Libesman, became "Zosia and Danka Wisnewska."

THE FAILURE of Germany's Blitzkrieg against the U.S.S.R. and the consequent prolonging of the war created severe manpower shortag-es. To partially fill the gap, laborers from the occupied areas were con-scripted under duress and sent to work in Germany.

For their own safety, Cecilia, Nadia and the two Polish girls wished to exploit the fact that they were now official, card-carrying gentiles, by utilizing the most ambitious hiding place from the Nazis, right un-der their noses! Their daring plan was to work directly for the German war machine. There was, however, no recruitment office for these jobs; workers were enlisted by force.

In the kind of irony that only war could produce, the girls were *for-tunately* captured and earmarked for deportation to the home front. But there was one final hoop they would have to jump through: the physical exam.

Cecilia naively believed that the Nazi's well-known anti-Jewish and racial theories were rooted in fact. Would they really be able to discern her true identity by her skin pigment, skull formation, the size of her nose and other physical traits? She was so nervous that she struggled to keep from shaking violently, but the exam proved to be extremely cur-sory. The four girls were deemed eligible for labor and sent to Vienna.

After the squalor of the Vilna ghetto, the staggering beauty of the Austrian capital caused their heads to reel. For Cecilia, especially, whose life was bound up with music, the city's architectural grandeur (a mélange of Biedermeier and Renaissance revival) was a revelation. She well understood why odes and waltzes had been written as paeans to its splendor.

But this is a story of disharmony. Vienna was magical, but its heart was dark: a repository of rabid and murderous Jew-hatred. It was red-olent of culture and elegance, but the four girls were relegated to an underworld that was impoverished and bleak.

They were assigned to a factory where the work was exceptionally monotonous, and in Cecilia's case, equally hazardous. She had to pack stacks of small metal containers used for armaments into boxes. The edges were often sharp and there was the constant threat of cuts and subsequent infection to her delicate fingers and hands. Cecilia had to work quickly and uncomplainingly despite the pain.

All of the workers were housed dormitory-style and fed meager rations. The labor pool was comprised of individuals who had been forced from their homes to slave for German industry. As an occasional diversion, a local civic organization would periodically supply the various factories with free tickets to local movies, plays and other cultural events.

One day a representative came to the plant with an assortment of giveaways. The workers eagerly snatched tickets to the latest screwball comedy from France and an array of ribald stage shows. Only one pair of tickets remained. Clearly, the program held no appeal for the bedraggled, unsophisticated proletariat: an evening of chamber music at the *Wiener Philharmoniker.*

Except, that is, for one laborer whose heart hammered and who wished nothing more than to leap from her workstation for the chance to hear "Beethoven's Quartet" in a world-class venue. Walentina Pawlowska, a.k.a. Cecilia Gradis, master violinist, star protégé of Adolph Metz, and prodigy of the Riga Conservatory of Music, began wildly flailing her hand. *"Yes, YES, over HERE!"*

The ever-cautious Nadia sternly gesticulated to Cecilia to put down her hand. "Zosia" and "Danka" hissed that the dangers of such an outing far outweighed its pleasures, but to no avail. To Cecilia, music was like air … and she had been suffocating for years.

She grabbed the tickets and gasped when she saw that they were for superb seats at an opening-night performance! Subscriptions to Vienna's Philharmonic remained in families for generations, and tickets for premiere performances were virtually impossible to obtain.

Cecilia's excitement was not shared by her most reluctant companion for the evening. "Helena Pawlowska" had also inherited a love for classical music, but her passion for this or any other cultural pursuit was outweighed by her determination to survive. She agreed to venture out for the evening only to be a hyper-vigilant chaperone for her sister. She was terrified of what might happen to Cecilia on her own. Their lives depended upon rigorous self-concealment; one false step, one careless word—could be their last.

Cecilia was beside herself with unbridled joy from the moment they entered the *Musikvereinsaal*. It was one of the most celebrated concert halls in the world, acoustically superb and magnificently adorned with opulent chandeliers and winding staircases, fabulous artwork and plush carpeting. This was the world that Cecilia had known and loved, and she thirstily drank in the moment.

Nadia could not appreciate the aesthetic beauty that surrounded her. She could only see the swastikas and eagles emblazoned upon the uniforms that occupied nearly every seat and the plentiful Nazi flags sullying the walls.

Cecilia marveled at the list of past chief conductors: Otto Nicolai, Hans Richter, Gustav Mahler, Felix Weingartner, Wilhelm Furtwängler and Clemens Krauss. These were the masters whose works she had studied, whose orchestral accompaniment she had performed, and whose symphonic tradition she had revered. To Nadia, they were nothing more than accursed Germans.

THE SOUND of the quartet was inimitable. The musicians played two compositions by Beethoven with exceptional finesse. Cecilia closed her eyes and was transported by the music as though she was in a celestial chamber. Nadia's eyes remained wide open, and surrounding her were more than enough reminders that she was in hell.

When the concert was over, Cecilia felt compelled to compliment the consummately proficient violinist. Nadia tried in vain to dissuade her. "Why stir up a hornet's nest?" she pleaded. "You are lucky to be alive, why, WHY must you always push your luck to the extreme?"

Another argument began to unfold, but Cecilia had no time to quarrel. She had been bitten by the music-nirvana bug and just *had* to speak to the first violinist, Margaret Kolbe!

Cecilia approached the woman, and even the Nazi insignia pinned to her bodice did not deter her from waxing eloquent about the performance. By this point Cecilia's German was quite good, although she was afraid to employ it at the factory. Foreign workers—composed primarily of uneducated Slavs, Poles, Croates, Lithuanians and the like—typically conversed in their native tongues; if they spoke German they were suspected of being Jewish.

The violinist was tickled by the girl's enthusiasm. "Since I see that you enjoyed yourself so much," said Frau Kolbe affably, "I must arrange for you to be treated to another performance!"

As Cecilia continued to gush, she could no longer conceal that she too was a violinist. "Where do you perform?" Frau Kolbe asked, quickly becoming irate when she learned that a fellow *artiste* was working in a factory. "Our Führer does not want talented musicians to toil in a factory!"

Cecilia struggled to maintain her composure. If only Margaret Kolbe knew where the Führer *really* wanted her. It was neither in a factory nor in Vienna's celebrated *Musikvereinsaal*. He wanted her dead and buried in a place like Ponar.

"Leave it to me, young Walentina," said Frau Kolbe grandly. "I shall get you out of that factory and into the orchestra pit, where you belong!" She gave Cecilia her address and telephone number, and insisted that they stay in touch.

Even without her sister's recriminations, Cecilia already harbored profound misgivings over her encounter with Margaret Kolbe. To the best of her knowledge, a musician had to be part of the union, the *Musikkammer*, in order to perform in public. Membership in the Musicians' Union required a rigorous screening process that was likely to arouse the sort of scrutiny that could be her undoing.

And so that very same night, with the music still resounding in her ears, Cecilia grimly resolved to banish the matter from her mind. As much as she yearned to perform once again on a real concert stage, involvement with the union was too risky. With the war nearly over, this was no time to jeopardize her safety or that of the other girls.

But the next morning at the factory, she stared down at her swollen, bloodied hands, with fingers cracked and blistered by the sharp metal discs. Were these hands already too far gone? Or maybe it was still not too late to avoid irreversible mutilation? In her short life, Cecilia had already endured so many agonizing losses; was her beloved vocation *another* dream that would have to die?

Against her own better judgment, Cecilia telephoned Margaret Kolbe, who was delighted to hear from her and promptly invited her to lunch.

Frau Kolbe prepared a sumptuous multi-course meal the likes of which Cecilia had not tasted since the outbreak of the war. She was hardly prepared for such hospitality. As she sat in the gracious parlor, she could not stop asking herself: how could such a cultured, educated people as the Viennese—whose raison d'être was Gemütlichkeit—commit such sadistic, barbaric acts of genocide?

Her reveries were interrupted by the great musician thrusting a violin in her direction. "Now, dear girl," said Frau Kolbe. "Let me hear you play the very last piece you learned."

The very last piece she learned? It seemed like a lifetime ago, but it was the stuff of her dreams, the melody she had played in her head all these years to cope and to hope and to block out the ugliness that surrounded her. It was a Max Bruch concerto she had performed at the Riga Conservatory. But how could she admit this to Margaret Kolbe?

Although Bruch was a German and a non-Jew, his work had fallen sharply out of favor because he had composed a score for *Kol Nidrei.* Cecilia's mind raced, but any composition she thought of seemed to have a Jewish connection. "Max Bruch's Concerto …" she blurted out, afraid to meet the eyes of her patroness.

"Fine," replied Frau Kolbe evenly. "A very delicate arrangement. Are you ready for your audition?"

CECILIA'S HEART POUNDED as she raised the instrument to her chin. Her hands shook and sharp needles of pain shot through her fingers as the open cuts pressed against the bow. *So many years*, she thought, *such a cacophony of sorrows.* Her mind was blank. Her arms felt leaden and lifeless.

The first notes were shrill and discordant. She watched Frau Kolbe flinch. *"Steady Walentina, deep breath, elbows straight!"* Cecilia summoned up the voices of her beloved maestros, Professor Kruminsh and the great Max Bruch himself. Suddenly, with her brown eyes closed and dark hair gleaming, her violin once again became an extension of her very soul. From a place inside her, rather beyond her, it came.

The Max Bruch concerto: stirring and majestic, enabling her to block out the bleakness and gnawing hunger of the Vilna ghetto, the squalid barn, Philomena's damp dungeon, the torturous night in the Ohr Somayach Synagogue, the wrenching loss of her parents and her home.

Her breath, her entire being, was one with the notes that rose from her very soul.

"*BRAVO!*" cried Frau Kolbe, when Cecilia was through. "A magnificent talent that mustn't be wasted in a factory!"

Before Cecilia could even respond, Frau Kolbe was on the telephone to the Musicians' Union. She had already inquired about the procedure for foreigners seeking membership, and now, having first-hand proof of the young woman's superior musicianship, she knew exactly whom to contact in the union's German liaison office.

This was, of course, the kind of place that no Jewish fugitive should dare to enter. But Cecilia had no time to demure. "Off we go, dear!" said a beaming Frau Kolbe, thrilled that she had personally discovered Vienna's newest virtuoso. "The director is waiting for us!" There was not even a chance to mumble thanks and escape. Margaret Kolbe pinned her hat to her head as she personally escorted Cecilia to the union's headquarters.

The director was a courtly fellow who was clearly pleased to meet the anxious young prodigy. "Due to the war, we are naturally in short supply of violinists," he declared. "So we are delighted to have you on board and will review your application without delay."

His brisk efficiency did anything but put Cecilia at ease. "Is the registration done here in Vienna?" she asked.

"Oh, no," he assured her with great officiousness. "Your papers will be sent immediately to our central office in Berlin for processing."

Cecilia's rich lunch suddenly rose in her throat. If her fake identity card reached Berlin, even the most incompetent clerk would smell a rat. Even the address of the issuing office on the card was fictitious.

"Is something the matter, young lady?" Frau Kolbe asked as the color drained from Cecilia's face. "You don't look well."

"Ah, it's … nothing," Cecilia stammered. "Nothing at all."

And in fact, her *own* downfall, at that moment, felt of little consequence. Once the authorities discovered that her documents were bogus, her fate would be shared by her sister and the two Polish girls. The four of them had arrived together and their papers were identical. The manager of the factory could accurately surmise that what applied to one, applied to all.

With an overwhelming sense of dread and remorse, Cecilia understood that her own hubris had placed all of their lives in serious peril. For the next five weeks, Nadia and the two sisters glowered at Cecilia and barely spoke to her. She could neither sleep nor eat. She prayed constantly that her headstrong behavior would not destroy the innocent girls who were her daily companions. One day blended into the next, with terror and guilt grinding away at her spirit. Her fear reached a crescendo when the manager of the factory handed her a large envelope mailed from Berlin.

What a cultured people these Viennese are, she thought listlessly. *In Latvia, the death squad broke down your door and hauled you off. Here, you receive an envelope apprising you of your extermination...*

Her mangled fingers fumbled with the clasp before she was finally able to break open her notice of execution.

"*Pawlowska, Walentina,*" the letter read, "*as you are still a minor, you are not required to be a member of the Musicians' Union in order to perform publicly.*"

The other contents of the envelope were propaganda fliers about the contributions that various musicians had made to the Nazi cause.

Cecilia looked up from her reprieve and was finally able to meet the eyes of the others. Once again, God had held his right hand over her. And in her own hand, she held the ticket to a new life.

EQUIPPED WITH OFFICIAL PERMISSION, Cecilia went overnight from assembly-line worker to concert violist. The very first week, she performed with the outstanding orchestras of the Volksoper and the Raymund Operettentheater. From the squalid factory to the orchestra pits of concert halls constructed in the style of the early French Renaissance, from abject poverty to acclaim—it was as if Cecilia was now living on a different planet.

But even on this grander terrain, her true identity had to remain strictly concealed. In some ways, this had become more challenging than ever. For in Viennese high society, in which Cecilia was now fully ensconced, enormous attention was lavished upon family background. The simple folk with whom she had rubbed elbows until recently displayed no interest in the juicy details of one's boarding-school escapades, holiday jaunts or brushes with nobility. These ubiquitous topics were ones that Cecilia Gradis could not discuss truthfully, and they would be her undoing should she be caught in a lie.

With her days in the factory behind her, Cecilia needed to find a new place to live. She was accustomed to searching for shelter—but never had she done so alone, and never ... openly. She feared the inevitable barrage of questions, and declined her superiors' offers to help her find a residence.

Cecilia mentioned her housing needs to a shopkeeper, Frau May, who had often provided her with a slice of bread or two beyond the ration quota. She sensed that this kind soul would not inundate her with the usual questions but deal directly with the issue at hand.

Cecilia was correct in her assessment, and the shopkeeper put her in contact with a woman who had only one child at home and whose husband was stationed on the western front.

Frau Wolf, her new landlady, was delirious with the honor of housing a border who was a professional musician and a rising star, and she treated Cecilia a bit like royalty. She even welcomed Nadia (who continued to work in the factory) to share Cecilia's room. Frau Wolf reminded Cecilia of the Latvian matrons that she had known growing up. Latvian, German and Austrian societies had a close affinity, the girl thought sardonically—mostly in their vitriolic anti-Semitism. How quickly her enthusiastic hostess would change her tune, were she to learn the truth about her celebrated tenant!

Cecilia hurtled rapidly towards the zenith of her career. Each night the curtain would open to a young performer whose artistry was breathtaking, and whose gifts far exceeded technical skill. Cecilia's heart and voice poured out through her strings; all that she dared not say exploded from her instrument. She received thunderous ovations and was the darling of every audience.

The audiences were not alone in their appreciation. One of her fellow musicians cast his eye upon Cecilia and began to flirt with her unceasingly, badgering her to share his lunch and go for walks with him after every performance.

Even without Nadia's hawk-like eye, Cecilia knew that such a relationship could only bring trouble. And despite the other women in the orchestra pleading with the man to leave young "Vally" alone, he would not desist and continued to make her life miserable.

At her wits' end, Cecilia turned to the agent in charge of placing the foreign musicians. She tearfully explained that her parents had been sent to Siberia for being anti-Communist (saints, from a Nazi perspective), so she was alone in the world in dealing with this unrelenting harassment.

As the father of a teenage daughter, the musical agent was very sympathetic. He quickly seized upon what he called "the ideal solution" to her problem. "I shall arrange for you the most perfect job, that will not only free you from this nuisance," he announced, "but will also place you in an environment in which you will *always* feel secure.

"What could be a more secure position for a concert performer in uncertain times," he exulted, "than performing for National Radio!"

Cecilia could scarcely believe her ears. As it was, she already had to associate with more Nazis than she could ever countenance. But working for this hotbed of Nazi propaganda would be tantamount to working inside Gestapo headquarters.

She insisted that she was not good enough to perform for the radio, which employed only the most elite musicians in the Reich. The agent cheerfully maintained that she was perfect. There were three different orchestras that performed over the radio, he explained, assuring her that she would be recommended for the third one, which played "very light classical music."

On the spot, the agent drafted a letter for her to present to the secretary at the foreign workers' desk at the National Radio. To ensure that everything went smoothly, he would speak with his contacts there immediately.

THE SCHISM of Cecilia's life deepened by the minute. She had achieved her childhood dream, remnant of a simpler time, to play among the finest musicians in Europe. Alas, this now meant using her God-given gifts to entertain the Germans as they pitilessly sought to destroy the remnant of her people and the very soul of Europe.

With mounting torment, yet resigned to her fate, Cecilia headed off to the National Radio's headquarters in a labyrinth of streets that she had never walked before. As she approached the address the director provided, panic overtook her.

It was as though she was about to enter the Third Reich's most sensitive military installation. Encircling the building was a phalanx of the cruelest detachment of SS men Cecilia had ever laid eyes upon. The troops were dressed entirely in black, with skull-and-crossbones insignia on their uniforms. She felt as though she was teetering on the very knife-edge of mortal danger. There was only one source of comfort: though she walked through the shadow of the valley of death, the Almighty had never forsaken her.

With a sharp intake of breath, as though she was about to plunge into icy waters, Cecilia presented her letter to the sentry. Brusquely, he waved her on. On every floor and at every door, another military attaché stood guard, but her letter got her past each inspection.

The clerk had been notified that she would be coming and was awaiting her arrival. "So, you're the foreign musician," she greeted Cecilia. "Everyone is on lunch break now, but they will be back in a few minutes. Tell me, where are you from?"

"Latvia."

"What a coincidence! We have a man who plays in the very same unit that you will be assigned to, who is also from Latvia. Let's see, umm, what's his name?..."

As the clerk rifled through her desk for the roster, Cecilia's heart sank. If by chance this fellow knew her, she was moments away from being delivered into the hands of the rifle-toting SS men who patrolled every corner of the building.

"Ah, here it is!" said the affable clerk. She opened a notebook to a page that displayed a photograph of the Latvian musician. Cecilia recognized him instantly as a fellow student from the Riga Music Conservatory, and she was positive that he would remember her. Though that period in her life felt like a million years ago, in reality, it was fewer than four. There was no doubt that the man would also recall that she had been one-half of the Jewish student body enrolled there.

Cecilia realized that her life depended upon getting out of that building within the next five minutes. But how could she suddenly escape the most heavily guarded facility that she had ever encountered, without arousing the clerk's suspicions? In nanoseconds, the woman could organize a search committee with deadly efficiency.

Cecilia had to think fast. "Could you tell me where the lady's room is, please?" she asked urgently. The Germans were widely known to be punctual, and might even return a minute or two before the end of their lunch-break!

Cecilia was given explicit directions, but once she made it down the hall she never entered the second room on the left, but kept on going. And going. And going. Even after she was out of the building, she didn't stop, but raced along Vienna's streets, constantly glancing over her shoulder.

Cecilia slowed down only when her legs could carry her no farther. She rested, and then returned home late at night. Nadia was waiting for her, worried sick. As much as she tried, she could not get Cecilia to reveal what had happened.

THIS WAS CECILIA'S closest call in her escalating peril of being recognized. Even had this fellow alumnus from the Riga Conservatory not recognized her, there was a great chance that someone else soon would. Latvia had already been liberated by the Russians, and many German collaborators fled from the oncoming troops into the German protectorate. Among this influx were musicians who had made their way to the state orchestras for employment. At least one of them was bound to know Cecilia.

For two days following her traumatic experience at the National Radio, Cecilia, uncharacteristically, remained sequestered inside her room, seized with apprehension. She knew that soon she would be forced to search for another job. She feared, too, that the agent would come looking for her, angry that she had not kept the coveted appointment that he had taken the trouble to arrange. Or perhaps he would forgive and forget her faux pas, and press her to return to the orchestra and translate musical instructions for some of the new Baltic recruits— another route to her undoing, should one of them recognize her.

What to do, when the world gets smaller and smaller? Sometimes, there is nothing left to do but wait, and pray.

And sometimes, a prayer will hit a perfect note, and will be answered.

IN APRIL OF 1945, about five weeks after Cecilia's incident with National Radio, the Russians entered Vienna. Within a week, all of the city's theaters and concert halls were boarded shut, as Germany retreated further and further from the steady rain of Allied bombs.

EPILOGUE

Notwithstanding their exhilaration over the long-awaited unraveling of the German-Nazi machine, Cecilia and Nadia continued to live in fear. The Russians burst upon the city in an orgy of drunkenness, violence and anti-Semitism. They menaced the few surviving Jews at every turn, and chaos and intimidation reigned, even in the air-raid shelters.

The girls joined a contingent of Poles who left Vienna via horse and buggy. Their first stop was a Hungarian town called Sopron, where they remained for two days. As they resumed their journey, a Russian demanded to come on board. When he saw there was no place for him, in a drunken rage he began hurling people's possessions from the cart.

One of the items that he smashed to the ground was Cecilia's violin. She was inconsolable—a girl without parents, without a home. And now, this.

They remained a caravan of the lost and the despised. From Sopron they traveled to Celldomolk where Cecilia and Nadia were placed in a huge camp with hundreds of homeless Ukrainian men, women and children. A Jewish commandant, Major Nuremberg, felt sorry for the two girls and placed them in a Hungarian home where they were fed and treated well. But the word from the camp was that they would all be sent to Siberia.

Once again, with the help of inside information, the permission of the commandant, and a constellation of Jewish organizations (often operating in secret), the girls fled—this time to Budapest, to a crowded building where Jews were being secretly housed. From the "Russian zone" of the city, the girls were eventually transferred to Stuttgart, under the British zone, and still, anti-Semitism ruled. The refugees pleaded to go to America or to Palestine-*Eretz Yisrael*. The powers-that-be would not hear of it.

In a cold, cruel spring, the first glimmer of warmth came from the Italians. Despite the absence of any identification, Cecilia and Nadia were invited to join approximately two hundred Italian men and women who were returning home by train via the town of Mestro. Aided by the Communists, the girls crossed the bridge to the Venice ghetto where Jews had lived for almost five hundred years. They were overwhelmed by the ethereal beauty of the city ... and by their first taste of living in freedom in many years.

Hampered by struggles with the language and a dearth of Jewish agencies, the girls eventually found their way to Rome. Cecilia became part of the city's celebrated conservatory, coincidentally named St. Cecilia Academy, where she studied under Professors Julius Benyami and Raemi Principe. From the government of Italy and the American Joint Distribution Committee, she received a new violin—a Joseph Klotz German Violin, crafted in 1792.

She still uses this violin today.

In 1947, in the Great Synagogue of Rome, Cecilia married Salomon Boruchowitz, a survivor of Dachau. Salomon was a student at the Hebrew University in Palestine-*Eretz Yisrael* in 1940, when he traveled home to Lithuania to visit his ill mother and was arrested by the Germans. After the war he worked for the *Aliyah Bet* organization in Rome, where he met Cecilia.

In 1949 the couple moved to Johannesburg, where Salomon's brother lived. Initially, Cecilia played violin in the orchestra of the South African Broadcasting Corporation, but after her first child was born in 1950, she limited her playing to participation in amateur orchestras, which she continues to this day.

The Boruchowitz's oldest son, Phillip, is a Supreme Court judge in Johannesburg. Their daughter, Ralene, is a specialist in remedial education who teaches at the King David primary school in Johannesburg. Colin, the youngest, is a businessman. Cecilia and Salomon have seven grandchildren. The two youngest are students at the King David School, and the older five, all graduates of Jewish day schools, are professionals in the fields of law, education, business and journalism. Cecilia is the great-grandmother of five.

Nadia married an American, Sam Vovsi. After a battle with cancer, she passed away in 1985 in the United States. Her only child, Gregory Vovsi, lives in New York.

Lisa, the oldest Gradis sister, perished in Auschwitz along with her two-year-old daughter. Cecilia was told by two survivors she met in Rome that Lisa had been given the chance to live or to be killed with her child. She chose the latter.

"Zosia" and "Danka," the two Polish sisters, were eventually reunited with their mother in Poland after the war and moved to Melbourne, Australia in 1950.

Heroic Cecilia Children

The child prodigy who performed on stage at a tender age. This exceptionally rare photograph (on the left) was miraculously discovered (everything from Cecilia's life up to and during the war was destroyed) when Cecilia made a trip to Israel as a middle-aged woman. She providentially met another woman from Latvia who was friendly with Cecilia's oldest sister, Lisa, who was murdered in Auschwitz. This friend had departed Latvia for Palestine prior to the war and had this picture of Cecilia in her photo album—bringing to light the one memento of a life and a career that had been nearly erased.

Cecilia, Johannesburg, 2000.

Cecilia with her great-grandchildren, Johannesburg, 2013.

Heroic Michael Children

Fanny and Michael, age 16 months, Brzeżany, Poland, 1939.

One-and-half year old Michael with his mother in their home town of Brzeżany, 1935.

Family portrait (paternal side) shortly after Michael's birth. Aside from grandmother (who died of natural causes in 1938), all—but Michael and parents—were murdered by the SS and Ukranian police in the summer of 19 Middle row: (L-R) Michael's father, grandmother, grandfather, and mother w Michael on her lap.

Children's choir in the Bindermichl DP camp where Michael's father was one of the leaders and the head of th rightist *Poalei Zion* party. Front row, second from the right, is Michael.

...ildren and their music instructor on the occasion of a performance at the ...dermichl DP Camp near Linz, Austria, 1947. Michael is on the far right.

Michael rendered the *Shehecheyanu* (Who has kept us alive and maintained us...) blessing upon the opening of the Jewish Cultural Center in Linz, Austria. Second from the right is Michael's father, far right Simon Wiesenthal, 1947.

...ss of Holocaust survivor children in the Bindermichl DP Camp. Michael is ... second boy from the right.

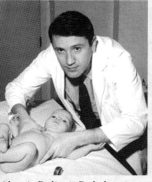

...sident in Pediatric Pathology in ...ronto's famous Hospital for Sick ...ildren, 1963.

On the occasion of Dr. Michael Thaler's 80th birthday, 2014. Included are wife, sister-in-law, daughter and son and five grandchildren (son-in-law, the photographer, behind the camera).

Family after the War. Front row: (L-R) Shlomo, Esther, Bella. Back row: (L-R) Mariette, Albert. Rome, 1945.

Wedding of Alter and Sidi, St. Martin Vesubie, 1944.

Lynn and Albert Sharon (Hebraized Sjazdholc), Jerusalem, 1985.

Heroic **Albert** Children

Bella and Mariette, Rome, 1944.

House on the left is where the family hid in Andonno, Italy.

View from St. Martin Vesubie, where the Szajdholc, Templer and Wolfinger families were assigned "forced residence."

Heroic Srulek Children

Three-year-old Srulek in his family's backyard in Munkacs.

Srulek after liberation from the Ebensee slave labor camp in Austria, 1945.

School photo in Munkacs. The chassidic boy on the far right on his knees is Srulek. He is the only Jewish child in this photograph to have survived the war.

Heroic Srulek Children

Hershel and Chana Pessil Storch, Srulek's parents.

el Stark with his wife and family celebrating their 50th wedding anniversary in Chicago.

Esther, center-top with the white hair ribbon, after liberation.

The Belz Shul, painstakingly completed in 1843, was destroyed by the Germans in 1939.

Porch of the Kinderheim. In the center-background are Madame and Monsieur Yona Tiefenbrunner, Antwerp, circa 19

On the occasion of a visit by Chief Rabbi Isaac Herzog to the Kinderheim.

Youthful Spirit

ALBERT

This is a story of youthful spirit that five years of wandering, struggle and displacement could neither douse nor diminish.

"Children, wake up!" bellowed Shlomo Szajdholc (pronounced Shaidholtz). "WE'RE AT WAR!"

It was five o'clock in the morning on May 10, 1940, and the sky over Brussels was filled with an ominous rumble that grew louder and louder.

"The Germans are bombing us!" roared Shlomo, even louder. "Get up! Get up!"

But the four Szajdholc children only pulled their bedcovers over their heads.

"Papa, it's only thunder," called out seventeen-year-old Alter—the oldest of the children, as his name indicated—while his brother Albert, not yet sixteen, groaned in agreement.

Suddenly, in the wake of the "thunder" came sirens and the din of exploding shells. Still the sleepy teenaged brothers did not stir, nor did the "women" of the household: mother Esther and the two younger girls, Mariette and Bella. War, to them, was little more than a page in a newspaper. A frightening affair that, until now, was mercifully far from Brussels, from their door and from their consciousness.

Shlomo alone paced the floor of the Szajdholcs' Brussels apartment, in the gathering light of dawn. As the family's patriarch and a successful manufacturer of leather goods, his responsibilities weighed heavily upon him. He had been following the news almost obsessively as the Germans moved inexorably closer to Belgium, and he viewed the shifting winds of war with utmost seriousness. He was determined that his family would not be caught in the maelstrom.

Shlomo's first move was to try and salvage some merchandise and machinery from his factory. He commanded his second son, Albert—the more rambunctious of the Szajdholc boys—to assist him, which made the lad decide from the outset that he did not like this new turn their lives were taking. At the very first opportunity, he decided to abandon his father's grim "war preparations," and ran to a cousin's house to play.

With the foolishness of youth, Albert was unperturbed by the fiery battles waging in the distance and in the sky above. As he blithely made his way across town, anti-aircraft shrapnel rained about him. Suddenly, a scrap of steel landed at his feet, missing him by just inches. Eagerly he reached for it, only to toss it in the air after crying out from the searing heat. Albert waited until the sizzling shrapnel cooled down, and then put it in his pocket. He was thrilled by all of the action, and insisted upon showing everyone he knew the "souvenir" that had nearly killed him.

With the war front getting closer and closer to Brussels, Shlomo Szajdholc decided to relocate his family to France. His wife resisted, insisting that the war would be brief and did not warrant uprooting the children, or abandoning their comfortable home and lucrative business. Her position was bolstered when British troops were spotted advancing in the direction of the Albert Canal. Seeing these soldiers lulled many Belgians into the false belief that it was just a matter of weeks before the Allied forces would evict the Germans from their soil.

This pipe dream was further enhanced by the arrival in Brussels of a contingent of stalwart soldiers with Jewish stars embroidered upon their uniforms—members of the Jewish Brigade from Palestine. The presence of these troops assured an admiring crowd that the German advance would be quickly crushed.

The Szajdholc brothers and their friends derived enormous pride from these rugged young fighters, their chests almost bursting when even gentile onlookers cheered, "*Vive les Juifs!*"

The bubble of Allied superiority was decisively burst within a day when all but one of the bridges over the Albert Canal were detonated by Nazi commandos. There was no longer any doubt that the Germans were on the verge of marching into Brussels.

Shlomo activated his evacuation plan, calling for an immediate departure.

Everyone was ready except for Esther, who would not budge until all of the dishes were washed and the apartment was spotless. Shlomo's patience was pushed to its extreme, and he ordered young Albert ahead to the train station, to purchase the family's tickets to Paris.

When Albert arrived there, he found that the station was a mob scene, filled to the rafters with desperate citizens vainly attempting to reach the ticket booth. Alone and unencumbered by luggage, the wily youth managed to thrust himself into the front of the line—and not a moment too soon. The train to Paris was about to depart.

Albert's eyes anxiously scanned the platform until, to his relief, he saw the rest of his family rushing toward him, laden with as many suitcases and bags as they could carry. They were all about to board the train together when a neighbor, who had come to the station with the same intentions, grabbed Shlomo by the shoulders. "Szajdholc, don't board!" the man said urgently. "The French have closed their borders to refugees, and no trains are being allowed in!"

But after a moment's hasty deliberation, Shlomo ordered his family onto the train—not an easy task as every car was already overflowing with passengers and their belongings. He reasoned that whatever might happen, it would be better than remaining in Brussels, helplessly awaiting the Nazi onslaught.

THE TRAIN to Paris should not have taken more than five hours, but even after a full day's journey they had not reached their destination. As darkness began to settle, someone called out the name of a station they had just whizzed past, jolting everyone from their slumber. They were headed in the wrong direction!

The frantic buzz of questions and theories quickly trailed off as the passengers somberly contemplated their uncertain futures. Albert sorrowfully reminisced about the pranks he had played, the teachers he would miss, and those he wouldn't. His older brother Alter was mostly

focused on his sweetheart, Sidi Templer, who, with her family, was escaping in the same car as the Szajdholcs. Innately, the brothers understood that what they had left behind, they would most likely never see
again.

All night the train chugged toward the unknown, until some time
the next day it came to a stop and Red Cross volunteers boarded with
food and water. Afterwards the journey quickly resumed, its destination
remaining a mystery. About an hour later, they passed Dunkerque—a
city whose name would later become historic—which is not far from
Brussels! But few passengers were focused on the fact that it had taken
a day and a half to make a three-hour trip, because outside the windows they could see large concentrations of British soldiers in fortified
trenches equipped with machine guns and anti-aircraft cannons.

The sight of troops poised to halt the Nazi advance greatly boosted
the passengers' flagging morale. No one realized that these soldiers were
engaged in an ignominious retreat that was preparing to depart from
Dunkerque to England.

The ugly truth quickly came to light. Further along the route, car-
nage from the German assault was visible for miles and miles alongside the tracks, dashing any fantasies of a hasty Nazi retreat. The grisly
"scenery" did not let up until a day and a half later, when the famished,
weary refugees arrived in Castagnede du Salat in the dead of night.

Remarkably, the Szajdholcs slept through the tumult of all the other passengers disembarking, and they alone remained on board. At
daybreak they awoke and frantically tumbled off the train. Standing
huddled together on the deserted platform, they had absolutely no idea
where to go or what to do.

It felt like an eternity before an officious-looking man, without ever
stating his name or position, approached the frightened family and announced, as if he were performing on a stage before a large audience:
"Our government has made provisions for refugees to be sheltered
throughout southern France. Follow me!"

The Szajdholcs were fortunate to be housed by a gracious family of
Spanish immigrants by the name of Fonseca, who vividly recalled their
difficult adjustment to France and were eager to spare others what they
had endured.

Notwithstanding the kindness of their hosts, the Szajdholcs

suffered from restlessness and sheer boredom, anxiously pondering what lay ahead. When Monsieur Fonseca suggested they visit the mineral spa at the nearby Hotel de Pyrenees, famed throughout Europe for its natural springs, they jumped at the opportunity, and invited two other families to join them: the Wolfingers, whom they had met on the train from Brussels, and their old friends the Templers. Alter's ardor for the Templer's oldest, Sidi, remained as strong as ever, so for him—even with all the uncertainties of wartime —the continuation of their teenaged courtship was sheer bliss.

The families hiked up to the hotel, which had been abandoned due to the war, rendering the curative waters free for the taking. Eagerly they availed themselves of the once-in-a-lifetime chance to benefit from the water's healing powers, downing copious quantities to gain strength for whatever was to come.

Soon after, however, they all learned the hard way that if one glass was good, five glasses were not better. The water's powerful purgative effect on their digestive systems transformed a pleasant outing into a painful memory.

OTHERWISE, life in the Pyrenees in June 1940 was placid and picturesque, albeit monotonous—until it was reported that the Germans were heading south. The Szajdholcs prepared to flee at once; rumor had it that military and civilian traffic was departing to England daily from the port of Bayonne.

They arrived in Bayonne the very day that France signed an armistice with Germany, significantly frustrating their escape plans. The city teemed with thousands of Jewish refugees, all lodging in the synagogue. The overwhelming sense of being trapped loomed ominously over each family as they weighed every possible plan of escape. The Szajdholcs decided to try to reach Spain.

The first step was to update their documentation. Shlomo was a Polish national living in Belgium, and had never envisioned he would encounter any difficulties in either having his Polish passport renewed or obtaining one for Albert. His assessment changed the moment he entered the Polish consulate, which had just relocated to Bayonne.

While non-Jews obtained whatever they requested, whether or not they had the proper documents, Shlomo was immediately ordered out of the building. He protested his eviction by displaying his passport. The consul declared brusquely that it was no longer valid.

"I know that, sir," Shlomo replied politely, "I am here to have it renewed."

"Since you allowed your passport to expire, you are no longer a citizen," sneered the consul with anti-Semitic vitriol. "You should have had this taken care of beforehand; now it is too late!"

"You could not have expected me," Shlomo protested "to rush to the consulate the day the war broke out. We have been running for our lives ever since—just today we arrived in Bayonne." Desperate for a morsel of compassion, he added, "If you do not renew my passport, I will not be eligible to receive a visa to Spain. There is nothing that I need more right now!"

The consul was unmoved, and curtly waved Shlomo off the premises. "If you will not validate my passport," Shlomo persisted, "at least issue a passport to my son!" And with that, he presented Albert's birth certificate.

"How old is he?" the consul inquired, not even deigning to examine the document.

"Almost sixteen."

The consul glared at Shlomo and replied smugly: "The law is unequivocal on this point. If he is over fifteen and does not possess a passport, then he is no longer a citizen. OUT!"

Without proper documentation in hand, the Szajdholcs were in an awful quandary. Should they risk boarding a train bound for Spain? They had heard that some Jews who had attempted the crossing without transit visas were stopped at the border, while others had succeeded in making it through. The Szajdholcs and the other members of their Jewish community genuinely didn't know what to believe, or how to tell the difference between a real danger and a perceived one. At this early stage of the war, their survival instincts were just developing.

When Shlomo and Albert returned to the synagogue from their disheartening visit to the consulate, they found everyone in a panic. The Germans were marching toward Bayonne! The Szajdholcs raced to the port, where several small boats were filling up with passengers.

They got in line with the other evacuees and their hopes surged, until they encountered a Polish officer who was supervising the evacuation.

He greeted Shlomo with a mighty shove, solely intending to inflict bodily harm. In the most vile language, he lied that only Polish soldiers were permitted to leave on the boats.

Rather than remain helplessly on the dock, Shlomo and Esther and their children trudged back to Bayonne's synagogue. They could think of no other place to go and it seemed like the logical site for what they feared might be their last night together—perhaps their last night alive.

Hours later it dawned on them that the synagogue was probably the most *unsafe* place for them to be. Throughout Europe—from the tiniest hamlets to the grandest cities—synagogues were always the focal points for gathering, interrogating, torturing and deporting the local Jewish population! In some communities, the shuls where families had gathered to celebrate life's most joyous milestones were the very places where they met life's fiery, disastrous end.

The Szajdholcs grabbed their parcels and, with the Templers and Wolfingers, fled to the town square. Suddenly a rainstorm of unprecedented fierceness began. With no shelter anywhere, they stood helplessly in the downpour, stranded, waiting for a miracle.

After only a few minutes, their miracle appeared.

Emerging from the blinding rain was a half-empty intercity bus whose driver motioned them all to climb aboard. No one hesitated. Where the mystery bus had come from and where it was headed were, for the moment, merely technicalities.

The bus traveled through the night until finally stopping at a village in the Pyrenees. The passengers were then transferred to a different bus. For several days they continued on this indeterminate, free-bus-ride-to-nowhere—courtesy, it became increasingly clear, of the French government—until arriving in the pastoral mountain village of Buziet.

The refugees were taken to an erstwhile monastery that was quaint—in both appearance and size—and overrun by rats. The Szajdholcs and their friends soon discovered they were not up against a garden-variety infestation. They were battling behemoths that had been grazing for months on corpses that the Germans had abandoned throughout the countryside, rodents that had evolved into mammoth creatures, unafraid of man.

Conventional traps proved to be useless. Even when the springs did clamp shut, the rats still managed to scamper away—cheese, trap and all. The three families put their heads together to figure out how to outfox their ardent adversaries. The result was a contraption that would never win any prizes for design, but was definitely lethal—with industrial-sized enhancements that could put a wolf out of business.

FOR THE JEWISH REFUGEES ensconced within the crumbling monastery of Buziet, the approaching High Holidays seemed surreal on every possible level. Without synagogue or community, Shlomo Szajdholc feared that the Days of Awe would be reduced to days of emptiness, devoid of meaning. He vowed to himself that this must not be the case. If he did not survive, Alter and Albert—both on the cusp of adulthood—would become the patriarchs of the Szajdholc family. Shlomo needed to safeguard not only their lives, but also their souls.

Arrangements were made to bring Jews throughout the region to the Buziet monastery for Rosh Hashana. The Szajdholcs' quarters were converted into a temporary sanctuary, and Mr. Templer arranged for a friend in Switzerland to send a shofar.

On Rosh Hashanah eve, the group gathered in utmost solemnity, but the shofar had not arrived. Nor did it arrive the next morning. Templer clung desperately to the hope that its redemptive wail would still be heard. Midway through the service, he lobbied strenuously for a break. The congregants expressed their sharp opposition, but Templer would not be deterred. "Let us be patient," he pleaded. "The mail will arrive soon."

But patience was in short supply among those crowded into the makeshift shul, and tempers began to flare. "For God's sake, we are refugees in a strange land in the midst of war!" someone protested. "No one knows when the Germans will conquer us here, or what tomorrow will bring. The Lord will understand if we don't blow shofar this year!"

"Would it be too much," Templer countered quietly, "if I were to ask you to have a little faith?" Gazing at the sea of angry faces, he realized he really was asking too much. Templer then spoke from his heart: "In all our lives, our prayers were never more needed than on this New Year. Everyone here wishes to be inscribed for a year of life more fervently than ever. A shofar can only help."

Templer vowed that if there was no delivery by eleven o'clock, the morning service would resume. It was a Pyrrhic victory for Templer, for he had strong-armed his position upon a nervous assemblage that was eager to emerge from its clandestine, underground service as soon as possible. Thus at eleven o'clock there was a roaring, practically deafening, "We told you so!" in the air, tinged with animosity.

Just then a postal messenger arrived, bearing a thick envelope. Everyone arose from their chairs and the tension reached a flash point as the multi-sealed package was carefully opened. True, the timing was dramatic, but whoever heard of a shofar squeezed into an envelope? Some suspected that Templer was playing for time.

The whole room stared expectantly at the envelope, and then ... a tiny, sacred shofar slipped into his hand. Shock and wonder filled the air.

It was a rather small and undistinguished-looking ram's horn, but its soaring, intense sound filled the room and each of their hearts.

The angst and foreboding did not recede throughout the ten-day High Holiday period. When the daylong fast of Yom Kippur concluded and the shofar was blown to its fullest, shuddering crescendo, the tension and release for the youngsters was so great that they launched into an impromptu, ecstatic dance.

Totally forgetting themselves, Albert and his friends whirled with frenzied abandon, and blessedly, for those few minutes, war, danger and displacement were the furthest things from their minds. Likewise, no consideration was given to the fact that the "dance floor" was at least three hundred years old, and had been termite-feed for the duration.

And so it was quite a shock when the floor caved in and the dance troupe plunged along with it. Miraculously, the only thing that broke was the floor itself. The youngsters' ribs did ache for several days—from their unexpected fall, and from their unrestrained, riotous laughter.

FROM THE TIME the German Army entered its territory in 1940, France was divided into occupied and non-occupied zones. The new rules specified that Jews and foreigners were not authorized to live within fifty kilometers of the demarcation line—rendering Buziet off-limits for the Szajdholcs and their friends.

But where could they go now? The officials in the Ministry of the Interior icily declared that their sole options were either jail or Lamayou, a distant village that no one had ever heard of. While they realized they had no other choice, the anxious wives still refused to travel there until they received some sort of report about the locale. To that end, teen-aged Shalom Templer was hastily dispatched.

Several days later, Shalom sent back a glowing description that gave them all a much-needed feeling of hope. Based on his boyishly enthusiastic report, the Szajdholcs and the others imagined that the bucolic village would have all the comforts of home, maybe even of a luxury hotel.

But the trip to Lamayou turned out to be a bleak, seemingly endless bus ride through vast stretches of uninhabited fields. They arrived late at night, and their initial impressions of the silent, gloomy village did nothing to assuage the trepidation that had resurfaced during the exhausting, all-day journey.

Shalom Templer was waiting dutifully for them at the bus stop in the darkness; not a building, not a streetlamp, not another soul was visible. It was going to take some rather convincing sales talk on his behalf to explain what was so appealing about Lamayou. It hadn't occurred to anyone that the factors a teenager uses to evaluate a situation might differ from the criteria of an adult.

"So what is so great about this place?" Shalom's bleary-eyed mother inquired dubiously.

"Lamayou is the food capital of the war!" the always-hungry teenager proclaimed enthusiastically. "It's nothing like Buziet, where we were starving. Here there's an endless supply of chickens, turkeys, ducks, geese..."

"And what about accommodations?" she pressed.

"Oh, nothing to worry about," Shalom assured her. "If you continue in this direction," he pointed, "away from the center of town..." The very implication of an urban presence as they stood in an unpaved, sans-civilization "crossroads" caused everyone's eyebrows to creep upward in astonishment.

"Just down this path," Shalom continued, "is a spacious barn."

"Do you mean to tell me," Mrs. Templer bellowed, "that we're staying in a barn? What about the Szajdholcs? And the Wolfingers?"

"Oh, the Szajdholcs have a really nice house," he declared, as his mother's eyes grew large with envy. "The mayor said that the larger family gets the barn and the smaller one gets the house. And the Wolfingers will be living about a kilometer away."

The Szajdholc's residence, though it lacked electricity, turned out to be sufficiently roomy for the Templers to move in with them. This left the Wolfinger family somewhat isolated from the others.

It was quickly apparent that the families' first impressions of Lamayou were correct; although picturesque, it was an isolated and provincial burg. Young Albert Szajdholc, however, received a bit of an education there. A local farmer named Basil, whose son had been taken prisoner by the Germans, recruited Albert as a farmhand. The work was arduous and commenced at 4:30 AM, but for urban Albert it opened up a new world.

Basil taught Albert all the ways of the farm, and in general was kind to him, showering him with almost as much affection as he lavished on his prize sow. On rainy days Albert had to husk corn in the barn, which meant keeping company with the pig, whose snorting drove him mad. Every time Albert tried to do something to silence the offender, Basil caught the boy in the act and reprimanded him. If the pig got annoyed he was liable to lose weight, which, Albert learned, was nothing less than a felony in that region.

The day the pig was slaughtered and weighed was a festive occasion marked by the serving of the day's kill. Albert was an invited guest at the gala supper, but he was not thrilled by the menu. His father, Shlomo, kept kosher even during the most trying times. Although he never insisted that his children maintain his high standard, Albert still could not bring himself to eat pork and was relieved when he saw that there were other options.

The feasting peasants decided to have a little fun at the boy's expense. They saw he was a novice drinker and made sure his glass was always filled. When the meal was finished, Albert got no farther than a few inches from the table before he collapsed to the ground. His parents were horrified when their stone-drunk son was delivered to their door.

WITH THE APPROACH of winter 1941–1942, the three families moved to nearby Coarraze, a town that was far less isolated. This gave them greater proximity to other Jews and greater access to the urgent news of the day, which was crucial if one was to stay a step ahead of the enemy. Often the information was merely gossip or hearsay, but nevertheless, there was always a chance that there was a kernel of truth in what they heard.

Greater accessibility to information came at a price, as the anti-Semitism in Coarraze, fostered by government policy, was palpable. Even though some areas were deemed safer than others, anti-Semitism permeated the whole of France. Families like the Szajdholcs always did their best to meld into the general population by posing as non-Jewish refugees.

Soapbox orators in the spirit of Pierre Laval, France's rabidly anti-Semitic prime minister, routinely broadcast their hateful message from Coarraze's town square. "Jews have brought about the ruination of France!" it was proclaimed, and although the local farmers did not seem overly agitated over the supposed Jewish influence, there was plenty of talk as to the consequences the Jews would face for their crimes.

Rumors both frightening and contradictory spread through the anxious Jewish populace: Jews—but only physically fit, grown men—would soon be rounded up to aid the Nazis in the war effort; anyone who had served in the French Army or Foreign Legion would not have to fear deportation; everyone—man, woman, or child—who had immigrated to France after 1936 was in imminent danger of arrest.

Once again it was Shlomo Szajdholc who took every rumor seriously in order to assess the risk for his family. He remained the undisputed, stalwart captain of their ship. From that fateful morning when he pulled the sleeping children from their beds as the bombs began raining over Brussels, he plotted, as best he could, to spare his family from deportation.

In the months that followed, Shlomo learned of a forger in nearby Pau, and hired his services for the creation of false papers and identity cards. His next step was to send away his youngest child, Bella, who was suffering from measles and whooping cough, to a summer camp sponsored by a Jewish welfare organization.

It did not take long for Shlomo Szajdholc's fears to be corroborated by fact. Talk of a roundup was on everyone's lips, and police presence in the neighboring town of Nay suddenly increased heavily over the standing force of four. Albert and his friends frequently visited Nay, and one day they saw that something was definitely out of the ordinary.

With an air of insouciance, Albert asked one of the officers what the show of force was all about. "Oh, no...nothing, nothing at all," he stammered hollowly, "we're just here on maneuvers."

To get a handle on the situation, the teenagers turned to a newly acquired friend who happened to be the niece of Nay's mayor. She confessed she was in the dark, but headed to City Hall to investigate. The mayor showed her a confidential communiqué revealing that a roundup was to take place at 4 AM the very next day. He impressed upon her that the contents of the communiqué were "top secret," but his true intent was clear. The girl sped off to alert her friends before it was too late.

The youth understood that they were no longer dealing with mere rumors and conjecture. Albert hurriedly telephoned an uncle in Toulouse to find out if the situation was any safer there. Because his phone lines were tapped, the uncle responded with a carefully phrased "forecast": "Now the weather is very hot here, and everyone is searching for a cooler climate..."

The teenagers realized that their time had come to search for a cooler climate as well. And this would have to occur before four o'clock the next morning. Unlike their parents, they spoke French fluently and could pass easily for locals. And so they clambered aboard a train at a whistle-stop in Dufai—a tiny station that was used exclusively by the rural populace and had few police patrols. They figured that in a small town, strangers were conspicuous; in transit, no one stood out.

The elder Szajdholcs, Templers and Wolfingers, hardly as fluent in French as their offspring, quickly went into hiding along with other adults in the region. Thanks to the mayor's courageous niece, they all had been warned.

THE SLOW-MOVING TRAIN went only as far as the sleepy little town of Tarbes, seventy miles southwest of Toulouse. There, the youngsters hastily informed some local Jews about the imminent roundup. No one there had heard the news yet ... and the information could clearly save lives.

They then boarded the next local "inter-urban," trying to spend as much time as possible among strangers immersed in transit. This train delivered them to Auch, another small town that is the capital of the grape-growing region of Gascony.

Disembarking there, the youth (Albert, Alter, Sidi and two friends)

quickly forgot the hazards of milling about conspicuously in an unfamiliar town in broad daylight. Indeed, they forgot the precarious-
ness of their situation altogether when they chanced upon a massive
monument to the swashbuckling hero of the region, the inspiration for
Alexandre Dumas' *Les Trois Mousquetaires*: the great d'Artagnan.

There, in the center of Auch, with his bronze sword held aloft, was
the statue of their childhood hero, the hotheaded country boy who
could match wits with Cardinal Richelieu. The real d'Artagnan was
born in Gascony during the seventeenth century, and they had stumbled upon his old stomping ground.

The statue threw them into such gaiety that they forgot why they
were in Auch, and impulsively began to act out the comical escapades
of the Three Musketeers. The play-acting was a welcome respite from
their dreary reality and uncertain future. Merrily they whooped and
hollered, and it was many minutes before Albert emerged from his
childhood reveries long enough to notice a newly erected grandstand,
bedecked with banners and flags, in the town square.

"So, what are we celebrating today?" Albert asked a passerby, with
characteristic irreverence. The man gazed slowly at Albert and the other youths. His grim expression made Albert's blood suddenly run cold.
In a barely audible tone, he cautioned, "Boy, any 'Bretons' (a euphemism
for Jews) must disappear from this town at once! The police are everywhere rounding up strangers. Admiral Darlan is on his way here right
now!"

Darlan was the lieutenant of Pétain who had established the Vichy
regime. The very name was enough to make Albert's knees buckle beneath him. The teenagers disappeared in the direction of the bus station, glancing over their shoulders and dodging every shadow along the
way.

They boarded the first bus to leave, which happened to be heading
for the dangerous "hotspot," Toulouse. When the bus stopped to refuel
en route, the passengers had a chance to step outside and stretch their
legs. The kids disembarked just in time to witness the arrival of a caravan of trucks. Each was heavily guarded, and crammed with Jewish
men, women and children. The pitiful sight made the young people
quake with fear, shattering their illusion that the Germans would do no
harm to the young, old, or infirm.

When they arrived in Toulouse, Albert secretly established contact with the local Jewish Committee so that he could keep abreast of news and also be eligible for the stipend the Committee distributed to refugees. He then called a friend in Coarraze—the daughter of the local grocer, a contact whom they trusted—to convey that he and his comrades were safe and sound. She relayed back, in turn, that his parents were hiding in a hayloft, and had escaped a number of early-morning roundups in the homes of their non-Jewish neighbors.

RABBI CASSORLA, the Chief Rabbi of Toulouse, was strongly connected with Palestine's underground. He was a tremendous resource for the many Jews who lived or sought shelter in the region, offering practical assistance as well as spiritual guidance. Rabbi Cassorla also worked in tandem with the local Jewish Committee, which put Albert and Alter to work in their documentation agency—a small operation devoted to forging documents, a skill that Alter had picked up during the time that he received his false papers in Pau.

Meanwhile, the families left behind in Coarraze were struggling to live day by day. Shlomo and Esther Szajdholc and Mariette, who had stayed behind to aid her parents, were being hidden in the hayloft of a Monsieur André Bon, a prominent citizen who often supplied police with wood in the wintertime.

Ever-vigilant Shlomo sought a contingency plan in case the situation worsened and they would have to flee from Coarraze. To that end, he ordered new papers from his sons the moment they stepped into their new line of work, and instructed them to send the new documents to him via a Mr. Schwartz.

Schwartz was a clever man who had outsmarted the Germans at their own game. In 1941, France's Jews were compelled to fill out a form listing their antecedents. Schwartz invented a family tree complying with the Nuremberg Laws' definition of a non-Jew, but he did not stop with merely submitting the form, as everyone else did. He mailed his lineage directly to Pierre Laval, the infamous Commissioner for Jewish Affairs in the Vichy Government.

The ploy worked and Laval confirmed in writing that Schwartz was an Aryan. The day that Coarraze's Jews were deported, they also came for Schwartz—who was able to produce documentation proving that any earlier assumption that he was Jewish had been mistaken all along.

Shlomo's precautions were not a minute too soon. A neighbor of Bon's notified the gendarmes that their model citizen had a secret. On the frigid morning that the police came to investigate, the Szajdholcs had miraculously decided to remain tucked under their blankets, and, in order to conserve fuel, decided not to kindle their tiny stove.

The gendarmes explained why they had come, and Bon thought fast. "What!?" he bellowed at them, enraged, his neck cords popping. "I, of all people, you would dare accuse of harboring Jews?" The officers apologetically beat a hasty retreat.

When the informer (a woman who lived across the street) saw the police leaving empty-handed, she doggedly intervened. "There are Jews hiding up there in the loft!" she insisted, pointed to a space above the carriage house. "Get closer and you'll see smoke coming out of the chimney. Where there's smoke, there's fire!"

As uncomfortable as they were with their mission, the police could not ignore an explicit tip. They returned to Bon's house to examine the chimney but indeed, on that lone morning, not a lick of smoke emerged. With a clear conscience they could now leave, having done their duty, as well as avoided another unpleasant encounter with Bon.

Bon was not about to tempt fate again, however. He quickly found temporary accommodations for the Szajdholcs, and a few days later, the false papers that Shlomo had ordered from his sons arrived in a disguised package. Once again armed with new identity cards, Shlomo, Esther and Mariette departed by train, this time to Nice.

They knew that the most dangerous leg of their journey would be the stop in Marseilles. There, the Germans would surely cut a swath through the train, as this city was the heart of the French underground resistance, and it was also adjacent to the Italian occupied zone, a sought-after refuge for Jews. French collaborators were on high alert throughout the area to bring into custody anyone who even resembled a Jew. Nowhere in Vichy France was there greater scrutiny of the civilian population.

Polish-born-and-bred Shlomo and Esther Szajdholc still spoke very little French, and Shlomo also had a distinctly Jewish appearance. Esther, at least, could visually pass for a native. Aboard the train she wore the attire of a common peasant woman with a scarf over her head, careful to have wisps of her blonde hair visible. Shlomo also wore peasant garb, and both husband and wife feigned sleep—Shlomo, with a newspaper covering his face, and his wife, slumped against his shoulder.

In Marseilles, just as they feared, the police boarded the train, searched through everyone's luggage, and demanded to see the travelers' documents. Inside the Szajdholcs' valise were Shlomo's *tefillin*; and in case they were overlooked, underneath the white-knuckled patriarch's newspaper was his tiny book of Hebrew Psalms.

The family's fate fell squarely upon the trembling shoulders of fourteen-year-old Mariette, who was blonde and blue-eyed, and looked decidedly Aryan. Inspired by the proactive behavior of their benefactor André Bon, Mariette decided to haul the bull by the horns and approached the policemen. Placing her finger to her lips, the girl motioned towards her "sleeping" parents, and thrust the family's documents, and the key to their luggage, at the officers.

"Gentlemen, do you wish me to open up our valise?" she whispered dutifully.

The French policeman took a cursory look at the papers and glanced over at the sleeping parents. "No, *jeunne fille*, that won't be necessary," he replied, patting Mariette on the head before exiting their compartment. After the door shut, Shlomo and Esther finally resumed breathing.

In every other car on the train, panic and chaos reigned, as the soldiers began to pull off terrified individuals and families who would never reach their destinations.

THE FIRSTBORN SZAJDHOLC, Alter, possessed an innate streak of altruism that persisted even while he and his family were submerged as fugitives in a squalid Nice hotel. Thus, when a handicapped fellow whom the brothers had met in Coarraze asked him to forge a document for a friend, Alter could not refuse him. The more suspicious Albert had a bad feeling about this from the outset, and pleaded with his brother not to get involved. But Alter's magnanimous nature made it difficult for him to say no, and he would pay the price.

The "friend" for whom he was seeking the document turned out to be an informer, and all it took was a beating of the invalid for the identities of the forgers to be revealed. The next day, as Albert entered his hotel, the concierge first gesticulated madly, and finally hissed, "Run away, boy! The police are upstairs, the young woman has already been arrested!"

Albert turned on his heels and ran down the street, buying a newspaper for camouflage and positioning himself at a safe distance from the hotel. Peering above the paper, he shuddered as he watched Alter being led away in handcuffs.

Albert immediately reported the dreadful turn of events to Rabbi Cassorla, who advised him to leave Toulouse at once. But Albert refused to depart as long as his brother and Sidi were in jail. He did, however, acquire new papers that changed his name and his birthplace, so as not to link him to his "criminal" brother, and he moved from the hotel to a safer location.

As Alter sat in jail, listlessly awaiting trial, it was Albert who faced constant danger on the streets. He routinely risked his life to bring food to his brother (despite Alter's vehement protestations), as the prison rations were both meager and barely edible. It was insanity for Albert—who was, after all, considered a fugitive—to venture inside the lion's den. But it was impossible to reason with Albert about his own safety while his brother was in peril.

One day, a member of the Underground brought a secret message to Albert from the prison. It was a note from Alter, instructing him to deliver a carton of cigarettes to a particular woman. Her boyfriend was a prison guard whom Alter had befriended. The jailer had agreed to relay the cigarettes to Alter, who would then barter the precious contraband in exchange for food, thus obviating Albert's risky forays.

Albert quickly set out to procure the cigarettes and bring them to the address he was given. To his astonishment and fright, this brought the seventeen-year-old to a house of ill repute in Toulouse's red-light district. Albert timidly entered the establishment and was approached by a heavily rouged madame whose smile contained enough sensual allure to redden *his* face.

This unfamiliar and seedy environment was definitely a first for him, and Albert realized that the madame had assumed he had come for a different purpose. He hardly knew how to break it to her that he was only there to deliver a parcel. Hoping with all his heart that she was the designated contact, he handed her the carton of cigarettes and whispered that it was to be transported to the prison. She accepted the parcel, and assured its delivery with a lazy wink.

Albert muttered his thanks and ducked out as quickly as he could. He was hurrying through the town square when a shrill whistle filled the air, and at that very second an army of policemen swarmed into the area. It was a police roundup!

Albert ran for his life to the only refuge he could think of nearby: the brothel. The madame quickly led him inside a tiny room, and locked the door from the outside. It was empty except for a bed.

Moments later, the gendarmerie entered the establishment; doors opened and shut, and muffled shouts filled the air. Albert had never dreamed it would all be over in a place like this. The heavy footsteps drew closer, and right outside his door he heard the lady of the night whisper to the officers that there was an "important police investigation" taking place inside the bedchamber. The policemen clearly had second thoughts about barging in on a superior, and hurriedly took their leave. Albert could only imagine the wink that she had landed upon them...

NOT ONLY ALTER relied upon Albert for his cunning and bravery. Though still only seventeen years old, Albert was viewed within the extended family as a man who could be relied upon.

Not far from Albert's lodging lived their Uncle Isaac, whose original apartment had been sealed by the police the night of the roundup. Isaac and his family located another roof over their heads on the outskirts of town, near a Luftwaffe airbase. But this shelter was of nominal benefit as it was a house under construction, without any electricity or method of heating. Isaac's family would freeze to death unless he could sneak back into his former apartment and retrieve their winter clothing.

Uncle Isaac was a rather anxious fellow, and a stickler about abiding by the law—a fine trait in normal times. But in a time when shrewdness and covert maneuvers were essential for survival, Uncle Isaac—also frail due to a lung disease—required an accomplice with steelier nerves. He could not have found a more accomplished partner in this realm than his young nephew Albert, and beseeched him for assistance.

Their mission would have had the makings of a comedy routine had the stakes not been life and death.

The two of them set off late at night to avoid detection, and Albert stood guard as his uncle got to work on the door. After a short while, Albert sensed something strange transpiring, and saw his uncle struggling to remove the door from its hinges.

"But ... don't you have the key?" Albert asked.

"Of course I have the key," replied Uncle Isaac. "But the door is sealed."

"So?" Albert persisted.

"It is against the law to break the seal, therefore, I must not use my key!"

Albert opened his mouth in protest, but realized that there was no sense in arguing with a man who believed it was illegal to use a key in the lock of his own front door, but not illegal to remove the door.

For interminable minutes, Albert waited outside standing guard, cringing each time he heard a footstep or a noise in the vicinity.

After finally removing the door from its hinges, Isaac bobbed underneath the police seal and crept inside the apartment. Albert continued waiting in the hallway; the few times he heard a door open to another apartment, he would duck down the hall and into a stairwell. But it was taking meticulous Uncle Isaac far too long to pack the winter garments; everything could have been flung inside his suitcases in less than a minute! Fuming, Albert remembered how his mother—Uncle Isaac's sister—had refused to flee their Brussels apartment until she had washed every last dirty dish.

The next hurdle came when Isaac finally finished packing; the overstuffed luggage could not fit through the narrow police seal, even with the door off of its hinges. Albert looked at him incredulously, whispering frantically that he should just break the seal and be done with it. But Uncle Isaac would not hear of it. His plan entailed hoisting the incredibly heavy valises through the tall bathroom window, which opened up into the hallway.

This was an extremely delicate operation, for if just one suitcase escaped Albert's grasp and fell, it would awaken the other tenants in the building, who would certainly alert the police. Furthermore, even if they managed to carry out the operation silently, any passerby who witnessed luggage emerging from the officially sealed doorway would definitely perform his or her civic duty as well.

Blessedly, all four suitcases were removed and the door reattached without a hitch. But because of the wartime gasoline shortage, no taxis operated at night. This meant that uncle and nephew had to shlep the backbreaking valises to the nearest streetcar stop, which was many blocks away.

There was no trolley stop near Isaac's new residence, either. But there was one close to where their friends, the Wolfingers, were staying. As he listened to his uncle wheeze and felt his own energy ebbing away, Albert suggested that it would make the most sense to park the suitcases there, and pick them up in the morning by taxi. This would be much less risky than two baggage-laden foreigners huffing and puffing their way through the darkened streets, especially since their route would entail passing a pub frequented by *Luftwaffe* airmen all night long.

But Uncle Isaac refused to be parted from his possessions for even a minute. He gripped the handles of his luggage as though its contents were diamonds! Albert had no choice but to follow, struggling mightily to maneuver the oversized bags. What was in these suitcases, anyway?

As Albert had feared, a group of German soldiers staggered out of the bar just as they were passing. The drunken airmen offered to help the older man and the youth, and without waiting for a reply, raised the suitcases upon their shoulders. "*Gott im Himmel!*" they shouted. "What do you have in here?!"

The Germans carried the suitcases right to Isaac's door, which meant that they now knew exactly where he lived. They were so inebriated, however, that it was unlikely they would have much memory of the encounter. Mopping the sweat from their brows, they did not seem in any great hurry to depart, and Uncle Isaac—his lung condition exacerbated by the anxiety-producing presence of rowdy German soldiers at his doorstep—was not holding up too well. He was in no position to reward or host them, yet they hung around waiting for some sort of remuneration, soon singing loudly as drunken men do. After several tense minutes, they finally shuffled off in search of further entertainment.

To cap off the nerve-wracking evening, Uncle Isaac invited Albert to spend what was left of the night, rather than return to his own lodging. Albert deeply regretted accepting; the house was so cold that he would have been warmer out on the street.

As the question would not go away, the next morning, Albert finally asked what was inside the valises.

"Tablecloths and bed linens," Isaac replied casually.

Albert was incredulous. For this he had broken his back, nearly frozen, risked imprisonment and his very life? He looked around Uncle Isaac's pitiful domicile, bereft of beds, table or furnishings to speak of. "Why, in heaven's name," Albert roared, "did we have to shlep sheets and tablecloths?"

"Oh," Isaac responded, as if it were the most obvious thing in the world, "these are good, really fine, quality linens. When I saw them, I thought, what a pity it would be to leave them behind! And tonight, my dear nephew, you can help me get the winter clothing!"

But Uncle Isaac had the wrong man. Albert would never serve as his accomplice again.

RABBI CASSORLA helped procure a lawyer for the trial of Alter and Sidi. Forgery was a serious infraction, and the young couple's attorney deliberately rallied a weak defense. He wisely reasoned that the safest place for anyone over eighteen was in jail, to avoid the all-too-frequent deportations of able-bodied workers to Germany.

The law dealt with the two as common criminals, since the authorities had remained unaware of their much graver offense of being Jews. They were sentenced to an additional six months in the Toulouse jail, to be followed by internment in a nearby concentration camp.

But just months after their sentencing, Alter and Sidi were aided by the Underground in a daring and successful escape. Finally, with his brother no longer in captivity, Albert felt he could leave dangerous Toulouse.

There were few parts of Vichy-France that were safe for a Jew with a criminal record for forgery, so Albert headed to Nice, which was under the jurisdiction of the Italian Occupation Forces, who were much more sympathetic to Jews.

But it was there, in the lush French Riviera, that Albert would finally lose his own freedom.

THE UNDERGROUND instructed Albert to report to Nice's Jewish Committee immediately upon arrival. The Committee paired him with Simi Templer, Sidi's brother, on a risky mission to obtain ration coupons for bread from the black market in Lyons. Passover was approaching, and the Committee had information that a local bakery would clandestinely supply matzohs to the bearers of these coupons.

Albert and his co-conspirator checked into a hotel in Lyons. In the dead of night, two policemen broke into their room, demanding to see their identification. Presumably looking for deserters from the French Army or other illegals, the officers scrutinized their expertly forged papers with a magnifying glass, and although they appeared genuine, the fact that both boys' birth dates were given as December 25th aroused suspicion. For this coincidence alone, the officers barked that they were under arrest.

Just as the officers brusquely ushered the youths into the street, Simi Templer made a run for it. One boy's escape automatically stripped the other of any semblance of innocence.

Albert was hauled into the police interrogation room, where he was shoved onto a stool and a steel ruler waved in his face. "Who are you, boy?!" an officer roared at him. Albert removed his identification papers from his pocket, and the back of his skull was swiftly struck by the ruler. "Not those papers," the officer snarled. "Your real papers!"

Though reeling from the blow to his head, Albert insisted in the strongest voice he could muster that these were his genuine papers. He maintained he had no idea who the other boy was, that they had only met that day and had agreed to split the cost of a night's lodging.

The cop wasn't buying a word of it. The disappearance of his frightened accomplice was irrefutable proof that Albert was a liar. "I'll have to beat the truth out of you, then!" he declared, giving Albert a few more sharp whacks as a painful preview of what was to come.

But more terrifying than any beating was the surge of fear Albert felt when he was ordered to empty his pockets. At that moment, he nearly stopped breathing. Buried deep inside his pants-pocket was a letter he had written to his parents but had not yet mailed. It would not only incriminate his parents, but also identify Mr. Schwartz (his contact in the Underground who had officially proven himself not Jewish) to whom it was addressed—and all of Coarraze's hidden Jews.

Albert tried to gain control of himself, and feigned elaborate trembling and disorientation as he emptied the contents of his pockets onto the desk, careful to leave the letter where it was. He was then frisked by the officers, but miraculously his pockets were not examined.

The interrogator was bitterly disappointed by the innocuous contents of his young suspect's pockets, and resumed his beating with even greater brutality, the metal stick vibrating in his fist each time it met Albert's head. Finally, the boy snapped. With his last ounce of strength, Albert arched upwards to his feet, menacingly raised the stool above his head, and threatened: "If this man takes one more step toward me, I will smash this over his head!" And with remarkable presence of mind, he added, "I shall also report him to the District Attorney for assaulting a minor!"

Albert's loud outburst attracted the attention of a more senior officer in an adjoining interrogation room. The supervisor was eager to restore order. "Take it easy, kid," he cajoled. "You put that chair down, and I'll call Montpelier, where these papers were issued, and see if you're on the level."

The supervisor did indeed check out Albert's documents and, blessedly, got word that they were authentic. But the ordeal wasn't over.

"It appears you are telling the truth," the officer said levelly, "so you are now under arrest for vagabondage."

"For what?" cried Albert.

"Your papers say that you are a minor. Wandering about without your parents is a criminal offense, and therefore we will keep you in jail for twenty-four hours while we thoroughly check out your story."

Albert's shoelaces and belt were confiscated, and he was frisked a second time. Once again the letter mercifully avoided detection. He was then tossed into a filthy, fetid-smelling cell, with a group of fearsome-looking Algerians.

The other prisoners were the dirtiest human beings he had ever seen in his life. Their tattered clothing was soiled with excrement and urine. There were no beds or mattresses, and an overflowing pail served as the latrine. On the floor were chunks of what Albert assumed at first to be human waste—but it turned out to be the putrid slop that was fed to the prisoners.

The boy feared for his life, but since he was clearly bruised and bloodied, his cellmates—it appeared—took compassion upon him, and left him alone. Eventually, one of them asked him what happened, and Albert recounted the tale, telling the men he was to be released in twenty-four hours.

Until that point, the prisoners had listened quietly. But suddenly it was as if he had cracked the funniest joke in the world. Their reaction started with a few snickers, and then escalated into a chorus of loud guffaws that echoed through the cellblock, as prisoners gripped their sides and slapped each other on the back.

Albert failed to see the humor. Finally one inmate explained: "Twenty-four hours means at least a week. And then a week stretches—"

"Can't be," Albert protested. "They said that the law only allows them to keep me for twenty-four hours!" This line triggered an even louder explosion of laughter.

While it was no laughing matter, the inmates were correct. A harrowing week elapsed before Albert was even summoned before a magistrate. Then the judge demanded to know who he "really" was and why his "accomplice" had run away. Several times during the proceedings, the judge warned Albert to tell the truth, or he would be sent to "the hospital;" Albert assumed that this was a euphemism for prison. But the boy stuck to his original story, reasoning to himself that it would be difficult for the court to verify information from the location given as his birthplace.

The case was a legal conundrum. Although Albert was actually eighteen (an age subject to deportation to Germany), his falsified papers listed him as seventeen, a minor—and a minor could not be released to anyone but his parents. The defendant was claiming, however, that his parents were dead.

After the brief hearing, the judge ordered that Albert be returned to jail while claims were investigated.

For weeks, the young "vagabond" was rotated through several appalling blocks of the prison complex. Warehoused with an assortment of murderers, thieves and other lowlifes, Albert found himself sinking into deep despair. To maintain his sanity, Albert began to write poetry. One day a guard observed him writing, and in a rage, ripped his small cache of papers to shreds.

For Albert, this was an indescribably low moment and he could not hold back his tears. But his anguish only made him wiser. He realized

that the prison staff was made up of semi-illiterates who deeply resent-
ed anyone who displayed any intellect or education; it weakened their
sense of power and authority. He now understood how critical it was to
fit in in prison—both in the eyes of the other prisoners and the guards.
A prisoner with high-minded, intellectual pursuits went against the
stream, and the inevitable consequence was trouble.

Albert used this lesson to improve his own lot, and to ease the suffering of another. In the prison library—a place rarely frequented by
the rank and file—he met an anguished youth who was being picked on
mercilessly by the guards and routinely beaten by his cellmates. Albert's
gut feeling was that the boy was a Jew, and gently put forth the question.
He denied it, until Albert whispered the Hebrew code word, "*amicha*
(of your nation)," frequently used by Jews at that time to secretly determine kinship.

After Albert received the frightened boy's reply, "*amicha*," he took
him under his wing. The boy, who was in for a minor offense, maintained that he was not guilty, and this infuriated his cellmates and his
guards—who could deal with felons, but had no patience for a babe
in the woods. "You mustn't tell a thief who is sharing your cell that
you're innocent—that's what you tell the police and the judge," Albert
instructed him urgently. "Everybody is in here for some reason, and the
more criminal it is, the worse the offense, the better you'll be treated in
this society. A 'goody-goody,' or someone suspected of being a spy, will
be beaten to a pulp."

The boy understood, and emulated Albert's swagger. From that day
on, his situation improved drastically.

But as days turned into weeks and months, Albert did not know
how much more he could stand of this hellhole. When a new prisoner
was tossed into his cell and raved about his erstwhile stint in "the hospital," Albert's ears perked up. So there really was such a place, and it
wasn't just a euphemism! And the conditions sounded far better than
where he was. Albert penned a desperate letter to the judge describing
how an innocent minor was being corrupted by unfettered exposure to
hardened criminals who conducted daily seminars on how to murder,
rob and defraud. To support his argument, he outlined the techniques
he had learned to force open a locked door. Citing the unbearably

subverting pressures of his environment, Albert pleaded for immediate transfer to "the hospital."

The judge granted his permission, and Albert was remanded to a vastly better situation. Sister Marguerite and the priest who ran the penal unit known mysteriously as "the hospital," provided nourishing incentives to all those prisoners who attended mass or volunteered as altar boys. This turned Albert, almost overnight, into an extremely devout Catholic—at least outwardly. For Albert had learned how to work the system.

BY THE TIME Albert was finally called to trial, the state had evidence that his papers were fraudulent. As Albert grappled with what his next prevarication would be, a spectator in the courtroom suggested he be placed in the custody of the Salvation Army, the Christian humanitarian organization. The prosecutor countered that a proven liar like Albert should be punished with the full severity of the law.

The final word came from the judge. "Even if we believe that he is lying, the issue is vagabondage and not a criminal act," he intoned, wielding his gavel. "If the Salvation Army is willing to assume responsibility for him, I am prepared to release him to them!"

The Salvation Army made earnest attempts to save youths from the detrimental influence of prison and other harmful environments. Albert's induction began with a stern warning: "We are totally responsible for you and have given our solemn word that you will not run away. If you escape our custody, the courts will never trust our organization again, and future convicts will be denied the break that you have been given."

Albert was not oblivious to his moral obligation, but he was keenly aware of another reality: that he would soon turn eighteen (at least, according to his papers), and that this age, coupled with a police record, would render him a choice target for deportation.

Accordingly, he immediately began plotting his escape from the Salvation Army camp, where he worked as a dishwasher. Leaving would be easy—but he knew that without papers he would not get very far.

Now the brothers' roles were reversed: Alter was on the outside working frantically for his younger brother's release. He sent word to

Albert that the Szajdholc family was safe in Nice under the Italian Occupation, the best place for a Jew to be under the circumstances. Sidi would be bringing him new papers to the home of her aunt who lived in Lyons. Once Albert secured what he needed he penned a letter to the Salvation Army apologizing for going back on his word.

With all of my appreciation for what you have done for me, I have no choice but to flee for my life. As a Jew, the situation is far too perilous here for me and my people. I deeply regret that I may jeopardize the chances of others, and I hope that you will forgive me and accept my gratitude for your help.

Albert realized that his letter would be immediately turned over to the police, so he added some false details to throw them off the track. Sidi explained to Albert that the safest route from Lyons to Nice would be via rail to Grenoble, and from there, by bus through the Italian Occupied Zone. This way Marseilles and Toulons, which were crawling with police, could be avoided. But all of this was predicated upon Albert getting through the Lyons train station—a favorite site of police dragnets—undetected.

Sidi purchased two rail tickets for Grenoble, while Albert bought one to Ortez, via Paris, which departed Lyons at almost the exact same time.

The Paris trip was a decoy, and Albert carefully left his footprints on the trail. He knew the police would follow him, so he cleverly allowed himself to be stalked, but not caught. His letter to the Salvation Army had said when he would be leaving for Paris, but he knew that if he were not found on that train all the other trains in the station would be inspected, sealing his fate.

Albert waited until the last call to board, and then conspicuously asked every railroad employee he encountered—including a conductor flanked by two plainclothesmen—if he was headed in the right direction for the Ortez-via-Paris train.

By this juncture of the war, Albert could smell a policeman a kilometer away, so in their honor he inquired a second time as to exactly which track the train was departing from. By the time Albert boarded the Paris train, *everyone* in the railroad station was familiar with his itinerary.

He now had less than a minute before the departure of his actual train to freedom. Albert jumped out a different door and from a different side than the one he had entered, and sprinted across the platform to the train to Grenoble, leaping aboard as it was already in motion. Gasping for breath, he stared out the window at the other train beginning its own departure from the station. With indescribable relief he watched the furious plainclothesmen race through the cars of the train he had just exited.

ALBERT separated from Sidi in Grenoble and arrived in Nice two days later. Life was completely different under the Italian Occupation. After years on the run, Albert now sought to be interned, and happily exchanged his perfectly forged card bearing a French governmental seal for a paltry slip of paper with a Jewish star, issued by the Jewish Committee.

The reason? False papers in Nice were cause for arrest, and while the French did not recognize the Committee's note it was perfectly legal to the Italian authorities who were in charge of the protectorate. Still, French police continued to swarm the area, and were always eager to assert their authority. If anyone was apprehended by a French official, their safety depended upon getting the attention of an Italian policeman who could pull rank.

The wisest policy, then, was for a refugee to keep a low profile— inside and out of view—until being assigned "forced residence" by the Italian Protectorate Authority, which invariably took a while.

Sidi had informed Albert that he should look up Shlomo Granat when he arrived in Nice. The pious and hospitable Granats were natives of Nice, and had become the respected benefactors of all the Jewish refugees in the region. They received Albert royally, and fed him the best meal he had eaten in years. They apologized profusely that they could not accommodate him overnight, because other refugees still awaiting homes took up every centimeter of floor space.

It was there that he received his first bit of news about his youngest sister, Bella, who had gone from summer camp to living with a Christian family, until dangerous conditions forced her to be transferred to a convent. He was overjoyed to learn that the Granats' son had rescued Bella from the convent, and had delivered her to Nice.

When the meal was over Shlomo Granat escorted Albert outside

and begged him to be careful. But Albert was not known for his pru-
dence. The very next morning he was driven by the balmy temperatures, spring blossoms and fragrances to take a leisurely stroll in a park.
What a luxury, after the bleakness of his prison cell! Before he knew it,
two French policemen swooped down upon him, forced him inside a
building and demanded to see his identification card.

"This is not Palestine," the officer reproached him snidely, after
Albert produced the slip of paper with the Jewish star. "See here, you
are in France!"

Albert was ordered to the police station, but he refused to budge.
He had had his fill of the French police, and tremulously declared he
took orders from the Italian Command—*only*.

There were no Italian soldiers in sight at that moment, so the French
policemen did as they pleased. But Albert began shouting for help,
louder and louder, and there was no way of quieting him. He knew
that he had some leverage, for if the French abducted a Jew, the Italians
would threaten to expel the head of the French police from Nice until
every Jew was accounted for; it had happened before. An Italian officer
soon heard Albert's cries and promptly set him free

The very next day, Albert became eligible for forced residence, but his
assignment was not to the same village as his family. Albert appealed to
the Jewish Committee, and a reassignment was immediately arranged.

Off he went to St. Martin Vesubie for a glorious reunion with his
parents, his brother and two sisters. The family's joy and relief was
indescribable.

Indescribable, too, was the beauty of the mountainous resort.
The cherry trees were heavy with fruit, and the tulips—in a dazzling
array of colors—were in full blossom. Most of the mountain peaks
were enveloped in clouds, and a pristine blanket of snow covered their
mid-sections.

"Forced residence" was the greatest oxymoron that Albert had ever
heard. The chalet assigned to the Szajdholcs was comfortable and im-
maculate. Outside the windows were postcard-perfect views of the
French Alps.

The only requirement was an early morning check-in with the police each day. Failure to report resulted in a typically lenient punishment, Italian-style. A member of the *carabinieri* would be dispatched to

determine if the perpetrator was ill, in which case he or she would be excused. Absence without an excuse resulted in 48-hour house arrest. There were no restrictions on visitors for those under house arrest, and invariably each "punishment" turned into a marathon party.

Under the rules of "forced residence," however, the Jews were forbidden to hold an assembly, and this ostensibly precluded prayer services. But seeing that this was so important to the Jews, the Italian marshal for the area announced he would permit a one-time convocation, which he would personally attend to verify that the gathering was religious and not seditious in nature.

A celebrated cantor from Antwerp, Chazan Dim, led the prayers, and his exquisite tenor rang out like a powerful bronze bell. Not only did the marshal give his go-ahead, but he attended every week from then on, because of his love of *bel canto*. A place of honor was reserved for the marshal.

Now that public prayer was permitted, Sabbath observers who attended synagogue were permitted to check in with the police at their leisure after the services.

In addition to the synagogue, the refugee community of St. Martin Vesubie established a medical clinic, a kindergarten and a Talmud Torah (school for religious instruction). Other activities included a swimming tournament and a boxing league. All athletic competitions were held in the presence of the marshal, who took pride in the industriousness of his internees.

The childhood romance between twenty-year-old Alter Szajdholc and Sidi Templer had blossomed into a genuine love that had transcended the separations and displacement of war. In St. Martin, it culminated in marriage, bringing sorely needed joy and hope to two families bound together by their struggles. The uplifting music of a violin and an accordion accompanied the procession to the *chuppah* (wedding canopy), which had been set up outside the synagogue. Cantor Dim chanted the special blessings, and a rabbi who had also been interned in the village conducted the ceremony. The marshal was a guest of honor, and attended both the ceremony and the modest reception with unabashed curiosity, enjoyment and respect.

For a brief, tender moment, as the bride and groom gazed adoringly at each other, and the guests raised their glasses to them, and the

Szajdholc and Templer families were united in joy, life seemed almost normal to those who had wandered and suffered for so long.

ON JULY 24, 1943, the Italians finally unseated Mussolini, and following the Italian Armistice in September 1943, their soldiers and *carabinieri* were ordered home from the protectorate. This opened the door for the German invasion of Nice, bringing a swift end to the ephemeral moment of serenity the Jews had clung to there.

The Jews of St. Martin appealed to their trusted marshal for help. "We cannot take you with us," the official replied with regret, "But if you wish to follow ..." he continued, with an expansive wave of his arms, and left the rest unsaid.

Convinced that freedom—finally!—lay over the Alps in Italy, nearly eight hundred Jewish men, women and children hastily gathered their meager belongings, and began a dramatic exodus on the heels of the Italian army. Even the hard-hearted French police and populace displayed a rare surge of compassion, waving misty-eyed farewells as the anxious caravan fled the village.

Hardly dressed or equipped for the rigorous trek in the autumn chill, the refugees hiked up the mountains, with the elderly and the handicapped valiantly struggling to keep pace. After two grueling days, they crossed a small bridge that marked the Italian border, and a communal sigh of relief reverberated through the crowd. They truly believed they were free. Why would the Germans bother to follow them there, after Italy had already signed an armistice with the Allies? Still, to create more distance between themselves and their dreaded enemies, the exhausted procession trudged along, deeper and deeper into the Italian countryside. Finally, when they reached the village of Valdieri, they set up camp for the night in a school.

Once again, the Szajdholc, Templer and Wolfinger families were united in a race to freedom.

BUT THE NEXT MORNING, they all awoke to a nightmare. A German mechanized division had encircled Valdieri, and Nazi guards were posted outside the building. No one was permitted to leave. The orders were for all the refugees to report to the village square at 10 AM.

In sorrow and resignation, the frightened assemblage began

preparing for their departure. But the ever-prescient Shlomo Szajdholc had a different notion. As everyone solemnly shuffled down to the square, he ordered his family to sit on a ledge, and wait. He convinced the Templers and Wolfingers also to hang back and assess the situation.

Every exit of the town was guarded. Ten minutes before the deadline, Albert turned to his father and said, "I think it's time that we join everyone else." Shlomo Szajdholc set his jaw and stated firmly, "It is not yet ten, there is still time, remain where you are!" One passerby urged the small group to hurry and join the others, but Albert's father motioned for everyone to stay put.

At ten o'clock, the officer in charge commanded the guards standing at the village exits to abandon their positions and reinforce the contingent in the village square. One soldier who had departed his guard-post passed by the group and ordered them to march down with the others. They all stood up, but as soon as the soldier passed, Shlomo pointed to a narrow path and whispered, "It is now clear to leave Valdieri. One by one we will escape up the mountains!"

The determined patriarch knew who must be the first: nimble young Albert. "Do not stop or turn around, even if you are shouted at," he commanded his reluctant son. "Stop only if you hear shooting."

Only one individual refused to accede to the elder Szajdholc's plan of action—the Templer's impetuous boy, Shalom—and a heated argument, in hushed tones, erupted between them. Shalom declared it was madness to return to the mountains, where death from starvation or hypothermia was almost certain. Try as they might, no one could convince young Templer to remain, and as the others launched their unsteady ascent, he broke away to join the mass descent to the village square.

Wearily they trudged up the steep mountain path, knowing not what lay on the other side—knowing only that they were not among the doomed captives in Valdieri's center.

Suddenly, as the road began to flatten, a farmer came running towards them, frantically flailing his arms and shouting a word they did not know: "*Tedeschi, Tedeschi!*" Alter saw that the man was about to block their passage, and gesticulated to his brother, "Let's jump him!" Just then, they heard the nearby rumbling of a tank. Their path led to a main road, and into the hands of the Germans.

That was the moment they realized that *Tedeschi* is the Italian word for "Germans."

Most of the group lunged behind some bushes while the Szajdholc brothers sprinted over to a shed farther up the hill to get a better view and determine their next move. From there they caught sight of a pitiful procession of heavily guarded Jewish prisoners, whose faces they could recognize in the distance.

Apparently their presence was perceived, as they saw a commanding officer point to the shed, thundering, "Bring me a hand grenade!" But mercifully, no grenade was forthcoming, and the column moved on.

Albert and Alter reported back that there was no way to proceed up the mountain other than the main road. The group dared not venture any farther during daylight. Huddled behind the meager bushes, they prayed for nightfall. Even a fierce, torrential downpour did not induce them to seek shelter in the shed until full darkness had enveloped them.

The following day, the rain receded and they continued their upward trek deeper into Italy, which they had (erroneously) assumed would be free of Germans because of the Armistice. In the sparsely populated mountain terrain, they came upon three shepherd's sheds, and were stunned to discover Cantor Dim and his wife in one of them. The Dims, like themselves, had decided to risk escape. And they, too, were starving.

Esther Szajdholc reasoned that with all of the greenery on the mountain, there had to be a source of underground water. She began to burrow until she uncovered some moist soil that led to a tiny mountain spring. They also discovered that the mountainside was dotted with chestnuts. The menu was sparse, to be sure—but the essential nutrients were there.

WITH WINTER fast approaching, life in the mountain shed was becoming unbearable. It was an especially chilly Friday afternoon with fierce, steady, bawling winds that caused Alter to finally break. He announced that he and his young bride were leaving, that they would find their way back to France, where they at least had some contacts and knew the language.

His father gave him a withering glance. It was Shlomo Szajdholc's position that it was the Lord's will that had brought them this far, and to retreat would be flouting a Divine directive.

Alter would not back down. "Papa, take your eyes out of your prayer book and look at us!" he railed bitterly. "What in the world do you expect—for us to stay here and freeze, or starve to death? Sidi and I are leaving tomorrow, no matter what, and whoever wishes to join us is welcome!"

Shlomo mustered every ounce of his waning strength for his reply. "My son, I beseech you to have faith in the Almighty. He has brought us this far and never failed us. I don't believe that turning back into territory that is totally dominated by the Germans is His plan."

Alter looked away guiltily as his father's eyes spilled over with tears. In a barely audible tone, Shlomo whispered hoarsely: "Ah, children, perhaps your way is best—who can know the right answers in such times? But I ask of you one last favor. Tomorrow is God's holy Sabbath. Surely you can wait one day longer to depart."

Many pent-up emotions were unleashed in Alter's reply. "What 'God' are you referring to, Papa? Where have you been for the past four years? And where has He been? God and His 'day of rest' have no more meaning to me!"

"I fully understand your pain and confusion," Shlomo said quietly. "It is all part of this great test of faith. All I pray is that you can hold onto some kernel of faith, for man cannot fathom the Almighty's ways."

While no ill will remained between the father and his firstborn son, Alter would not budge from his position. He and Sidi would begin their journey on Shabbos morning, and the Templers, not wanting to be parted from their daughter, would join them. Shlomo promised his family that they, too, would finally abandon the isolated mountain shack—but only the following day.

That night, Albert tossed and turned on the hay-strewn floor of the shed. The wind howled outside its thin walls, but more than that, he was deeply unsettled by the words of his older brother. Alter had always been so "good," so dutiful—the model Jewish son. If his pious brother's faith was gone ... how would he cling to his own?

Finally he fell into a fitful sleep, only to be awakened by strange sounds coming from outside the shed, and he braved the whipping night air to investigate. Scaling terrain that was by now familiar to him even in the dark, Albert crept slowly towards the source of the noise and what he saw froze him in his place.

Swaying back and forth, with the moonlight shining eerily on his face, was his father. His eyes were shut, and his arms stretched upward, like those of a Biblical prophet.

Shlomo Szajdholc called out to the heavens in a quaking voice, "*Master of the Universe, what have we done wrong—what have I done wrong? I have tried to live according to Your commandments. My greatest priority in life remained steadfast, that our children be raised as God-fearing Jews.*"

For a few moments, his voice gave way to wrenching sobs, a sound that broke Albert's heart as he crouched motionlessly nearby. And then Shlomo pressed on. "*My Father, I have never left you. I beg You, have mercy, do not forsake us now! We suffered every imaginable indignity, lost our home, our livelihood, everything we ever owned; we have scaled mountains and crossed valleys and are hunted and driven like animals, but we cannot continue fighting the elements.*

"*Please, Almighty One. I can no longer shoulder responsibility and assert leadership. I cannot direct which road to take, when every road may lead to death. I ask only that You give us a sign so we will know what to do. If You wish us to stay here, unleash a torrential rain. And if Your will is for us to return to France, let the sun shine upon us.*"

As tears streamed down Albert's face, he lifted his eyes to the clear night sky. Though the wind blustered, there was a dazzling canopy of stars. His poor father had obviously lost touch with reality.

Albert stumbled back to the hut, but sleep was now even harder to come by. Seeing his father pleading nakedly to the heavens for mercy, so alone and so bereft, shook him to his core.

Finally Albert drifted off, and once again awoke with a start—this time, at the crack of dawn. His eyes roamed the hut—his father was not there! Albert leapt to his feet and found him outside, rooted in the very same spot. His eyes remained shut, and his lips moved in silent prayer.

Suddenly, the sky turned as black as if the lights had been switched off. A blinding downpour erupted, and great flashes of thunder and lightning snapped in the sky.

For three consecutive days, torrential rain imprisoned them inside the shed. When the storm finally let up, there was no way out of the mountains. Massive flooding had rendered every road impassable, and mudslides coursed down the mountainside. Higher up on the mountain, a route that would have been the surest escape from the Germans was no longer even discernible as the storm had deposited an impassably deep snowfall.

Even Alter had to admit that there was no way to misread "the signs."

But enduring an icy winter inside the mountain shed was not an option; even the simple act of kindling a fire would alert the Germans to their presence. Albert and Mariette were sent to Andonno, the town carved into the base of the mountain, about two hours away, to seek aid from one of its most influential citizens, Father Antonio Borsotto. Albert and Alter had met the Catholic priest on an earlier occasion through a couple they knew who lived in the town.

The sympathetic cleric saw the terror and exhaustion in the eyes of the Szajdholc children. "If the Germans even suspect someone of sheltering an 'outlaw,' they burn down his house, sometimes the entire village!" he said fretfully. "But no one could survive on the mountain through the long winter."

Father Borsotto handed the children the key to a small building next door to the church that had a sparsely furnished spare room. "Move in at night," he instructed them. "I will alert the villagers that you are living there, but we must be very, very careful of strangers."

The Szajdholcs gratefully inhabited the tiny quarters, and the Wolfingers, Templers, Alter and Sidi found other nearby accommodations. Their next-door-neighbors, Usebio and Anna Giordano, were kind people who gave what food they could spare. It was a vast improvement over the conditions on the mountain, but their problems were far from over. Even with the Giordanos' generosity and that of the other villagers, the meager rations were not enough to feed five mouths. Andonno was blanketed in snow, and their meager woodpile offered only the mildest relief from the frigid temperatures. And in some ways, life in the village was more hazardous than in the mountains. The Germans made routine incursions to sweep the town for partisans, striking fear into the hearts of the Jewish fugitives, and the good people of Andonno.

ON CHRISTMAS EVE 1943, just before midnight, the church bells of Andonno echoed through the mountains, enveloping the village in an aura of tranquility. The Szajdholc family huddled together for warmth, and tried to think about anything but their gnawing hunger.

The night was shattered by an insistent pounding on the door that filled them with terror. For many tense moments no one moved, but the knocking would not cease. As they heard no sounds of an army truck or jeep—signals of a Nazi raid—Albert opened the door a crack. There stood a wizened old peasant woman wrapped in a shawl. "*Buon Natale*," she whispered, "Merry Christmas."

She handed Albert a parcel of cheese and disappeared into the night. Soon after, another villager came bearing a large bundle of firewood, and then another with some loaves of bread. The knocking at the door continued practically through the night, resulting in a large cache of desperately needed supplies.

The Szajdholcs were deeply touched by the generosity of the poor peasants who had so little of their own. The next day they learned that Father Borsotto had preached during midnight mass about how the infant Jesus and his family were alone and friendless in a manger in Bethlehem.

"Just like our Savior was isolated and rejected, so, too, are the Jews of today," the priest had thundered. "They are all by themselves living in mangers and often far worse. In our own village there is a Jewish family, hungry and dejected—hunted for no other reason than that they are Jews, and afraid for their very lives. Everyone here can be the Magi, and bring gifts and hope to the Jews of Andonno!"

And so, for this one day, the frightened inhabitants of the little room next door to the church were reminded of what it was like to be human. And then, just as quickly, their lives reverted back to a fierce, primal struggle for survival.

AS THE FRIGID DAYS and weeks passed, the quest for a plan of escape became ever more frantic. The Templers seized upon the idea of obtaining Hungarian citizenship papers. These documents would be an invaluable travel asset, as Hungary was an ally of Germany.

The Templers had never even lived in Hungary. But since the family's roots were in Czechoslovakia, which had once been part of the Austro-Hungarian Empire, they spoke Hungarian. In a fit of desperation, they figured that it was worth a try.

As far-fetched as this option seemed, it was more than the Szajdholcs had going for them, and their future looked very bleak. But blonde, blue-eyed Sidi, who looked anything but Jewish, undertook the mission of traveling to the Hungarian Consulate in Rome, and she was determined to acquire documents for everyone. There was no dissuading this strong-willed, exceptionally brave, young woman. Before she departed, she insisted on taking individual photographs of each of them, to affix to their papers.

The journey from their perch in the Italian Alps would be a rigorous one, accomplished via a train that departed from the valley to Florence, and from there to Rome. It would be even more rigorous for courageous Sidi Templer Szajdholcs. For what only she and Alter knew, was that she was pregnant.

There was another new life to fight for.

Sidi left not a moment too soon. The Germans razed the neighboring village of Boves because of suspected partisan activity. Two days later, Andonno was engulfed in artillery fire heralding a German sweep. Father Borsotto came pounding on the door and ordered the family to flee immediately into the mountains. If Jews were discovered in Andonno, it too would be burned to the ground.

As they frantically layered on their clothing, they received word from their kindly neighbors, Usebio and Anna Giordano, encouraging them to return after nightfall. The Giordanos knew it was impossible to survive a winter night in the mountains. They would leave their barn door unlocked, but cautioned that the premises would have to be vacated before daybreak.

As German bullets rained randomly throughout the village, the hapless Szajdholcs scurried up the mountain path they knew so well. Alter and Albert led the expedition, and located another shepherd's hut in the distance. As they approached the structure, it was obliterated by mortar fire. The Germans knew that the mountain huts were used by the partisans, and they were determined to eliminate any possible shelter.

They had no choice but to huddle together in a mountain thicket, and the temperatures dropped with each passing hour—how they prayed for nightfall!

The Giordanos kept their word. After the Szajdholcs snuck back into town, they found a pot of hot soup waiting for them in the unlocked barn, where they were able to spend a few hours protected from the elements. The neighbors also provided a pile of fresh straw for them to take back up to the mountain, to gather around themselves as insulation.

Albert was sent back to their old lodging to gather a few belongings, and what he saw there made his blood run cold. The place had been ransacked for evidence of partisans. Strewn on the floor were the black leather boxes and unfurled straps of Shlomo Szajdholc's precious *tefillin*. Had the Germans realized what these objects were, had they closely examined the boxes and recognized the Hebrew characters, they would have surely done in Andonno what they did in Boves: set fire to the house, to the adjacent church ... and to the priest himself.

When Albert returned to the barn and breathlessly reported what he had found, they all knew there was no choice but to return to the mountain each day. And each night, they would creep back into the barn, and gratefully guzzle another pot of hot soup. The Giordanos, like Father Borsotto, were well aware of the huge risk they were taking. But they would not budge from doing what they knew was right or what they perceived as their duty.

THE HUNGARIAN CONSUL in Rome was highly skeptical of the "other" family that Sidi was representing, though the young woman argued passionately, and in fluent Hungarian. Suddenly, in the course of her oration, she fainted dead away. It was clear that this was not a stunt staged for compassion.

After regaining consciousness, Sidi revealed tearfully that she was pregnant. The consul was deeply taken with her and her plight. He immediately prepared documents for every person on her list.

Now the trick was returning safely to Andonno. If the Fascists inspected her bag, which was standard procedure, the thick pile of documents would likely arouse suspicion and jeopardize everyone's welfare.

The solution to Sidi's problem became apparent as soon as she boarded the train. The car was crowded with Wehrmacht officers, who were eager to engage a good-looking girl who spoke German. A seat was grandly vacated for her, and nobody bothered to examine the bag of such a comely "friend" of the good officers.

It was a day of rejoicing, that day in the dead of winter, early 1944, when the Szajdholcs saw Sidi strenuously climbing up the mountain smiling broadly and waving. Her jubilant expression revealed that she had been successful in her mission, and she was greeted with a hero's welcome. Now, documents in hand, they could move on to a safer haven. Rome was their destination, because there were reports of a number of helpful bishops there, making it the best refuge.

The plan was to avoid Andonno's main train station, where Jews had been arrested in the past, in favor of a tiny station a few kilometers away. There, the Giordanos informed them, they could catch an early-morning train to Torino, the first leg of their journey.

The Szajdholcs planned to go to the distant station on foot, but Anna Giordano—a very large woman with a very strong personality— would not hear of it. She commanded her reluctant husband to drive them in his horse-drawn cart, and to stand in line to purchase their tickets at the station, lest they draw undue attention.

And so, on the morning of January 7, 1944, the Szajdholcs piled onto the Giordanos' primitive wagon. With Usebio at the reins, Anna presented them with a package of food, and they hastily said their goodbyes.

Anna Giordano, a simple woman who was not educated, or even literate, would hardly accept their tearful thanks. "We have no choice," she said matter-of-factly. "You are innocent people, hounded for no reason! If I were in your place, I dread to imagine what would happen if no one came to my aid. If one human being doesn't help another, what kind of world would this be?" And then she and her husband spread a pile of hay in order to conceal them, and they were on their way.

The bumpy, skittering ride to the station felt like an eternity. Finally, after meticulously fulfilling his wife's instructions, Usebio Giordano offered his closing words of caution: "No matter what, stay away from Florence, where the German army is headquartered. Your safest route to Rome is via Genoa."

THE TRAVELERS arrived in Torino late at night, and despite a great deal of tumult in the station, located the track for Genoa. Yet again, they climbed aboard an overcrowded train that did not even have seats for its passengers. But the family's exhaustion, coupled with the steady rocking of the train, lulled them into a deep slumber.

They were awakened in the morning by the booming voice of the conductor: *"Florence— final stop! Everybody off!"*

Florence? How on earth did they get to the one place they had been warned to avoid?!

The station was teeming with German soldiers and had the air of a military installation. An Italian traveler saw their consternation and explained what had happened. In their rush to board in Torino, they had not noticed a sign indicating that only the first three cars were going to Genoa, and the rear of the train was Florence-bound. During the night, those cars were uncoupled.

The mysterious Italian traveler seemed to be their guardian angel through a dizzying series of frightening twists and turns. As Shlomo Szajdholc tried to steer the group clear of the swarm of German soldiers, a police patrol appeared and began checking everyone's papers. Shlomo surveyed the scene and instructed everyone to quietly and ever-so-casually follow him—one by one—to the side of the station that had already been checked by the police. Their defection worked without a flaw. Then the mysterious Italian man briefly reappeared to inform them that no trains were departing for Rome because of track damage from Allied bombings.

They had no idea what to do or where to go. Before they knew what was happening, their nameless guide began heaving their packages onto a truck that belonged to the Wehrmacht and then he literally pushed them on just before it barreled out of the station. Shlomo Szajdholc and his family were terrified at being in such a dangerous place, disoriented by the pandemonium of the station, and utterly baffled as to where they were now heading. They had not intended any of this, and seemed helpless to avoid what appeared to be their most illogical move since the outbreak of the war.

Their destination? The panic-stricken family knew only that they were driving into the night, taking detour after detour to circumvent bombed-out roads. At one point, an air raid siren pierced the air, followed by a barrage of explosions. The driver turned off his lights and propelled the truck full throttle in a zigzag course of sudden starts and stops, dips into ditches and hairpin turns on fewer than four wheels— all in the pitch darkness.

When the bombing finally subsided, the truck pulled into a quaint village square. The other passengers marched off as if they knew exactly where they were going. The Szajdholcs, however, stood helplessly root-ed to the spot. Mercifully, again their Italian guide came back to steer them—this time, to a crowded inn where they received free food and lodging.

Public transportation was clearly no longer an option. In the days and nights that followed, they took every ride they could find to get closer to their destination—even going as far as flagging down German army trucks.

With steely determination, they recalled the proverb that was so thoroughly ironic at that place and time: all roads lead to Rome.

For a restless youth like Albert Szajdholc, life on the run—though endlessly perilous and grueling—was preferable to being trapped inside the tiny room in Andonno, or on the lonely mountain. His risk-taking nature and penchant for human connection would either be the key to his and his family's survival—or their demise.

One hitch took them straight into Bagnaia, a town about sixty miles north of Rome, and a regional headquarters for the Luftwaffe. Although curfew was imminent, they were reluctant to stay overnight in a hotbed of German activity, so they planted themselves in the village square and waited—to no avail—for a ride.

Eventually a young airman approached them, warned them that only a few minutes remained, and pointed them in the direction of a nearby inn. Shlomo Szajdholc conceded that there was little chance of finding a ride at that point, and ventured inside the establishment— only to be brusquely told that there were no vacancies. Once again they returned to the road, risking arrest for flouting the strict laws of the wartime curfew.

Just then the same airman passed by, accosted them and demanded to know why they were still on the streets. Albert spoke up and re-ported that they had been turned away from the inn. The two stood eyeball to eyeball, and it was obvious they were practically the same age.

"You just come with me!" the irate soldier commanded. Followed by the hapless procession, he burst into the inn and shouted at the startled innkeeper: "*I order you to vacate a room— your own room!— this instant, for my friend's family!*"

The innkeeper cowered and stammered his apologies, and then followed the airman's directive to the letter.

The Szajdholcs could not remember the last time they had laid down their heads in such comfort—they could not even remember when they had last slept in a real bed.

The young soldier introduced himself as Hans. The family never really understood why he had interceded so vociferously on their behalf, but it was obvious that he had taken an instant liking to Albert. He even invited the youth to accompany him and his Luftwaffe cronies to a movie being screened just for the military, which Albert—though sorely tempted—politely declined.

But when Hans came to the door again, insisting that his newfound friend join them for drinks, Albert felt he could not say no. Shlomo shot his son a glance that required no interpretation, but Albert followed his new "chum" to the inn's common room. As risky as it would be to hoist a few glasses with the Luftwaffe, it was even riskier, he believed, to refuse.

The scene that followed was surreal. Hans' comrades, who happily made room for him at the crowded table, greeted Albert boisterously. The boy's prior alcohol consumption had been strictly ceremonial (Sabbath and Passover), until earlier that year when he had been tricked into drunken revelry by the peasants of Lamayou. This time, he had to do everything within his power to stay sober—he was toasting with the Luftwaffe, and the stakes were life and death! He gamely partook of every round, all the while being excruciatingly careful in speaking German, lest he accidentally intersperse it with Yiddish, of which he had a better command.

They even solicited Albert's opinion on current events. It was rather remarkable that at a table full of Nazis, he was the only one convinced that Germany would ultimately win the war.

The next morning, the innkeeper had little trouble remembering who had booked the Szajdholc's room and offered the accommodations "on the house." Albert's family was about to resume their uncertain journey, when Hans swooped down again to offer his assistance.

The next thing Albert knew, he was being ushered into the regional army headquarters and brought before a highly decorated commander. He quaked at the sight of the swastika flags and other Nazi paraphernalia that adorned every centimeter of the room. But at Hans' behest, after quizzing Albert in German, the busy commander summoned another officer and ordered, "When your convoy leaves for Rome, Lieutenant, you are to take this boy and his family with you."

A captain within earshot had yet other plans in mind for Albert. "I am also looking for a translator and I can make it very much worth your while!" he gushed. "I'll put you in Florence's finest hotel, you'll eat the most exquisite cuisine, have an endless supply of cigarettes, and other perks..."

A return to Florence was the last thing on Albert's agenda but every excuse he came up with, the captain dismissed. Suddenly, a soldier on a motorcycle roared into the square and sprinted inside with a new set of orders. Albert had no clue what they contained, but all hell broke loose in the compound. The lieutenant told Albert that his convoy would not be leaving for Rome after all, and the captain ceased extolling Florence.

Albert happily rejoined his family, but Hans spotted him and revealed, "Don't go to Rome! The Allies are breaking through and you'll be taken prisoner by the damn Americans." Albert tried his utmost to conceal his joy.

Hans, however, still sought to keep Albert in the entourage. "Look, the convoy that's forming now is about to leave for Florence! Jump aboard and I'll see how I can help you over there."

Shlomo Szajdholc had permitted his bold son to take the lead, but now he put his foot down. "This Hans is too good for our own good," he declared to the family through clenched teeth. "Let's get out of here before he does us any more favors!"

In all the chaos, they managed to make a run for it, ducking into a nearby field. Obscured by the tall grass, they barely moved a muscle until they heard the last truck pull out.

When they finally dared to return to the road, they managed to find a ride to the nearest railroad station and, at long last, boarded a train for Rome.

Like everyone else who entered the city, they were methodically searched, but their papers were found to be in order.

Was their long ordeal finally at an end?

Word of mouth, which governed the refugees' every move, guided the Szajdholcs to check in at the Salus Hotel, where they were briefly reunited with Alter and Sidi, whom they had not seen since their parting in Andonno. They were also thankful to see the Templers and the Wolfingers and other families from their Alpine sojourn—it had been a long and eventful time since they had all been together. Yet since it was far too risky for all the families to travel to Rome together, they had split up, as they had several times in the past, always managing to find each other in the end.

Only Shlomo Szajdholc, who always had a nose for danger, could not bring himself to rejoice. The situation in Rome was volatile, roundups were commonplace, and even the most minimal quantities of food were at a premium. Allied bombings exacerbated the desperate food shortages in the city. The Szajdholcs had to trek to the soup kitchen run by nuns in the distant neighborhood of San Lorenzo. The Catholic clergy there obtained their food via Vatican convoys, and trucks bearing its insignia were rarely bombed.

One day as Albert and Alter waited in line outside the soup kitchen, a sack of lentils split open while being unloaded from the truck. Throngs of hungry people pounced upon the treasure, and Alter and Albert filled their berets to overflowing.

It was a gold mine for their undernourished father, who still adhered to the laws of kashruth. But how would they prepare these precious morsels, when pots were not to be had?

They innovatively hit upon a solution by converting enamel chamber pots into cookware. For the ravenous Shlomo—who had not consumed any cooked food since the outbreak of the war with the exception of beans, chestnuts and rice—and for the rest of them, it was a veritable feast.

SHLOMO SZAJDHOLC'S reluctance to celebrate prematurely was once again well founded. Hopes for the speedy liberation of Rome were dashed by a spate of stiff German counter-attacks that broke the Allied momentum. Moreover, being transplanted into a teeming metropolis created a host of temptations for the younger Szajdholcs. Alter and Albert were beset by boredom, and frequently disregarded their father's

stern warnings not to wander the streets. They had several frightfully close calls in movie theaters, a popular target of plainclothes police
in search of Jews and other illegals. Once they were even roped into a
German army camp, yet still nothing could persuade the brothers to
desist from their folly.

On one occasion, their sister Mariette joined them in an outing to
the movies. When the film was over, they realized that all the exits to
the theater had been sealed, and a commotion outside indicated a major
roundup. Once again, God held his hand over them, and a black-shirt-
ed, Fascist guard allowed them to slip out a rear door.

They later learned that the Germans were exacting revenge for the
partisan killing of 32 of their troops. Everyone from the theater was
loaded onto a truck in order to pay the price. Their standard "quota" for
retribution was ten-to-one, and when they could not gather the requi-
site 320 civilians, 70 Jews were taken from jail and shot with the rest of
the innocent victims.

A few days later, Italian Fascist police raided the Salus Hotel. Albert
refused to go with them, insisting he was not a Jew, and handed over his
"Hungarian" papers. The official threw the document to the floor, and
demanded: "Lower your pants!"

"I don't have to listen to you!" Albert retorted. "We are Hungarian
nationals—our consulate is our only authority here!"

His indignation was not convincing enough. The Szajdholcs, the
Templers and a handful of other "criminals" were herded inside a van
and taken to police headquarters, where they were forced to spend the
night in a filthy interrogation room. In the morning, the heart-thumping interrogations began.

The Szajdholcs were called in as a group and made to stand before
a police official, an SS officer, and a distinguished-looking man out of
uniform. The families shuddered as the SS officer slowly looked them
over from head to toe, one by one, with an icy gaze.

The dignified-looking gentleman was the Hungarian consul, and he
demanded the family's release. "But they are Jews!" the policeman ob-
jected. The consul declared that their documents were authentic and a
heated debate ensued until the intensely suspicious SS officer relented
and let them all go.

Upon their return to the Salus Hotel, Shlomo declared that they would not spend even one more night there; he sensed the place was being watched. The weary Templers said they would move the following day, but Shlomo ordered Albert to go in search of new lodgings immediately.

Albert's moans, groans and protestations that it was half-an-hour until curfew in no way dissuaded his father. "When God provides you with a sign you do not delay," said Shlomo Szajdholc sternly. If the Almighty wanted us to leave tomorrow, He would have given us the sign tomorrow. Go and find us another hotel at once!"

The headstrong boy did as he was told and the Szajdholcs relocated. The next day, they learned that there had been a wave of arrests at the Salus Hotel, and that the Templers had narrowly escaped by climbing out onto the roof and down the fire escape!

Now veritable prisoners in their new hotel rooms, the Szajdholc and Templer families commemorated Passover and the Exodus from Egypt. Alter and Albert were recruited to bake matzohs by jerry-rigging a heater with a piece of tin and the heads of both families reconstructed the text of the *Haggadah* (*Seder* liturgy) by heart. The ritual cups of wine were substituted with tea, and the traditional salt water used to commemorate the tears of suffering, was replaced with the real thing. The focal question of the liturgy, "Why is this night different from all other nights?" could not have been more appropriate, or poignant.

A few nights later, German soldiers once again broke into their rooms, this time—fortunately for them—in search of army deserters. Nevertheless, to Shlomo Szajdholc, it was another "sign" to keep moving. The most ominous sign was occurring to the northeast, where Germany had occupied Hungary, rendering their papers worthless.

They were in more danger than ever. It was time to go even deeper into hiding.

Sidi and the youngest Szajdholc, Bella, would take refuge in a convent. Mariette Szajdholc, blond and blue-eyed, elected to remain on the outside and tend to her increasingly infirm parents; the three of them rented a room in a private home.

ALTER AND ALBERT, as young men conspicuously out of uniform, were at the greatest risk of all. Their latest scheme was to become nationals of a neutral country, not an easy feat considering the scarcity of such countries, and their limited foreign-language skills. Switzerland was the most plausible choice for two French-speaking youths, but they could not concoct a story that would withstand the scrutiny of Swiss officials, who were known to meticulously verify every detail before issuing any documents.

Then they remembered their warmhearted neighbors in the Pyrenees, the Fonsecas. Spain! It had been four long years since the loquacious couple had regaled them with tales of their native *Espagne*, but they remembered enough to devise an elaborate yarn—one that included a convincing explanation as to why they didn't know a word of *Espagnol*. Next, they marshaled their skills in forgery to document that they were of Spanish nationality.

After meticulously rehearsing their story, making sure their dates and facts were in sync, they went to the Spanish consulate. The consul claimed that he could not help them. As if on cue, the brothers jumped to their feet and delivered a jaw-dropping performance. They railed about how difficult it had been to remain proud Spaniards among Belgians, about the humiliation and taunts they had been subjected to because of the nationality that had been bequeathed to them by their parents, who—though they were still in Belgium—had remained fiercely loyal Spaniards. "What did all of their sacrifices get them?" the brothers demanded. "A callous consul who has no compassion for them and no recognition of their family's suffering!"

No one could help but be moved by this emotional display; still, the consul had some reservations. He permitted them to spend the night in a well-appointed hotel under Spanish protection, before subjecting them to a full day of further interrogation. The consul asked if they were in touch with their parents. "We wish," they replied earnestly, further expounding on their phony tale of separation and woe.

The consul declared that he could get through to the Spanish consulate in Brussels using the Vatican phone lines. He dialed a series of numbers and began speaking rapidly in Spanish, but Albert could see that his thumb was holding down the phone's plunger. The consul was unable to call their bluff, and they had passed the test. Albert shared this vital observation with Alter and now they knew that they had him. From then on they were able to convey their plight with even greater gusto, resulting in them being issued Spanish papers.

Now convinced that he was facing constituents who had been tragi-cally separated from their parents, the consul offered in a fatherly tone: "These are uncertain times, young fellows, so stay in touch if you need anything. And take my advice: stay off the streets!"

Albert followed the consul's advice ... for about an hour. That night he came face to face with a German soldier who had once helped him avoid arrest by harboring him inside a military canteen. The Nazi now demanded that Albert hide him before Rome fell.

Albert Szajdholc didn't need to look for trouble; it invariably found him (even if he mildly assisted). Although he was tempted to repay the man's kindness, he quickly fled the scene. Shielding a German deserter would be sheer suicide at this juncture.

THE VERY NEXT DAY, leaflets fell from the sky declaring that the Allies were giving the German army twenty-four hours to evacuate Rome.

It was the ultimate thrill for Albert—indeed, for all the victims of Nazi subjugation—to watch the panic-stricken Germans run for their lives. Nothing could have been more foolhardy than to gloat as the van-quished army retreated, yet Albert, an impetuous youth to the very end, would not miss a moment of this glorious event. Eager to witness, from a bird's-eye view, the defeated Germans scurrying about and abandon-ing their wounded comrades, he scaled the Pincho, which offered a pan-oramic view of Rome.

Fully absorbed, at first he did not pay attention to the escalating rumble coming from behind. But when he finally spun around, his blood ran cold.

Moving in at zero range was a German tank with its guns aimed directly at him.

The thought of being gunned down hours before Rome's libera-tion—after years of one close call after another—was too much to bear. What should he do? Leap off the steep peak and risk serious in-jury—perhaps even permanent paralysis? Surrender to the Germans and risk even worse? For once, the wily young Albert was at a loss. He stood frozen to the spot, the hair on the back of his neck standing up like spikes, and he breathlessly watched as the tank came closer, closer ... and abruptly, veered away. It took long seconds before Albert could resume breathing and he had to muster every ounce of strength to avoid fainting; it was June 4, 1944.

His wise and pious father would have deemed it "a sign" for Albert to sit out the evacuation behind closed doors. But this was a boy who craved to see history unfold not outside his door, but before his very eyes.

The retreating Germans had blown up the electricity pylons that illuminated the city, and Rome was now enveloped in complete darkness. The absence of illumination only enhanced the mysterious aura that engulfed the ancient city. Then an unfamiliar sound began to reverberate in the streets. What began as faint applause swelled in volume until it sounded as though a million people were clapping.

Albert could barely see a thing, but his senses were overloaded by the cacophony. Delirious crowds swarmed the streets. There was the sound of marching, and the first column of Allied troops could be faintly discerned, carefully entering the city single-file on the sidewalks—a far cry from the goose-stepping brutes who had dominated these streets for years.

Albert, caught up in the euphoria of the moment, jumped up on the muddy tire of a troop carrier and hugged one of the soldiers by the neck, kissing him on both cheeks as the other soldiers in the vehicle smiled shyly.

EPILOGUE

From the time of Rome's liberation until the conclusion of the war, Albert volunteered for the Jewish Brigade of the British Volunteer Corps. In this capacity he served as a driver and aide to its Jewish chaplain in Rome. In August of 1944, Sidi gave birth to a son. In 1945, Alter, Sidi and their baby, Pinchas, along with the Templers, immigrated to Palestine.

At his father's bidding, Albert returned to Brussels to see if any of the family's possessions could be salvaged, but very little remained. He went back to Italy and missed by one day the eligibility to acquire a visa to the United States, as the rest of his family had, under the Displaced Persons Act.

Esther and Shlomo Szajdholc were not without regrets over leaving Italy. In fact, the Chief Rabbi of Rome, together with the Jewish community, appealed to the couple to remain, and open a kosher restaurant in the city. They had loyal friends throughout the country, including Father Antonio Borsotto, who was made a Canon of the Cuneo Cathedral. Indeed, it was a tempting proposal, for the elder Szajdholcs had learned to love their adopted country. For this very reason, Shlomo ultimately refused the offer. He feared that the Italians were such marvelous people that his children might assimilate and intermarry.

And so in 1949, under the U.S. Displaced Persons Act, they settled in New York. The American authorities refused to issue Albert a visa, claiming that by returning to Brussels, he had been repatriated there. It took another full year before he received a visa to the United States, and he was reunited with his family in 1950.

He met his future wife, Lynn, on a blind date in 1953 in New York. She was taken with his cosmopolitanism and ability to speak French, Italian and German; he was impressed, among many other attributes, by her ability to relate to the Holocaust.

After their wedding, the (Albert) Szajdholcs—soon to become the Sharons—lived in New York City before moving to Long Island. They became the proud parents of a son and a daughter. Albert worked first for a pharmaceutical firm until he assumed his father's line of work in leather handbags. In 1971 the family made aliyah (moved to Israel), and settled in Jerusalem.

The reality was that whoever stayed with Shlomo Szajdholc survived the war. All of their children left Europe for America, and eventually settled in Israel. Shlomo and Esther remained in America and died in Borough Park, Brooklyn, in the mid-1960s.

Albert dictated his memoir (the source of this story) to Lynn, and on the night of February 26, 1990, she finished typing his final sentence. At that moment the couple tearfully exclaimed together, "We did it, we finished!"

Five hours later, he passed away at the age of sixty-five.

Resistance

SRULEK

This is a story of resistance. Of a lone boy who bonded with his comrades and stubbornly refused to accept what seemed liked his inevitable destruction.

In 1941, as Germany was flexing its military muscles, 10-year-old Yisrael Storch (known affectionately to all as "Srulek") was growing up in Munkacs, Hungary (until 1938, the region had been part of Czechoslovakia), happily engaged in mischievous behavior that made him the nemesis of his teachers. Srulek and his spirited friends had an array of pranks that kept each other entertained, and their elders furious. There was the time when his Talmud teacher fell asleep in class and Srulek and company used the opportunity to practice their arts-and-crafts skills by gluing the man's beard to his desk. On another occasion, Srulek demonstrated his opposition to corporal punishment by spiking the teacher's ruler with a spice. As the instructor was allergic to the condiment, it put not only the ruler out of commission but also its master, and (not coincidentally) succeeded in delaying the administration of a test.

These were bright, good-hearted, boisterous boys, beloved by parents and rebbes and neighbors in this tightly knit, thriving center of Jewish life. They were boys like any other boys, with a bit of growing up to do before they would rightfully take their places—as their fathers and grandfathers had before them—in the religious, communal and commercial life of Munkacs.

But Srulek Storch and his cronies would have to finish growing up very soon. And soon, too, Jewish Munkacs would be only the stuff of dreams and memory.

AS THE BOYS approached the age of bar mitzvah, war raged only one country away. Although Hungary was still not in the Nazi crosshairs, with the number of Jews nearing 800,000 it was only a matter of time before the Germans took aim. The talk of war, which had previously been confined to private gatherings and hushed tones, was now on everybody's lips, on the radio, and in public announcements that blared through the city's streets providing instructions in the likely event of an aerial assault.

German strategists had thus far assumed that the Hungarian government and its gentile populace would enthusiastically implement the Third Reich's racial policies, without direct Nazi supervision. But it wasn't until the Germans actually occupied Hungary that they were able to get the job done according to their specifications.

By mid-1941, anti-Jewish measures had affected every aspect of political, economic and social life in Munkacs. By the end of March 1944, all Jewish businesses had been confiscated and Jews were forbidden to earn a livelihood. Unless families had money stashed away or desirable commodities to sell or trade, starvation became their lot.

Like so many other Jewish homemakers desperate to feed their families, Srulek's mother, Chana Pessil, became an expert at extracting the absolute maximum out of every serving; what was formerly a minor lunch component became the staple of numerous meals. Even scraps that had previously been discarded were now valued as delicacies, and savored for any nutritional value they might possess.

Chana Pessil and Hershel Storch had just experienced a personal tragedy—the loss of their seventeen-year-old daughter, who was mentally and emotionally handicapped from the time she was an infant. They were determined to do all they could to protect the rest of their brood, consisting of Srulek and his two surviving sisters, Gittel and Yolanda.

Much of the responsibility fell to Chana Pessil, as Hershel had been fired from his job as bookkeeper at a brick factory (this factory would later become the site of one of the Munkacs ghettos). The family's sole income was now derived from Chana Pessil's job managing a pub, which was part of the inn that was attached to their home. Thirsty non-Jews on their way to and from the market still frequented the pub, which had been owned by Jews before the war. But this business, too, had been expropriated—and its one remaining Jewish employee, Srulek's hard-working mother, was soon to be dismissed.

It was during these lean times that Srulek celebrated his bar mitzvah—not the most auspicious era in which to observe a religious milestone. His entry into manhood was a subdued affair, marked with some modest (and diluted) schnapps and a small cake that his resourceful mother had somehow managed to assemble. The guests had little doubt that this would be their last communal celebration together.

Hungary, everyone realized, hung by a thread. And yet, a sliver of hope—wishful thinking, perhaps?—remained. The Hungarians were methodical in demoralizing the Jews and in systematically depriving them of everything they owned. Nevertheless, government policy at that point did not overtly target the Jews for annihilation. Indeed, at the dawn of the German occupation of Hungary, Jewish survival—though it was antithetical to the Nazi agenda—was viewed by most as a distinct possibility.

Who could blame the Munkacsers for exhibiting the hopefulness and naïveté so typical of the Jews of Europe? By this final stage of the war, the Germans had perfectly honed their standard mode of deception. The SS would take hostages and post exorbitant ransom demands. When the ransom was received, the hostages were released. This fostered the illusion that the Nazis were true to their word, and that danger to life could be averted as long as their demands were met. Adolf Eichmann himself convened with the Hungarian Jewish Council and assured them: "Everything taking place on the Jewish question is only for the wartime period. After the war, the Jews will be free to do whatever they want and the Germans will again become good-natured and permit everything, as in the past."*

Eichmann further proclaimed that any Hungarian who harmed a

---

* As quoted in *The Holocaust* by Sir Martin Gilbert, page 663.

Jew would pay the price. He demanded to be informed of such violent incidents, pledging that he would "deal with the attackers."

And so again Nazi guile triumphed over Jewish innocence and decency, conning Jews into desperately believing what seemed to make sense. With razor-like precision, the groundwork for the future deceptions had been firmly laid.

The Germans' first imperative was to deport to Poland all Jews of Polish extraction currently living in Hungarian territory. The Storch family fell within this category, as Srulek's paternal great-grandfather had been born in Poland.

To Hershel Storch, "deportation" had an ominous ring, especially to Poland. Although no one in Munkacs yet understood the true extent of the horrors occurring in the bucolic Polish town of Oświęcim (in German, "Auschwitz"), or in the other "camps" that dotted the Polish countryside, there was no shortage of frantic whispers regarding the fate of Polish Jewry. One chilling tale, repeated with dread clarity, told of Jews being shot and tossed—dead and alive—into a river.

Determined to save his family from such a gruesome fate, Hershel Storch decided to take the rumors of atrocities at face value. After seeing to it that certain sums of money ended up in just the right official pockets, a number of records were falsified and the Storch family history was rewritten. For generations, on both sides, the family could now bureaucratically trace its roots to Hungary or to Czechoslovakia—exclusively.

THE CASE CAN BE MADE (as Lucy Dawidowicz so eloquently does in *The War Against the Jews*) that all of German military strategy was governed by the plot to exterminate Jewry. This is startlingly evidenced in the Nazi invasion of Hungary—the only instance in World War II that Germany invaded a country for the sole purpose of exterminating its Jewish populace.

Although Germany was losing the war on both fronts, the Nazis' priority was to abandon German troops on the battlefield and focus on the destruction of Hungarian Jewry, the majority of whom were still at large. Germany's leaders were resigned at this point (mid-1944) to the fact that they had lost the war, but they were determined, at all costs, not to lose the War Against the Jews. The Final Solution—*über alles.*

The Hungarian invasion was like no other. There was no massive show of force, no succession of bombings and strafings to hail the arriving conquerors. At this stage of the war, Germany lacked the manpower to mount a formidable occupation. More to the point, there was no need to inflict massive civilian casualties, as Hungary was an ally—an irritatingly incompetent one when it came to its "Jewish Problem," but an ally nonetheless.

From the day the Germans set foot on Hungarian soil, on March 19, 1944, it was made clear that incompetence would no longer be tolerated. The situation of the Jews rapidly deteriorated even further. Despite Eichmann's assurances, he employed every deception in the vast and experienced Nazi arsenal to ensure that the violence-free days were over.

The Germans marched into Munkacs on the eve of Passover. In the Storch home, the eagerly awaited *Seder* evening suddenly had the underpinnings of a nightmare. Most of the house was taken over by officers of the *Werhrmacht*. As the Nazis slept, the family conducted the *Seder* in an isolated corner, in whispers and trembling voices. Never were their plaintive prayers for freedom and liberation from the yoke of tyranny more fervent!

On the eighth and final day of the Festival of Freedom, Jewish history cruelly inverted itself in Munkacs. For the Storch family and hundreds of thousands of others like them, the process of freedom to slavery to annihilation had begun.

The roundup began early in the morning, even before the Jews had put away their Passover dishes. An SS officer accompanied by two Hungarian gendarmes arrived at the Storch home to determine how many were in the family and if all were present. When the investigation was concluded, the family was told they had exactly one hour to pack whatever they could carry—without suitcases.

Chana Pessil raced frantically from bedroom to bedroom, stripped the pillowcases from the pillows, and began stuffing them with clothing, matzoh and whatever other edibles could be packed within the prescribed time limit. Sixty minutes later, she, her husband and Srulek reported to the nearby synagogue. The girls escaped out the house's rear window and fled to the nearby forest.

The Storchs, along with all the other Jews in a three-kilometer radius, were made to wait in the synagogue for upwards of six hours. After the Germans verified that the entire area was now *Judenrein*, thanks to the information supplied by the local Hungarian gendarmes, they ordered everyone to stand outside in rows of five so that they could be counted.

Just then, Srulek's sisters—on their own—returned to the synagogue. No sooner had they escaped than they realized that they were not really free. They had nowhere to go, no place to hide, and everyone they knew was huddled inside the synagogue. Intuitively they felt that they would be better off sharing their family's fate.

The roll call continued. With the return of the sisters, the head count would be correct and the liquidation could proceed.

THE JEWS were marched to two factories in which bricks were manufactured—one named "Podhoryan and Munkacs" (also referred to as Kallush,* and where Hershel Storch had once been employed) on the outskirts of Munkacs, and the other, "Sajovics"—in the Jewish section of town, and the premises were cordoned off. To the Nazi mind, the austere buildings formed the perfect, ready-made ghettos. The minds that saw human hair and contrived mattress stuffing, the minds that saw boxcars and imagined human transport, could easily see a brick factory and envision a ghetto. There was easy entry, but no way out.

Every day, more and more Jews who lived within a 100-kilometer radius were rounded up and deposited into the makeshift ghetto. It wasn't long before its numbers swelled to almost 4,000. Trapped inside a too-small space with little food, inadequate sanitation and medical care, with the heavy Nazi boot pressed tightly upon their necks, the inhabitants of the Munkacs brick factory endured all the grisly components of ghetto "life" experienced elsewhere in Nazi-occupied Europe.

Young Srulek Storch had originally viewed the proceedings as something of an adventure, a reprieve from the usual return to school after Passover. But he and the other youths quickly lost their sense of intrigue. They were living a nightmare that worsened by the hour. Their fellow townsmen would disappear after being summoned by the SS, never to return. Those who did come back were mute and severely traumatized.

---

* Where Shlomo Zalman Teichman and his family were interred (see page 316).

From each group that was rounded up, a representative was designated as a one-way go-between from the SS to the prisoners. This spokesman was assigned to relay the Nazis' endless barrage of instructions and orders ("Sleep here!" "Be ready for assembly at dawn!"). No one had any difficulty identifying these individuals, for they were all badly bruised, with heads horribly disfigured from savage beatings.

The Jews were desperate to know their fate, but none of their frantic questions were answered—or even acknowledged. Then the Germans carefully planted rumors that the prisoners were being transferred to help gather the harvest at Hungarian farms. Under different circumstances, this would have been an exceedingly bleak thought, but after being piled together, practically suffocating on a crowded factory floor for nearly a month, farm work sounded like a vast improvement.

The rumors fed upon precisely what the Jews wanted to believe: that they would be freed from their abominable conditions and placed in a situation where they would become productive—hence, indispensable. This foolhardy conclusion was the predictable end product, once again, of Jewish innocence (and desperation) versus German guile.

THE TRAGICALLY naïve Jews responded to the departure orders with unabashed optimism. Full of hope, they reinserted their meager belongings into their sacks and pillowcases, and lined up to leave the ghetto.

What greeted their eyes was a contingent of heavily armed Hungarian policemen in far greater numbers than they had ever seen before. To the analytically minded, this was clearly much too menacing a force to oversee a routine transfer to farm employment. But for most of the befuddled prisoners, logic and reason had already been extinguished several weeks into their ordeal. They stood expectantly at the gates of the factory, clinging to their unsuspecting belief that their situation was about to improve, despite ample—indeed overwhelming—evidence to the contrary.

Not coincidentally, there was a rail spur to and from the very entrance of the brick factory. A caravan of cattle cars pulled up, and the human cargo was brusquely loaded.

Srulek Storch and his family were crowded into a single, airless boxcar with nearly one hundred other people. There was no room to move, to sit or to stand, leaving everyone frozen—in unbearable heat—in his or her position. The last sound Srulek would ever hear in the town of his birth was the door being rammed shut and the ominous clank of the lock.

The single source of illumination in the boxcar was a tiny opening near its roof. Several men who were crammed alongside Srulek managed to hoist his skinny body aloft, so he could peer through the fissure and report where they were headed. The train slowed down every time it approached another railway station, which was the indication for them to wedge him above their heads.

Srulek did as he was instructed and called out the names of the passing stations, but none of them were towns in the Hungarian countryside. Finally he announced a station that was recognized by many, but its familiarity brought no relief. "Košice" was the main rail junction between Hungary/Slovakia and Poland. The conviction that they were being transported to their own country's farm regions vanished with the harsh realization that they were on their way to Poland after all. This only exacerbated the horrendous physical and emotional distress aboard the train.

For Srulek and the rest of the captives, the lack of food was bearable compared to the torture caused by the lack of water. This was the single greatest factor that caused a number of deaths in Srulek's car and in the others. Yet the conditions onboard were but a grim prelude for what lay ahead.

After three days, the train slowed down to a crawl. And then, to a stop.

Once again Srulek Storch was lifted up to report on what he saw. This time, the terrified boy struggled for words to describe the indescribable, to make sense of the incomprehensible.

"We are entering a ... a place ... there are parcels lined up all along the tracks ...now I see suitcases and bundles piled along the track ... there are thin people— terribly thin, without hair, like walking skeletons!— in ragged, striped pajamas ..."

Even in their most unspeakable fantasies, the Munkacsers and their neighbors, praying for the end to their awful journey, could not have imagined an end like this.

German officers, steely-eyed and grim, had the "Kanada

Kommando"—a unit composed of Jewish prisoners—yank open the boxcar doors. Simultaneously the officers barked orders for all to disembark and leave their belongings behind. Numb with fear and confusion, hunger and exhaustion, everyone obeyed.

Srulek was blinded by the light of the afternoon sun and was caught off guard when his father pressed a pair of *tefillin* into his hands without offering any explanation. Srulek's mother motioned to her son to stay on board the boxcar. For the first time in three days there was room to maneuver, and Chana Pessil seized this opportunity to unpack her pillowcase and layer clothing upon her boy. In an urgent whisper, she commanded Srulek to put on two additional shirts and an extra pair of pants.

"But Ońu, I'm not cold!" the boy protested.

"*Now* you're not," she exclaimed under her breath, furtively thrusting at him a sweater to wear over the three shirts.

Chana Pessil now stood with her son in an empty car, desperately trying to foist the last of the clothing upon him. A *Kanada Kommando* who had been assigned to supervise the detraining, caught sight of the serious infraction being perpetrated by mother and son. "Out!" he ordered sternly.

"We won't be more than another minute, sir," Chana Pessil replied in a genteel, controlled voice. Her politesse in the vilest place on earth provoked an even stronger reaction from the *Kanada Kommando*. "Out, this SECOND!" he thundered.

"Just a minute, please, a minute!" she gasped, feverishly continuing to dress the boy.

The two of them froze with fear as they watched the irate overseer pull himself into the boxcar. They did not realize that the interchange that would follow, would save Srulek Storch's life.

"*Oy, Yiddeneh!*" murmured the prisoner bitterly, addressing Chana Pessil in the Yiddish they both knew so well. He pointed at the sweater she clutched to her breast. "*Yiddeneh*, none of this is necessary, you won't be needing this over here."

Then the man turned to Srulek.

"How old are you, boy?" he asked.

"Fourteen, if it's any of your business!" Srulek snapped, mustering some of his schoolboy insolence.

"No, you are not fourteen," he declared. "You are eighteen."

"Why should I be eighteen if I am really fourteen?" Srulek challenged.

The man looked straight into Srulek's eyes and poked his chest. "Here you do not ask questions," he spat. "I am telling you that you are eighteen, therefore you are eighteen. Now GET OUT!"

Mutely, Chana Pessil and Srulek descended from the car. She was immediately waved to join a long line of women, and he was shunted into the male formation.

What would that moment have been like, had mother or son understood that they would never see each other again? That this would be their moment of final parting—an event that the boy would replay over and over in his mind, for months and years and decades to come? One cannot even speculate.

But that is what the moment was.

SRULEK REJOINED HIS FATHER and other men from his town as they marched for a long time until they were ordered to form a single file. One by one they passed before an SS officer who pointed for them to go left or right.

The officer asked a middle-aged gentleman named Gelb, standing ahead of Hershel Storch, "What is your profession?" Gelb, relying on his service to the Kaiser to keep him in good stead, staunchly replied that he had been a decorated hero in World War I and was "75 percent disabled" from his wounds. The SS man made it clear that he had no interest in history. "I asked if you can work," he barked. Once again Gelb declared that he was disabled from his service in the German Army. Immediately, he was waved to the right.*

Next was Hershel Storch. When the Nazi asked him the same question, Hershel answered in a strong, clear voice: "*Jawohl!* (Yes, Sir!)" And he was sent to the left.

Now it was Srulek's turn.

"Age?"

The *Kanada Kommando* prisoner's words echoed in Srulek's ears. "Eighteen," he lied.

---

* There was no uniform policy. Sometimes the doctor assigned to determine who shall live and who shall die designated "left" as death, and sometimes "right" meant death.

"And are you able to work?"

"*Jawohl!*" he said, like his father; and like his father, he was sent to the left.

Years later, when Srulek learned that not a single boy his age or from his school had survived the selection, he understood that his life had been saved the moment he "became" eighteen.

Despite the instant maturity that had been conferred upon him, Srulek's childish impulses still reigned. As his row was given its marching orders, the agitated boy started to move toward the infirm Gelb. The crippled man would surely be assigned to less arduous labor, Srulek insisted, so it would be safer to be part of his group. "Look— over there!" pressed the boy, tugging at his father's sleeve. "Quick, let's cross. He's not too far away!" But Hershel, mindful of the phalanx of armed guards and savage dogs, quickly negated the plan. He, unlike his son, had begun to comprehend the monstrous reality: that any attempt to join Gelb would result in accompanying him to his ultimate destination. And that destination was extermination.

As dusk settled, the men continued their exhausting shuffle. Srulek managed to keep pace, but his mind was occupied with one and only one thing: water. His thirst was so great, nothing else mattered.

The group was led into a cavernous room resembling an airplane hangar. There, they were instructed to undress completely except for their shoes. Srulek peeled off his two sweaters, three shirts, both pairs of pants and, reluctantly, the *tefillin* as well. Then about thirty men arrived with large, dull clippers and proceeded to remove all the hair on their heads and bodies.

Standing naked—stripped of even their hair—they felt they had reached the very lowest degradation. Then, like cattle they were roughly herded into an adjacent room, where the barber crew began handing them their new clothing, assembly-line style. One man distributed shirts, a second furnished pants and a third provided caps. Those who were attired were ordered to line up once again.

Just then, Srulek noticed a rubber hose with a faucet-like lever in the corner of the room. He asked the closest *Kanada Kommando* if he could take a drink. The man panned the room, saw that no one was looking in their direction at that moment, and nodded.

Srulek sprayed the liquid down his parched throat and guzzled it until he gasped for breath. The *Kanada Kommando* leaned closer to him and asked, "How old are you?"

Again, the question! By now, Srulek knew the answer well. "Eighteen," he replied, unblinking. The man bent even closer, and sighed, "*Yingeleh*, you are only half-saved, your struggle for life is just starting..."

But Srulek had no idea what he meant. "What's going to happen to us?" Srulek pressed the man, but he could not elicit a reply. Then he asked a second *Kanada Kommando* prisoner, and then a third, but they both turned quickly away. And then Srulek asked the rest of them. But no one would answer. They were all Jews, they spoke the same language ... but they inhabited different planets.

Srulek and the others in his group had just arrived in Auschwitz. The *Kanada Kommando* prisoners had been there a long time. And what they knew and what they had seen and what they had done, could in no way be understood or assimilated by the newcomers. There was a chasm between them as deep and dark as the mass graves that had been dug into the Polish countryside.

Nearly two hundred prisoners were processed through the night, with each step in the sequence culminating in a protracted line-up. At dawn, just as they were marched to their barracks, it was time for the mandatory morning roll call, and there was nothing that could excuse them.

Srulek stood in the *Appellplatz*, the designated area for counting prisoners in front of the barracks. He struggled to keep his eyes open in the glaring sun. A group of prisoners filed past in the gray-striped uniform. At first he could not tell that they were women because their heads, too, were shorn.

And then—out of the corner of his eye—in the midst of the procession, he spotted his two sisters! His first impulse was to scream their names, to turn around and call out to his father, who stood wearily a few rows back, "Tateh, Tateh, look ... the girls!" But Srulek—justifiably—was too frightened to call attention to them, or to himself.

This was the first of the thrice-daily roll calls—early morning, afternoon, and night—each lasting sometimes as long as five hours. Their Nazi overseers had a sadistic, Prussian fascination with counting and cataloguing their captives. The prisoners' lives revolved around being herded from roll call to roll call, each day blurring into the next, punctuated by tedium, bewilderment, fear and a terrible, gnawing hunger.

In Srulek's group they asked themselves, what were they supposed to be doing while in Auschwitz? Their flesh was not engraved with numbers and they were not assigned work. Nor were they sent for—that terrible word!—*Sonderbehandlung* (Special Treatment), which everyone knew meant extermination.

And why, why, these mind-numbing, sadistic roll calls? There was no escape from Auschwitz. Thus the procedure was purely for the sake of imposing misery and torment. During the crowded, torturous *Appells*, Srulek was often in the presence of his father. In their weakened stupor, silence reigned between them. But the terrible pain in Hershel's eyes spoke volumes to his son. For Srulek, there was nothing more agonizing than this, even in comparison to the rest of Auschwitz's horrors. Such was the deep psychic connection between father and son.

Srulek soon witnessed some of the most gruesome sights of Auschwitz, including the open incineration pits into which Jewish babies were hurled, dead and alive; and he saw the chimneys devoted to the same awful end. He prayed that his depleted father had not seen what he had seen, although it would have been quite difficult to miss. Srulek knew that his father had inhaled the stench that emanated from the camp's crematoria—it was unavoidable; it permeated the prisoners' nostrils, their pores, their very being.

ONE DAY, no more than two weeks into their incarceration, Srulek, Hershel and about two hundred of their fellow prisoners were handed larger rations than usual, and abruptly lined up to be transferred.

But to where? The rumors and questions flew wildly. Nazi strategy was not restricted to physical torture and humiliation. Jews were subjected to equal measure of mental cruelty, which included never providing any information other than that which was designed to mislead.

The group was herded into boxcars for the far-off destination of Mauthausen.

In the macabre Holocaust Kingdom, where comparisons are beyond the ken of normative sensibility, this Austrian concentration camp was in some aspects worse than Auschwitz. The unparalleled savagery of Mauthausen was unleashed upon all of its daily arrivals.

Most new prisoners were immediately heaved into the jagged depths of the camp's quarry, or herded to its "Gates of Heaven" firing range. But

Srulek and his cohorts reasoned that they would be in Mauthausen for a long time (if they could only survive), as they had now been issued numbers, which they each personally had to write onto a white cloth and sew onto their shirts. Several prisoners were in charge of overseeing that the numbers were transcribed and affixed according to the camp's specifications.

Yet, just one week after their arrival, the morning roll call would be the final count for many of the assembled.

Hershel Storch was positioned two rows ahead of his son during this *Appell*. And it was precisely at his column that the roll call was suddenly aborted. Hershel and those who surrounded him were no longer property of Mauthausen and were being shipped out.

Srulek took one long, last look at his father as he shuffled away. Expressionless, eyes downcast, this stone man who had all but died the day he had arrived in Auschwitz bore no resemblance to the strong, mirthful father of Srulek's youth. Silently, his own heart like a stone, Srulek watched Hershel disappear into the departing crowd. He felt as though the earth had already begun to swallow him up, him and all the others, in a monumental quake that made not a sound.

Only after the war did Srulek learn that Hershel and the other prisoners had been transferred to Austria's notorious Gunskirchen slave camp. He would never discover the details of his father's final days, but for now the stark reality was that from that day forward, in the late summer of 1944, Srulek Storch was all on his own—an orphan in hell.

Later that very same day, Srulek's group was transferred to a labor camp in Melk, Austria, which was attached to a Luftwaffe barracks.

The tedium of the *Appell* quickly became a pathetically minor part of Srulek's endless days. All prisoners in Melk were slave laborers assigned to a task normally relegated to heavy equipment and to mules: carving a city within a mountain. Why should the Germans resort to conventional and costly methods of excavating tunnels, moving earth and blasting rock, when they had a thoroughly dispensable labor force that could be worked round-the-clock, at virtually no cost? The Jewish workers, in the course of their exploitation, simultaneously fulfilled two key Nazi goals: construction and their own self-destruction.

The sole sustenance of Melk's prisoners was a slice of bread in the morning—bread that was composed of about sixty percent bean flour and the remainder sawdust—with a cup of hot, colored water that tasted at times like caraway and at times like tea. Never did the liquid have any nutritional value. In the evening they were given an even smaller portion of the same bread, with a miniscule pat of margarine. The prisoners' pangs of hunger were so relentless that they could think of almost nothing else.

Many paid the supreme price in pursuit of nourishment. It was known that any prisoner caught lunging for a discarded apple core or carrot slice would be murdered immediately, but all the logic in the world could not quell the temptation to alleviate their desperate cravings.

Along with starvation, the most common malady plaguing the prisoners was lice. The parasites fiercely attacked every inch of their bodies, literally eating them alive. Every morning, Srulek and the others would thrust their hands up into their armpits and scoop out handfuls of the gnawing creatures, while the dreadful assault continued from head to toe. And every night, a full re-infestation would occur, as the filthy straw mattresses and flimsy blankets were crawling with vermin.

Where could youth—orphaned, starving, terrorized and totally without protection—possibly find hope in this abyss? For some, there was an answer, a dim ray of light. It was—as it has always been, and will always be—friendship.

Among the workers was a core of boys aged 14 to 18, most of them slightly older than Srulek. These lads united and made a solemn pact that they would survive—no matter what. This decision was in and of itself an august act of resistance. The Germans had no tolerance for the slightest inkling of a rebellious thought, let alone act, and alleged perpetrators were either shot on the spot, or beaten so viciously that they would never recover.

The result was a grim conundrum. Simply submitting to death was the easier option; avoiding it required an iron will and unrelenting craftiness. Alas, psychologically submitting to death made survival virtually impossible; if one did not commit to survival one would perish. Yet those who did decide to survive could be executed for that decision.

This challenge was not lost on the boys, and they devised an elaborate strategy that included psychological exercises to ensure that they did not abandon their will to live.*

The boys' pact entailed, for example, that they were required to sing while the other prisoners wept. Only when they were totally by themselves—and no one else could see them—were they permitted to cry. They tried to make sure that this situation would never arise, rushing to soothe any of their number whose morale was flagging. The adults around them could not fathom the cheerful and at times even playful behavior of these youths and viewed it as a sad indication of how clueless they were about their ineluctable fate.

When the pact members lined up for roll call they always stayed together. If one of them ever received an extra morsel—and there was no greater reward—they would share it among themselves. Children (as they were referred to, because they were the youngest of the prisoners) were often given preferential treatment if there was food "left over"— that is, if some slop remained at the bottom of the barrel. If the child was a member of Srulek's group, they would all reap the benefit.

To further bolster their spirits the boys developed a regimen that was rigorously followed. In the latrine there were ten taps of cold running water. Every day—except for in the dead of winter when the water was frozen—the boys improvised a kind of shower. The scrub-down

---

*   All on their own, and without the noted psychiatrist and philosopher Viktor Frankl (who was simultaneously developing this theory hundreds of miles away) to guide them, the boys had grasped the essence of that philosopher's "logotherapy":
    Everything can be taken from a man but one thing: the last of human freedoms—to choose one's attitude in any given set of circumstances, to choose one's own way. And there were always choices to make. Every day, every hour, offered the opportunity to make a decision, a decision which determined whether you would or would not submit to those powers which threatened to rob you of your very self, your inner freedom; which determined whether or not you would become the plaything of circumstances, renouncing freedom and dignity to become molded into the form of the typical inmate.... Even though conditions such as lack of sleep, insufficient food, and various mental stresses may suggest that the inmates were bound to react in certain ways, in the final analysis it becomes clear that the sort of person the prisoner became was the result of an inner decision, and not the result of camp influences alone. Fundamentally, therefore, any man can, even under such circumstances, decide what shall become of him—mentally and spiritually. He may retain his human dignity even in a concentration camp.
    —Viktor Frankl, *Man's Search for Meaning*, p. 66

helped them retain a modicum of self-respect, making it psychological as well as physical therapy.

During the freezing weather when this ritual was impossible, the boys' first priority was to promote their blood circulation. Wearing only threadbare prisoners' garb, they could fall victim to deadly hypothermia as easily as to starvation, work-exhaustion or infectious disease. Thus the brotherhood would massage each other's backs with pebbles or sand.

The backbone of the group's resistance was Koppel *de Callendarsh* (Koppel the Calendar), a Yiddish nickname given to this budding Talmud scholar who was a master of the Jewish calendar. The young genius always knew precisely what date it was—no simple feat, considering that the Germans withheld every shred of information from their captives. Not only were the prisoners kept ignorant of how the war was progressing, they didn't even have any idea what day it was. Because their work shifts often alternated between day and night, they were further confused in their efforts to keep track of time.

But neither food deprivation nor fear nor chaos could confuse the data bank in Koppel's brain. He always knew the first day of the lunar month (a supreme mathematical feat even under normal circumstances) and when every Jewish holiday would fall. Isolated from all news, the brotherhood's sole link to the daily rhythms of the outside world, to the Jewish world, to some semblance of normalcy, was through Koppel *de Callendarsh*.

What a pitifully small arsenal these boys possessed against the German juggernaut! Trembling voices, raised in muted song. A few morsels of shared, stale bread. The most elemental hygiene. The touch-stone of a calendar. The comforting touch of a friend. And yet these were the fierce bonds that kept them defiantly human ... and alive.

DAY AND NIGHT in Melk, under incandescent lights and punctuated by the deafening roar of the machinery, the backbreaking work continued. Srulek was assigned to the tunnel-diggers. They and the others—concrete workers, carpenters, and a host of specialized laborers—were supervised by a group of German civilian engineers, the so-called "masters." The Nazis considered this the perfect appellation for those who supervised Jewish slaves.

The masters were no more humane than their cohorts in uniform. If they witnessed what they considered to be an error, careless work, lack of alacrity or any other "crime," they reported the perpetrator, using the number that was prominently displayed upon his shirt. The SS knew how to exact punishment, and mistakes were never repeated.

The tunnels were dug with the aid of small mechanical hammers powered by air pressure. After the diggers succeeded in opening a cavity in the rock, the cement and carpentry divisions would take over.

The air-hammers were tipped with spiky steel heads that would become dull after being repeatedly rammed into the mountain. Srulek's job was to be a *Spitzenträger*, meaning that he had to remove the dulled heads and replace them with sharp ones. This entailed loading about ten of these heavy-grade steel rods on each shoulder. Each rod weighed several pounds, was 25 inches long and nearly four inches thick. He would then haul the rods through the long tunnel to the blacksmiths, who would sharpen them.

Outside in the blacksmiths' pit he would collect an equal number of pointed heads to return to the diggers inside the tunnel.

Day in, day out, staggering from hunger and exhaustion, Srulek would repeat this arduous ritual too many times to count. During the pre-dawn hours of one particularly grueling overnight shift, he was desperate for a moment of rest. He looked around surreptitiously and an idea tempted him unrelentingly. At that hour, aside from the diggers, the tunnel was virtually deserted and no masters remained at their posts. He still had nearly half a mile to shlep the heavy steel rods, and then start all over again.

His idea seemed foolproof. A conveyor belt churned beside him, removing sand and debris from the tunnel. Here was a chance to "hitch a ride" and give his weary bones a long-deserved rest. One last time, Srulek looked in both directions, verifying that the coast was clear, and then he hopped aboard.

No sooner had he ascended the conveyor belt, than its gentle, chugging movements lulled him to sleep. It wasn't a very long nap, but long enough to make him miss his "stop." Srulek didn't wake up in time to lift his frail form off the conveyor belt when it reached the platform.

What did jolt him into wakefulness was the sheer horror of what came next: as the belt curved down for its return trip into the tunnel, Srulek's entire body became tightly wedged in between the belt and the platform. Gravel and dirt rained down and began to bury him, filling his lungs. The belt ground into his flesh like sandpaper, ripping off the top layer through his thin clothing.

He was unable to free himself, and he knew that it was only a matter of seconds before he would be suffocated or crushed to death. Srulek screamed for help. But the enormous cavity within the mountain— large enough to house an entire village—contained a cacophony of ear-splitting industrial noises: the roar of the air-hammers, the grinding of the shovels, the creaking of the wheelbarrows—and the drone of the conveyor belt, which was now screeching in protest.

Srulek was being ground to pieces.

With all of his might, he let out one final yell. Suddenly a lone figure staggered towards him from the tunnel, rushing to his aid. His unlikely savior was Freind, a Satmar Chassid who had been reduced to a *Muselmann*—a zombie skeleton. With a miraculous burst of strength, the man, who was more dead than alive, heaved and shoved and managed to extricate him.

As Srulek lay in shock upon the ground, Freind gingerly began to peel away the debris and shredded clothing. It was clear that Srulek was gravely wounded. Even in the dim light of the tunnel shaft, they could see that the whole bottom half of one of his arms, from the elbow down, appeared barely attached, the skin rubbed raw to the bone.

Freind informed Srulek that one of the other night-shift workers was a doctor. Though Freind himself could barely walk, he took the injured boy, whose arm left a trail of gushing blood, to find the man he knew to have been—in another life—a physician.

The doctor's hands were caked with dirt and he barely glanced up from his toil. He knew what needed to be done, and he certainly knew how to do it, but declared with a defeated look, "But I cannot help, I have nothing with which to wash or dress the wound."

Srulek stood dumbfounded, partially from the pain but also from the helpless realization that his wound could be fatal. Too weak to speak, he looked at the doctor with pleading eyes.

"All I can suggest," the man muttered, "is that you urinate into your cup and then use it to clean out your wound as best as you can...."

Srulek was incredulous. "And this—this is supposed to help?" he demanded.

"It might," the doctor replied with a sigh of surrender as he returned to his work.

It was his only hope.

Srulek followed the doctor's prescription. With Freind's help, he found a cup, and used his jacket to swab the wound with the "solution."

This left the boy without an outer garment, which was against regulations. Besides, he had to disguise his wound. A Jewish slave who was not fit for work lost his justification for living.

Another prisoner magnanimously shed his jacket and handed it to Srulek. The donor would be able to replace his own garment with one stripped from a corpse—of which there were plenty. All that needed to be done was to ensure that Srulek's identification number appeared on his clothes. This could be surreptitiously taken care of later, by one of the tailors, before the numbers were inspected.

As Srulek lay that night on his straw mat, unbearably weak from pain and the loss of blood, he weighed his options—and there were not many. Admitting himself to the camp's hospital was akin to suicide. Whoever entered that hovel did not emerge alive, even if the ailment was simple dysentery, which was rampant. But how long could he show up to work with only one functioning arm, before he was discovered?

Within two days, the arm began to show signs of infection. In some ways, the exhausted boy welcomed this nearness to the end. And then he remembered the pact with his friends that they must never give up. This meant continuing to seek other options and never going to the hospital—even if he was on the road to developing gangrene.

Srulek's salvation came not a moment too soon, with a succession of sun-drenched July days. He was working the night shift and the day was to be devoted to sleeping, but Srulek was unable to close his eyes because of his acute pain. And those bleary eyes gazed upon a ghastly sight: of swollen, discolored skin draining pus from the gaping hole in his elbow.

Near-crazed with pain, Srulek crawled outside his barracks during his precious "sleep time" and exposed his wound to the strong midday sun. Instantly he could feel the radiating heat having a therapeutic effect; his pain was eased and the infection began to dry up. In the days that followed, he devoted every possible second to surreptitiously exposing his wound to the sun and praying that it would not rain. Narrowly, he managed to avoid a deadly infection—and a deadly hospitalization.

What did the boy have to live for, really? A boy without a home or family. A boy with a past that had been obliterated, a future that was uncertain at best, and a present that was in the depths of hell. He had only one thing: his friends, and the promise he had made them, to live another day.

ONE EVENING, returning from the worksite to the prison camp, Srulek encountered a commotion in the *Appell*. The news passed furiously from one prisoner to another: that night was Yom Kippur! Koppel *de Kollandash* had declared ten days earlier that it was Rosh Hashanah, but with minds and bodies so depleted, no one—until that moment—remembered.

Some of the young men in "the brotherhood" impulsively decided to hold a prayer service that night. According to the plan, when the lights were turned off by the *block ältester*—the Nazi appointee in charge of the barracks, who had received his favored status by being a stooge for the SS—the youths would swing into action.

The risks were clear to all. If the *Blockältester* reported them—and there was no reason to believe he wouldn't—the Yom Kippur of 1944 would be remembered as a day of mass martyrdom. Still, the boys made the commitment to go ahead. And there was nothing anyone could do, although many tried, to change their minds.

That night, like every other night, the *Blockältester* turned off the lights and then, like no other night—like no night ever before—over one thousand thin, fragile Jewish souls crawled out of their bunks and stood in the total darkness. At first, only a few barely-audible voices were heard—one of them, the heartbreaking wail of a cantor. And then the voices grew, like a great, rushing river of sound.

Not all of the barracks' inhabitants were Jews, and at first the uninformed looked around in bewilderment and consternation. Those in on the plan exchanged solemn, penetrating gazes. This could well be the last night of their lives, and the words of the holiday liturgy resonated as never before: "*And on Yom Kippur, it is sealed/Who shall live, and who shall die.*" A curious peace overtook the hollow-eyed congregation.

The cantor continued his prayers of supplication. *"From this Yom Kippur until next Yom Kippur, may it come upon us for good,"* he chanted in a plaintive tone, and virtually the entire barracks, a choir 250 strong, joined in the haunting melody.

The heart-stopping fear that the SS was likely to come crashing through the door at any moment was eclipsed by the classical liturgy—music of the synagogue, of the home, of the holiest of holies. Even the non-Jewish inmates were brought to tears, overwhelmed by the sanctity that had been introduced into their corner of hell on earth.

The climax was yet to come as the cantor launched into a crescendo of prayer. He raised his quavering voice in the *"Shehecheyanu,"* the centerpiece of holiday invocations: *"Blessed are You O God, King of the Universe, who has kept us alive, sustained us, and brought us to this moment."*

But he never completed the blessing. The irony, the poignancy of the message—who has kept us alive, sustained us, *for this moment*—in a slave-labor camp!—caused him to break down completely. Sobs wracked his body and the traditional melody could no longer be distinguished.

The inmates slowly climbed back into their bunks and returned to the world of darkness. Together they had soared high above the confines of Melk and gathered beneath the wings of the King of the Universe. Maybe He would see fit to sustain them until the next Yom Kippur. *It should only be for good...*

A WEEK LATER, as Srulek was emerging from the tunnel, Webber, a middle-aged prisoner from a different brigade, quietly approached him. "Come with me," Webber whispered.

"What is it?" Srulek wanted to know, but Webber's lips were sealed. He stealthily edged away from the worksite, with Srulek at his side.

"Where are you taking me?" Srulek persisted, but his companion would not reveal a clue. The diversion was getting more dangerous by the minute. The German masters knew exactly how long it should take to retrieve the sharpened drill-heads, and if Srulek exceeded the allotted time, they would surely report his number to the SS for severe punishment.

The two men managed to drift to a section of the work site that was off-limits to prisoners, and this was no minor misdemeanor. Webber ordered Srulek to join him in dropping to the ground, and the two crawled on all fours to avoid detection.

For all the mystery, Srulek had little doubt the journey would be worthwhile. Prisoners did not jeopardize their lives—or their friends'—on a whim. He was sure that Webber was about to unveil a stockpile of food.

The excavation of the mountain rendered the area thick with dust; still, Srulek's mouth watered even as the dirt particles clogged his throat and burned his eyes.

For about a hundred meters the two of them continued slithering furtively across the rocky earth. The longer it took, the more agitated Srulek became. He imagined the enraged masters shouting his number, with each digit reverberating throughout the tunnel. Suddenly, up ahead, Srulek spotted a disabled hopper car that had previously been used to remove large rocks from the tunnel. The rusty wagon was lying on its side, with a gaping hole in its lateral wall.

As they neared the wagon, Srulek saw his friend's expression change. A gentle smile blossomed on his lips and he appeared deeply at peace. Srulek understood that there was a treasure—a treasure worth risking it all—within the discarded wagon. Webber kept the lead and motioned for Srulek to follow him inside.

Srulek surveyed the cramped surroundings. He neither saw nor smelled a trace of food. "Webber, what is this?" he demanded.

Webber beamed. His eyes glistened as he gazed up at the open cavity of the wagon, bestrewn with branches and twigs. "Why, this," Webber pronounced triumphantly, "is our *sukkah'leh!*"*

Srulek looked up in disbelief. Based on information gleaned from Koppel the human calendar, Webber had found a way to reclaim his Judaism and his humanity. Risking his life to sneak away from his work detail several days in a row, Webber had cleared debris from inside the corroding wagon and added a canopy of broken boughs. By constructing this temporary dwelling, like the ancient Israelites did when they wandered in the desert, he had fulfilled the sacred commandment, the *mitzvah* of the autumnal festival of Sukkos. After all that he had gone

---

* (Yiddish) a tiny *sukkah*, the temporary dwelling with a roof of branches that the Bible requires Jews to dwell in for the weeklong festival of Sukkos.

through, Webber just had to share the fruits of his labor with someone else. The two of them reverently recited the blessing, "*Blessed are You, Lord of the universe, Who has commanded us to dwell in a sukkah.*"

Even to a starving youth, no food could have tasted sweeter than this moment. Srulek and his friend huddled together peacefully inside the world's tiniest and most clandestine *sukkah*. Both aloud and in their hearts, they quietly reminisced about the splendid holidays they had enjoyed with their loved ones. For a few minutes they were transported from the belly of the Nazi beast into the loving arms of Jewish tradition. Their eyes traveled upwards, through the *sukkah's* leafy cover, for a short, grateful glimpse of Heaven.

IT IS REMARKABLE how many defiant acts of religious fidelity the defenseless Jews performed, right under the noses of the Germans in Melk. This was so throughout Europe. Yet, not every potential encounter with the Divine had such a fulfilling outcome. Srulek once heard a rumor that one of the cement workers, Shalom Ostreicher, had found a *shel yad* (the portion of *tefillin* worn on the arm) among the bags of cement. Srulek ached to see the ritual object, so familiar and so forbidden, and to hold it in his hand once more. From the day of his bar mitzvah, when he had first clumsily wrapped the leather straps around his arm and head, and placed the box on his head as prescribed by his father and his rabbis and his teachers, he had expected that *tefillin* would be a part of his daily life. Now it all seemed like a million years ago, and somebody else's life.

Srulek's shift never overlapped with Ostreicher's, so he approached another inmate, Rabbi Shialah Greenwald, the esteemed Chuster Rav. The rabbi would not reply to Srulek's barrage of questions. It was clearly too risky to share this kind of information—if whoever had smuggled this "contraband" into the camp were to be caught, he would pay with his life. Srulek could see in the venerable rabbi's eyes that the rumor was true. Srulek was impatient for the day that his own eyes would catch sight of the covert, coveted *tefillin*. But the rabbi's silence was unshakable.

As fall gave way to winter, and winter to spring in the godforsaken slave camp of Melk, Srulek heard about another monumental act of resistance from the blacksmith who sharpened his drill bits.

This time the conspirator was Dovid Leib, an unassuming fellow who had been the Storch family's milkman in Munkacs. One evening, as Srulek and his barracks-mates consumed their pitifully meager portions of food, he noticed that Dovid Leib was not eating. Srulek reasoned the man was saving his scraps for later—but why? This was extremely unusual behavior and it caught Srulek's attention.

Later that night, a man from a different barracks quietly entered and approached Dovid Leib. Srulek was shocked to see Dovid Leib hand over his evening rations to the stranger in exchange for several cigarettes. Dovid Leib was not a smoker!

Srulek had no explanation for the most illogical behavior he had seen since his entry into captivity. "Dovid Leib, what happened to you?" he demanded, unable to contain his curiosity.

Dovid Leib pulled him away from public view and held open his shirt. There, secured in place by the string that held up his pants, were 15 or 20 cigarettes. The prisoner's uniform did not have any pockets, so smuggled goods were concealed in the only place that could avoid detection.

Srulek was certain that there was something terribly wrong with poor Dovid Leib. A non-smoker stockpiling cigarettes, and giving away his precious meals in exchange for useless contraband? Srulek had known the man all his life, and took advantage of their hometown familiarity to declare, "Dovid Leib, you're raving mad!"

Dovid Leib calmly stared at his young neighbor. "For ten cigarettes," he whispered, "I can get a cup of flour."

"So?" snorted Srulek, unimpressed. "You can't eat flour!"

"Do you know what time of year it is?" Dovid Leib challenged him, acting as if Srulek were the crazy one. Srulek truthfully did not know the time of year—sometime after winter, if he had to guess.

Dovid Leib answered his own question. "It is right before Passover," he said matter-of-factly, as if Srulek had forgotten to consult his pocket diary. "And a cup of flour is the essential ingredient for baking *matzoh*."

Baking matzoh? With no accessible oven, and with the death penalty as punishment for anyone attempting to hoard or devise a ritual object?

Dovid Leib was describing his plan as if it were the most natural thing in the world. Maybe he was expecting the SS to generously provide the other essentials of the *Seder* table!

Srulek no longer had any doubts as to whether Dovid Leib was out of his mind. What else did the lunatic have up his sleeve—four cups of kosher wine?

Srulek determinedly broke away from Dovid Leib to head back to his bunk. But Dovid Leib reached out to grab his arm and disclosed urgently, "Srulek, I need you!"

"You don't need me," Srulek protested. "You need Dr. Sigmund Freud. Let me go!"

"No, I need you," Dovid Leib insisted, looking into Srulek's eyes. "You are an integral part of the plan."

"Not me," Srulek stated as calmly as he could. "I'm not giving away my meals and I'm not imagining an oven that doesn't exist. And I'm not, I repeat not, going to get involved in a scheme that will mean my end!"

But Srulek's protests fell on deaf ears. Dovid Leib explained that Srulek was his only link with the all-important blacksmiths.

By the time the night was over, Srulek had agreed to do his part, which meant unearthing a tin can, mixing water with the flour that Dovid Leib would provide, and using a cigarette to pay off a blacksmith for baking the paste over his white-hot fire. The result would be a *matzoh*—the traditional bread of affliction, the symbol of slavery.

But in the depths of Melk, to those who blessed it and ate it in secret, it was the bread of Jewish heroes.

And one of them was surely Dovid Leib, the former milkman. A simple man—but one of the paragons about whom (as already quoted) Viktor Frankl wrote: "*They may have been few in number, but they offer sufficient proof that everything can be taken from a man but one thing: the last of human freedoms—to choose one's attitude in any given set of circumstances, to chose one's own way.*"

Dovid Leib was not especially pious, and hardly a scholar. But like so many other Jews throughout the Holocaust Kingdom who chose the way of the Almighty, he was a courageous resistance fighter. He led Srulek in performing a glorious act of defiance that enabled them both to overcome their miserable surroundings, and to feel, once again, the hand of the Divine.

SHORTLY AFTER that unforgettable Passover, the winds of war seemed finally to be blowing in the right direction. The Russians were advancing against the Germans and Vienna was within imminent reach. Since Melk was only 36 miles west of Vienna, the Germans were pressured to evacuate the camp before the Russians would arrive to liberate it. The last thing the Nazis wanted was for Allied forces to discover their camps filled with human cargo. Marching the prisoners to their deaths would solve this problem.

Hence, they were to be transferred to Ebensee, in the Austrian Alps, a picturesque location that stood in stark contrast to its use as a killing center of monumental proportions.

Boat and train were the two methods employed to deliver the prisoners. But neither conveyance would bring them even close to their destination. The remainder of the route would be traversed in a death march, which lived up to its grisly name. Significantly fewer than half of those who embarked on the evacuation would complete it.

Srulek was selected to travel by boat. The hull of the rocking vessel was crowded to the point of suffocation, and the conditions were just as horrific as those on the trains. Once again, just like on the journey to Auschwitz, Srulek found himself next to a window—in this instance, a small porthole. Somewhere en route, they passed perilously close to another boat—so close, that Srulek could actually hear Hungarian being spoken on board! Forgetting himself, he stuck his head through the porthole and called out urgently, "Hello! Hello! Where are we? Who is winning the war?"

He was still a boy. Impulsive, unthinking. And he had committed a capital offense. A guard, screaming obscenities, yanked Srulek on deck.

There, he was positioned to be shot.

As always, there was protocol to be followed, and an officer was summoned to do the deed. Srulek stood face to face with his executioner. It had all come down to this moment. He had suffered so much, survived so much! All along a small voice inside him had whispered that he would never die, that perhaps God had a better plan for him. But now ...

The military official, his hand closed around his weapon, stared at the emaciated youth. What ran through the man's mind at that moment? Images of his own son, perhaps, or of himself as an innocent teenager? Srulek would never know. But in a most atypical breach of Nazi behavior, the officer could not bring himself to shoot. "Go below, boy!" he whispered hoarsely to Srulek. And Srulek jumped into the hold, endeavoring not to show his face for the duration of the voyage.

The prisoners disembarked in Linz, a city approximately 40 miles from Ebensee, and were forced to march through towns and villages, in full view of the Austrian civilians, en route to the camp. Those too weak for this arduous trek, or those the guards decided to shoot for any arbitrary reason, met their deaths along the way.

Like Melk, Ebensee was a slave camp devoted to excavating tunnels through a mountain, only here the feverish digging had a different purpose. In Ebensee they were working to extract oil from coal to be converted into gasoline, in an effort to replenish Germany's dwindling fuel supply.

But the newly arrived prisoners from Melk were not put to work in Ebensee. They had been brought there simply to die. Accordingly, they were not fed and were given only water. Every day hundreds died of malnutrition and equal numbers went mad from starvation.

A number of inmates were driven to the most extreme measures to appease their hunger, and Srulek witnessed scenes that he could never bring himself to describe. His personal method of survival consisted of ingesting anything that could provide even the slightest nourishment, which had him chewing on leaves and sucking on bark.

In the beginning of May, liberation was in the air—literally. Artillery could be heard in the distance and Allied bombers owned the skies unchallenged. There was a sense among the starving remnant that liberation could not be more than a few days away.

But could they even manage to hold on until the Allies arrived? Everyone understood with dread clarity that what loomed ahead would be the greatest battle of their lives; if every day of survival was a test, this was the final examination.

Their resources—internal and external—had come to an end, and time became never-ending. They knew only one thing: the Germans were unlikely to let the war end with them still alive, for the world must be *Judenrein über alles.*

ONE MORNING the guards were no longer in their towers and there was a sense that things in Ebensee were not business as usual. One ritual, however, could not be abandoned. The prisoners were lined up in the *Appellplatz*, and their captors began their cherished rite of counting. They counted and they counted, as though they knew it might be their last opportunity; all day long the prisoners were forced to stand at attention as they were counted. The ritual was continuously repeated because a single prisoner appeared to be missing.

His name was Yisrael Forkosh, and he would later disclose his hiding place as the very bowels of the latrine. Of course, the incessant counting did nothing to reveal his whereabouts. The absurdity of it all! Just four days left to the war, and all this to ensure that not a single Jew would escape the Nazis' clutches.

As night began to fall, the Germans finally got to the original purpose of the assembly. The camp commandant had an important message—so important that he had translators present to relay his instructions in every language understood by the prisoners, ten in all.

"The Americans," the commandant announced, "are just 15 kilometers away." This was the first time the enemy had ever been mentioned by name. "But their days are numbered!" he blustered with false bravado. "We are about to launch a mighty counterattack that will pulverize them, and we do not want any one of you hurt!"

Hurt? The skeletal assemblage that swayed before him was already more dead than alive.

"Therefore, for your own protection, you are being ordered to take cover inside the tunnels, where you will be safe!"

No one budged. The Nazis' lies were transparent; their guardhouses were abandoned. They wielded no more power over these prisoners, the final remnant of Ebensee.

And all that night, and into the next day, the mighty SS fled.

After the liberation, the American army found more than one ton of dynamite wired throughout the tunnels, all connected to one fuse. Had the prisoners obeyed their captors, there would not have been a single survivor.

The SS's defection left Ebensee under the aegis of Austrian civilians, discernible by their white armbands. The change of administration in no way improved the camp's appalling conditions. Without a drop of food, the dazed inmates barely clung to life. Though liberation was literally around the corner, each day was an eternity. And each day, some lost the fight.

The "brotherhood" that had all but disbanded in Ebensee because of the acute starvation, managed to rally, somehow, for the final critical hours. Srulek and his comrades mustered whatever strength they had left to convince each other to hold on and not succumb. It was a crucial, vital, lifesaving directive that was fully vindicated.

Others used this time to settle accounts as anarchy reigned throughout the camp. The kapos—who had indiscriminately performed the behest of the Germans in order to enhance their own treatment—were now up for grabs. Srulek and his friends had no more sympathy for these collaborators than the other inmates, but they—unlike some of the other prisoners, especially the non-Jewish Russians—found themselves incapable of taking revenge against those who had buckled under such inhuman conditions.

The boys of the brotherhood roamed the camp, including areas that were previously off-limits. In one of them, they discovered a handgun and passed it around. Suddenly, a German civilian guard appeared, hauling a suitcase and frantically trying to make his way out of a prison that he no longer controlled.

The tables had turned. The German cowered before his former prey, seeing that the boys of the brotherhood were armed. But Srulek and his friends stood there, paralyzed. Even after all they had endured, with a loaded gun in their hands, and an evildoer in its sights, they did not have the internal makeup of killers. Time stood still as a wave of grayness passed over them all.

Out of nowhere a Russian inmate arrived at the scene, grabbed the gun, and shot the German without a moment's hesitation.

WHEN THE AMERICAN LIBERATION FORCE—consisting of only one tank and two jeeps—finally drove up to the camp, a surge of strength revived the wasted inmates, enabling them to break down its locked gate. Feebly, in a gesture that spoke volumes, they began hugging and kissing the tank.

An American GI peeked out of the tank's command hatch and beheld a scene far more gruesome and devilish than anything he had ever witnessed in battle. What he saw and what he smelled was beyond belief. Overcome with horror, he unthinkingly added to it, by tossing a box of crackers and two packs of cigarettes into the camp.

Pandemonium ensued, as nearly 150 starving men lunged, all at once, for the meager rations. An unknown number paid the supreme sacrifice, as they were trampled and asphyxiated in the rush of bodies. Tragic scenes like this one were occurring simultaneously throughout the path of the liberation, as well-intentioned Allied troops unwittingly finished off the work of the Germans. There was nothing—nothing!— in the psyches or training of these soldiers that prepared them for how to deal with the barely-human survivors of this apocalypse. Without even a common language between the liberators and the liberated, deadly mistakes were repeated over and over again.

Suddenly an American officer did manage to convey, through what he remembered from high-school German, that it was imperative that all remain calm for just a little while longer, as a better-equipped military presence was on its way with more rations.

Two hours later, a larger military contingent arrived and set up a field kitchen in the middle of the camp. The fetid air was soon filled with the pungent scent of rice and bacon.

After much hesitation, Srulek headed for the enormous queue of prisoners, several hundred strong, waiting for the serving. Those on the line, however, were the minority, as most of the inmates were so malnourished that they hadn't the strength to stand. Thousands of others were scavenging through the camp for receptacles of any form or fashion that would enable them to receive a helping.

Suddenly Srulek noticed a second, much shorter line. He could not see what the fare was, nor detect smoke or a recognizable aroma. As Srulek looked more closely, he became further confused, realizing that no one in the line was holding a bowl. What on earth were they serving?

There is food for the body, and there is food for the soul. Even a starving boy can understand this.

At the head of the line, Rabbi Shialah Greenwald, the Chuster Rav, was presiding over the rebirth of the Jewish People. In his hand he held the elusive *shel yad* that had been redeemed from the cement bags.

Two hundred Jewish men chose to forego the food, so that their first act of freedom would be a Hebrew blessing over a tattered fragment of *tefillin*. Their earthly reward was not long in coming...

All around them, a horrifying new wave of death and dying erupted. Stomachs that had contained so little for so many years—and had been totally empty for the past several days—could not tolerate the rapid introduction of rich foods. Altogether over 200 souls perished that day because of the woeful ignorance of the liberators. Those who had opted to bless the *tefillin* were spared this terrible end.

SRULEK and his friends from the brotherhood pulled through. It was as though their souls were intertwined—they would not let each other go. Every member of the pact survived, except for two who had been wounded in an Allied bombing and were subsequently executed by the Germans.

Freedom was something these boys would never again take for granted. Even the smallest freedoms; or freedom from the smallest creatures. Their final farewell to the camp came when American soldiers filled hoses with DDT and fired the white powder onto and into their clothing and blankets. The lice were annihilated on the spot.

That night, beneath the white mountains of Austria, Srulek and his friends would sleep the sleep of kings—for the first time in years, without pain or hunger or fear. And soon the brotherhood would go separately into the future, charting their own paths toward an uncertain new day.

EPILOGUE

After liberation, the Americans announced that the former prisoners had a choice of either remaining in the camp to be assisted by U.S. Army medical staff, or they could leave and fend for themselves. Many were eager to flee the premises as quickly as possible, and raided the adjacent houses for their needs. Srulek remained and began a slow process of recuperation.

He told the Allied authorities that he was a Czech national and wished to return to his home. The Americans got him as far as Pilsen, and from there he made his way to Prague and to the Jewish relief agencies that were active there.

Srulek never imagined it would take so long to get from Prague to Munkacs, but even months after the war ended, regular transportation had not yet resumed. The only way to his hometown and—he hoped—a family reunion, was via a train to Budapest. The route to Hungary was very complicated, as the railway was the exclusive domain of the military.

Thanks to military police who were willing to look the other way, Srulek, traveling on the roofs of freight cars, finally arrived. His greatest joy was to be reunited with both of his sisters in Munkacs and to spend the High Holy Days and *Sukkos* together as a family.

Soon after, they departed for DP camps in Germany at the urging of Jewish officers in the Russian Army, who warned them that Russia's borders would soon be closed. In Germany, their goal was to leave and settle in Palestine-*Eretz Yisrael* after the lifting of the British blockade.

Affidavits to travel to America arrived first and were utilized. Srulek spent his first year in the United States at Bellefaire Jewish Children's Bureau, which had been founded nearly 100 years earlier as the Cleveland Jewish Orphan Asylum. In the afternoons and when they had free time, Srulek and other residents would go to the nearby Telshe Yeshiva. Later, he was looked after by a family in Chicago.

Srulek's last name became Americanized to Starck as it was easier to pronounce than Storch. He married in 1957, is a successful diamond merchant and has seven children and more than forty grandchildren. Both of his sisters married and established their families in Brooklyn, New York.

As for the Chuster Rav, he resumed his court in New York and was succeeded by his son-in-law, Pinchas Dovid, the son of the Grand Rabbi of Boston, Rebbe Levy Yitzchak Horowitz.

Moral Spark

GUTTA

This is a story of a moral spark that burned at the core of a child. Gutta Eisenzweig nurtured that spark inside herself as a youngster during wartime. As a young teacher, she nurtured it in the hearts of other Jewish children engulfed by the horrors of the Holocaust. It was this unquenchable spark that illuminated the path of this brilliant, determined young woman, and motivated her to forge crucial associations with some of the greatest Jewish figures of her day. Young Gutta Eisenzweig instinctively understood that human connections were as essential to survival in the Holocaust Kingdom as food and water.

Propelled by fear, she hurtled through the campus as quickly as her legs would carry her, darting across its bucolic, tree-lined courtyards, past hallowed halls of science and civilization. White-faced, bathed in cold sweat, she dared not pause to massage a hideously throbbing ankle, or to catch her breath—or to consider what would happen if they caught her...

Actually, Gutta Eisenzweig knew what they would do. She had witnessed what befell Jewish males who had the temerity to study at the University of Warsaw during the 1930s; of this, there was ample bloody evidence in the classrooms and in the hallways.

Her hulking assailants—none other than two of her classmates—

were on her heels, cursing loudly, and terrifyingly close to grabbing her hair. That they had failed thus far to tackle her only infuriated them more.

Audacity, a sharp mind and a pioneering spirit were all requirements for a Jewish girl enrolled in a Polish university in 1939. But why was Gutta Eisenzweig running for her life?

None of the Jewish students—girls and boys alike, brimming with intellectual fervor and lofty goals—were prepared for the virulent anti-Semitism that was, for all intents and purposes, an integral part of the college curriculum. Jews were forced to sit together on the left side of their classrooms, and it was standard for the males to be beaten senseless by their fellow students. All too often it was the professors who provided the iron bars, blunt objects or other weapons of assault.

Jewish boys, if they valued life and limb, would attend class as little as possible. But in order to acquire a diploma—a prerequisite for earning a decent wage in hard times, and for the possibility of advancing above manual labor—they needed to pass their final exams. The eligibility to take those exams was contingent upon course attendance—verifiable only by the professor's signature in notebooks that the students were required to present at the end of every class session.

And so the hapless youths were damned if they set foot on the campus, and doomed if they didn't. The small number of Jewish girls who studied at the university, Gutta among them, conspired to help their brethren. These intrepid young women risked expulsion by nonchalantly placing more than one notebook on the professor's desk for signing.

On this particular day, one of the most outspoken anti-Semites in the class had uncovered their scheme. Enraged, he had lunged at Gutta, attempting to grab the three slim books she clutched under her arm, but she managed to duck from his grasp. Pandemonium ensued as she raced out the door, with her pursuer and a sidekick giving chase, screaming obscenities. As she bounded down the steps of the building, she twisted her ankle, but with the brutes closing in, she ran through the pain; she ran and she ran, past students jeering and faculty members who carefully averted their eyes, until she reached the outer edge of the campus and was able to take refuge in the streets of her birthplace, the once-grand city of Warsaw. It was home to some of the greatest minds and noblest souls of the Jewish people, who comprised over a third of the city's population.

Gutta ran with no premonition that it would be years before she could finally stop running.

INNOCENTLY, she had once trusted that the future could only get better, for she had been reared in times that were unprecedented in their harshness. Surrounded by the grinding poverty and squalor of Warsaw in the early 1930s, young Gutta Eisenzweig would never dream of drinking something so precious as a full glass of pure milk. Although her own family was not considered poor, the child would fill a cup with water and cloud it with just a drop of dairy, conscious that she had concocted a more protein-rich potion than most Chassidic house-holds could muster in those dark days.

Every day, Gutta would bring two sandwiches to the state-run "Chavazelet" school for Jewish girls: one for herself and the other to be placed in a collection box at the school's entrance. The excess food was quietly divided among the needy students so that none would know who were the sponsors and who were the less fortunate.

The watery milk, the extra sandwich—these were the early buds of a heroic, activist spirit blossoming forth in a desolate time and place. This was the essence of Gutta, whose very name bespoke "goodness." But no one could predict, then, that the winds of war would align her destiny with those of the most extraordinary characters of her day—and that with them, Gutta Eisenzweig would quietly save a piece of the world.

SHE HAD BEEN BORN into a world in dire need of saving. Long after the guns of World War I were silenced, Polish Jewry continued to inhabit a country in ruins far deeper than its razed buildings. The citizenry persisted in the plunder of Jewish homes and institutions as though it was part of their national duty. The desperate times produced a social climate antagonistic to Jewish tradition, with cities once cel-ebrated for producing geniuses of Torah, morphing into hotbeds of secularism.

In the renowned Jewish community of Warsaw, particularly in its once-stable and stalwart religious enclave, change was irrevocably in the air. Some of its children fled in the dead of night, as members of Zionist youth groups bound for the rugged homeland of Israel. But with such immigration held to a trickle by the British, many youths remained behind and, thwarted by poverty and lack of opportunity, they often turned to communism.

It was a world especially confusing for an observant Jewish girl on the brink of womanhood. While most of the boys remained cocooned inside their yeshivas, girls were enrolled in Polish *gymnasia*, becoming susceptible to secular and Marxist ideologies that were on the rise. In heavily Jewish neighborhoods, state-run schools bowed to the majority by offering classes in religious instruction—but they were taught by decidedly anti-religious Jewish teachers who took advantage of this opportunity to spout contemptuous views on "archaic" practices.

Young women in scandalously immodest fashions would sullenly appear at their parents' Sabbath tables, condescending of the rites. Matchmakers and arranged marriages were no longer willingly accepted, and yeshiva students—these girls' own brothers!—were regarded as pathetically unworldly.

Gutta Eisenzweig was somewhat insulated from this phenomenon, as a student at the Chavazelet school, a haven for girls from staunchly Chassidic families. And yet she was drawn to a path most uncommon for a Jewish girl, much less one from such a sheltered background: her burning ambition was to continue her education in college. Proud as they were of their daughter's passion for study, the Eisenzweig family tried to discourage her. They did not consider the University of Warsaw an appropriate place for a pious daughter of Israel, even without full awareness of the anti-Semitism mushrooming there.

Ironically, they were almost as skeptical of a newly established institution that offered girls the opportunity to study Jewish subjects: "Bais Yaakov," a religious seminary launched in Krakow by an educational trailblazer named Sarah Schenirer. For the Chassidim of the day, and for many of their non-Chassidic brethren, a women's seminary where Torah was taught was a radical notion to be shunned.

But Gutta persisted, and finally her family opted for what they deemed was the lesser of two evils. During her first weeks at Bais Yaakov, however, the letters she received from home were anything but supportive; her parents continued to cast doubt upon the entire notion of higher education, while her less observant friends cynically inquired how long she intended to remain at "the convent."

Then all of the naysayers were stunned into respectful silence. The Gerrer Rebbe, undisputedly the most influential Rebbe in all of Poland's many Chassidic courts, sent his granddaughter, Rivka, to the Krakow seminary. This one act awarded Bais Yaakov greater credibility than could have been conferred by a mountain of endorsement letters.

The arrival of Rivka Alter was a boon to the school, and not only because she carried the lineage of her father, the future Rebbe and of her grandfather, the "*Imrei Emmes.*" According to the dean of the seminary, Rabbi Yehuda Leib Orlean—himself a Gerrer Chassid—young Rivka was such a brilliant and deep thinker that her gifts rivaled those of her illustrious forebears. Similar to the Chassidic masters, who were famed for employing a minimum of speech, Rivka said little, allowing her actions to speak for her. She became the school's prize pupil and had a profound effect upon the entire student body.

She also became Gutta Eisenzweig's dearest friend, and would later be the comrade of her darkest hours.

Together they became pioneers in Sarah Schenirer's revolutionary educational experiment, plunging into their challenging studies with an intellectual zeal that would rival any male scholar's. In addition to deep friendship, Rivka Alter offered Gutta a life-changing perspective: through Rivka, Gutta began to comprehend the greatness of the celebrated Rebbes. Although Gutta, too, had been raised in a family of Gerrer Chassidim, she had never experienced anything at home that had given this way of life particular appeal. It was difficult for an inquisitive girl to sustain adherence to a spiritual leader with whom she felt no genuine connection—until Rivka entered her life.

Another young woman whose dynamic presence would impact Gutta was her teacher, Chanke Grossfield. This woman's superior gifts as an educator were seen as crucial to the future of the fledgling seminary—and to the future of the Jewish people. When she became betrothed to Rabbi Yosef Biegun, a rising star in the Lithuanian yeshiva world, rabbinical authorities ruled that he must sacrifice his leadership role and move to Krakow where his bride held court.

What Gutta learned from this vibrant young couple, considered one of the most brilliant matches in Poland, also went beyond the stuff of books.

One Rosh Hashana she merited the honor of an invitation to their home. She was taken by the sight of the beautiful teacher sitting close to her adoring husband throughout the meal. She had never seen a Chassidic couple interact this way before. They clearly shared a powerful bond that was both emotional, as shown by their loving gazes, and intellectual—because the passionate conversation in which they were immersed, revolved around the holiday and its laws.

At first Gutta felt as though she had stumbled upon some private moment, but the couple repeatedly interrupted their discussion to make sure that she could follow and be a part of it. For Gutta, this was a tantalizing glimpse of what her own future might hold, if she were so blessed: a remarkable union that could encompass mind and spirit, body and soul.

GUTTA THRIVED in Bais Yaakov, where the innovative curriculum suited both girls from little towns and villages, who seldom questioned their faith, and those from larger cities, who typically grappled with doubts and challenges. But ultimately, the school faced a dilemma regarding Gutta Eisenzweig.

Gutta had not given up on the idea of university studies. While this was not the route the school encouraged, Rabbi Orlean knew it was his duty as headmaster to counsel each pupil according to her individual needs. He also knew that Gutta's matriculation at the University of Warsaw could be a major coup for Bais Yaakov, if she agreed to return to them afterwards, as a teacher. Having just one college graduate on its staff would confer state accreditation, academic prestige and major financial benefits to the seminary.

Carefully, Rabbi Orlean helped Gutta to understand that he was not sending her to the university or even actively condoning it. The choice was hers; but if she returned to Bais Yaakov, the benefits would be everyone's. Gutta was devoted to her seminary and assured him she would be thrilled to join its staff after graduation.

But first, Gutta, like her fellow alumnae, had to complete a key requirement of the Bais Yaakov education: fieldwork as a teacher. Barely older than the students themselves, the recent Bais Yaakov graduates had to put up their hair and wear high heels in order to present the image of seasoned educators. Nevertheless, these young instructors, trained by world-class educators, had absorbed the seminary's burning passion and were eminently capable of spreading its message.

The impact made by these young women can be seen through the classic photographs that were routinely featured in Bais Yaakov publications, displaying large groups of grinning young girls surrounding their teen-aged teachers. These pictures spoke volumes about a bond that far surpassed the standard student–teacher relationship. Hundreds of them were framed and displayed in living rooms, over a bed, on a little shelf, or tucked inside a purse amidst its owner's dearest possessions … even unto her journey's tragic end.

GUTTA WAS SENT to student-teach in the village of Stopnitz, about two hours from Lublin. This impoverished townlet was more isolated and backward than any place she had ever seen. It was as though the clock had stood still a century earlier. There was no train station, nor any mechanized vehicles.

But this in no way dampened the spirits of Stopnitz's jovial and good-hearted Jewry. Gutta was ensconced in the home of the *schochet*, the ritual slaughterer, who boasted the town's finest accommodations: a real straw mattress. From the day of her arrival she was dubbed "the *Lerrerke* (female teacher)" and was a celebrated figure in Stopnitz, second only to the rabbi.

The citizens of Stopnitz were lavish in their appreciation of Gutta; whenever they encountered her on the town's muddy, unpaved paths, they would greet her with an enthusiastic curtsy or bow.

Gutta's classroom shared a stairwell with an impoverished cobbler who would display his wares upon the steps. This industrious craftsman could salvage footwear no matter what its condition. The cobbler was not especially fashion-conscious, yet his handiwork could transform a worn-out, discarded shoe into one that was wearable, its original design all but unrecognizable under layers of platforms and patches.

The effusive shoemaker would serenade Gutta with Gerrer Chassidic tunes whenever she approached his makeshift workshop, and his tunes escorted her all the way to the basement classroom.

And every Friday, there was a constant stream of little girls from her classes and older ones from her "*Bnos*"* group who would bring her delicacies for Shabbos—steaming pots of cholent and chicken soup, gefilte fish, and a variety of kugels and crisps—causing her hostess, the *schochet*'s wife, to put her hands on her hips in indignation and grunt, "You'd think they think we don't feed you!"

So great was their appreciation for the gifted *Lehrrerke*, that the residents of this exceedingly pious village were even willing to look the other way when Gutta's intellectual curiosity collided with their extremely strict social constraints. For example, she relished frequent visits to a local Talmudic scholar—a brilliant, blind sage named Nathanson, who happened to have an unmarried son. The villagers frowned upon an unwed girl entering a home where there might possibly be a single boy; the fact that young Nathanson did not live at home with his parents did not diminish their disapproval, but they would say nothing disparaging to their heroine.

When Nathanson's son finally did return from school, a new dilemma arose. The boy, a talented violinist, was invited to the slaughterer's house to perform at a *melava malka*, a traditional Saturday night party held in honor of the Sabbath's departure. In Stopnitz it was unheard of for a single man and woman to be in the same room, but how could they deny their beloved teacher the opportunity to hear the bravura performance? A creative solution was devised: Gutta would remain sequestered in her room, but her door was left open.

Gutta spent half a year dispensing lessons in Stopnitz; in the end, she felt she had learned far more than she could ever impart.

And so, only a few months later, as a student in one of Europe's most renowned universities, Gutta clung to her idyllic memories of Stopnitz: of living contentedly among its simple and kindhearted Jews, of being a respected member of its close-knit community. These were the thoughts that consoled her as she lay weeping in her bed, her throbbing, distended ankle propped on a pillow.

But the indignities that Polish Jews suffered on the college campus

---

*   Literally "daughters," *Bnos* is the name Sarah Schenirer gave to an educational youth organization for Bais Yaakov students. The organization was created in order to keep the girls occupied, and spared from outside influences, during after-school hours.

would soon pale in comparison to their plight upon the outbreak of World War II.

ON SEPTEMBER 1, 1939, Germany invaded Poland, blindsiding its army and its citizens with a surprise attack. Many initially believed that Warsaw would remain impervious to what was at first (and hopefully) conceived as a border conflagration. Just two days later this assumption was shattered by the approach of German forces, and the city's densely populated Jewish area becoming the target of unrelenting bombings, though it had no militarily strategic value.

Virtually no one realized at this stage of the war that the entire operation's key strategic value, from the Germans' standpoint, was the annihilation of the Jews.

The first days of the occupation would further divert Warsaw's Jews from this chilling reality. When the conquering soldiers—trained in warfare and not in dealing with the "Jewish problem"—did not, for example, remove Jews from the massive food lines, this was interpreted hopefully as a good sign. Members of the older generation insisted that they "knew" the Germans from World War I, and that they really weren't so terrible. Thus, even while Jewish homes were reduced to rubble and daily life was in a shambles, morale remained oddly high.

But as the Secret Police, the Gestapo and their cohorts became entrenched throughout Poland, all this changed. With bloodless proficiency, Jewish businesses and possessions were confiscated and their owners humiliated and tortured.

Forcing Jews to perform gymnastic feats in public, cutting and ripping off beards, and commanding the elderly to play "leapfrog," were among the Germans' sadistic games. Standard German procedure dictated that Jews be forced to shuffle in the gutters like farm animals, and display the utmost deference when an SS man passed on the street or sidewalk. Failure to comply immediately meant humiliation, beatings, and sometimes, death.

Corporal punishment could also be inflicted without any justification at all, and the Polish folk proved to be a willing audience that could not get its fill of Jewish degradation. Gutta's brother, who wore the flowing *payos* (sidelocks) and dress of a Gerrer Chassid, once made the near-fatal mistake of being spotted by a German while walking near the Eisenzweig home. The soldier aimed his rifle and began shooting wildly as he chased the terrified youth through the streets of Warsaw, shattering every window in the front of the family's apartment building as young Eisenzweig ducked inside.

Not long after, the Gestapo broke into the home of Gutta's esteemed grandfather, Berel Geffen, who in partnership with his nine children was one of the region's most prosperous leather merchants. Gutta stood by in horror as the steely-eyed soldiers loaded a truck to haul away every last bolt and shred of leather, and emptied the safe inside the office where Berel Geffen often received needy Jews seeking charity. In the safe, the intruders left behind a grisly joke: a slip of paper attesting that the German government had removed 200,000 zloty—as if any attempt to redeem this receipt at Gestapo headquarters would not cost the bearer his life!

Berel Geffen's large extended family, including Gutta's parents, lost everything in one fell swoop. Many others who had been beneficiaries of their largesse would now suffer as well. But the losses and degradation had only begun.

THE WARSAW GHETTO was established by order of Governor-General Hans Frank, on October 16, 1940. This decree did not arouse great consternation at first; in fact, some Jews felt a sense of relief, hoping it might reduce the unrelenting humiliation and torture to which they had been subjected in public, and also insulate them from the illnesses running rampant. At this point, their dread of the Gestapo paled in comparison to their fear of disease. This notion of an improved health situation was later dispelled, by posters announcing that entrance into the ghetto was forbidden due to a dangerous epidemic inside. The purpose of these posters was to frighten the non-Jewish population into avoiding all contact with the ghetto inhabitants. The Jews, once again, had failed to fathom the seriousness of their situation. That things could get markedly worse did not seem to occur to them, nor did the folly of finding "security" inside a place cordoned off by the enemy.

Crowded inside the ghetto, the Jews of Warsaw and the surrounding areas were either living in their original apartments (the Eisenzweig home fell just within the ghetto walls), in apartments that had previously belonged to Poles who were forced to vacate, or crammed inside the residences of relatives, friends or strangers. It was an abominable situation, but at least Gutta's family still slept on their own mattresses, unlike others who lacked even a roof over their heads.

As Europe's largest Jewish community, Warsaw had drawn Jews of every stripe. It was the capital of religious and Chassidic Jewry and headquarters of Zionist and Bundist* and Communist Jewry. And now they all lived on top of each other, with critical needs to be addressed: an absence of sanitation, schools, communal agencies, and most pressing of all, food. These shortages would have been somewhat less acute if not for the subsequent influx of an additional 150,000 Jews from outlying areas, swelling the ghetto's population to nearly half a million. The result was that half of Warsaw's population was squeezed into 2.4 percent of the city's area.

The latest arrivals suffered most of all. Some crowded into attics, others crawled into basements, but in the freezing winter these improvisations were futile. When the deportations began, they were the first victims, as they had nowhere to hide. Many actually lined up on their own volition when (in 1942) the Germans promised bread to those who reported for "relocation."

With the horrendous lack of sanitation and medicine, disease spread unchecked throughout the ghetto. Typhus, especially, was impossible to contain and often resulted in death. Among the thousands it claimed was Gutta's nineteen-year-old brother. Gutta too was afflicted, but managed to survive. She ignored the German directive to report to the hospital for quarantine, aware that whoever entered never emerged alive.

In desperate situations, human beings often resort to desperate acts. Yet the Jews of the Warsaw Ghetto—starving, disease-ridden, unprotected from the elements and literally gasping for air—did not rob each other or kill.

GUTTA, AS WAS HER NATURE, put aside her own frailty and was determined to aid the most destitute. What was needed now was far, far greater than the long-ago gesture of her "extra sandwich." She was thunderstruck by the indescribable dehumanization that had

---

* The "Bund" was Yiddishist in language and culture, socialist in politics and economics, and vehemently anti-religious.

overtaken the ghetto. In icy temperatures, barefoot and half-naked children wailed for milk, old people in rags mourned and prayed amidst their own waste and piles of emaciated corpses. Gutta would return home and vomit in revulsion and despair.

But this was a fiercely determined young woman whose strong faith and associations with some of the greatest minds of her day would not allow her to be paralyzed by hopelessness and fear. In fact, one of her longstanding associations—a childhood friendship—would catapult Gutta to center-stage in the daily workings of the ghetto ... and ultimately save her life.

A brilliant young historian by the name of Hillel Seidman was employed by the *Judenrat*, the ghetto-based Jewish council appointed by the Germans. The *Judenrat* attempted to assist its desperate population with the most pressing issues of survival, but was empowered only to comply with the Nazis' ruthless demands. Before the days of the ghetto, Seidman had been director of the "*kehillah*," the archives of the Warsaw Jewish community, a role which he continued behind ghetto walls. There were times he was able to free people from forced labor by registering them as employees of the *kehillah*—a temporary reprieve for most, but one that proved instrumental in Gutta's survival.

Of all of those affiliated with the *Judenrat*, Dr. Seidman was the most knowledgeable about his faith, and therefore the most sensitive to the needs of the ghetto's observant Jews. He became no less than a father to the scores of frightened and starving yeshiva boys who had traveled on their own to study in Warsaw, and were trapped inside—without their families—when the war broke out. Dr. Seidman struggled to keep these youths and their rabbis alive by securing ration cards that would entitle them to a daily bowl of soup. Knowing that they were favored targets of Nazi brutality, he tirelessly sought to boost their morale even while he himself appeared skeletal, dark circles rimming his eyes from lack of sleep.

Gutta had considered Hillel Seidman "a saint" ever since they had played together as children. In the grimly adult world of the ghetto, she would find him worthy of the designation many times over.

THE WINDS OF WAR would also cause Gutta Eisenzweig's path to intersect with that of a legendary hero of the Warsaw ghetto, the noble Dr. Janusz Korczak. Before the war, Korczak (a name adopted to disguise his Jewish identity) was a highly regarded pediatrician, a prize-winning author, head of a network of excellent orphanages (both Polish-Catholic and Jewish), and a beloved public figure.

The influential Korczak hosted his own daily radio program, titled "The Old Doctor," though he was not yet even fifty when the show first aired in 1926. The educational digest was broadcast during school hours, and for its duration Poland's classrooms would tune in and the schoolchildren became his rapt students; shopkeepers would put down their wares; machinists would abandon their tables; and housewives would pull up their chairs. An entire country—earnest young educators like Gutta, most of all—became riveted to Polish Radio's most popular personality.

Korczak's Jewish orphanage on Krochmalna Street afforded its residents a standard of care superior to anywhere else in the world. Even after the hardships of war drove the orphanage into grinding poverty, the children never knew that they were lacking. Korczak's progressive, visionary educational philosophy, shared by his longtime assistant, Stefa Wilczyńska, was to treat children with as much respect as adults—as he put it, "children are adults with small feet"—and to encourage them and give them tools to structure their own world.

It was Janusz Korczak who promulgated the belief of "the moral spark" that burned at the core of every child, a philosophy that would deeply influence his future protégé Gutta Eisenzweig. He once commented:

> Within each child there burned a moral spark that could vanquish the darkness at the core of human nature... Life threw me these children like sea-shells. I didn't ask where they came from or where they were going. I only wanted to be good to them so that their hatred toward man wouldn't harden into stone.
>
> (Betty Jean Lifton, *The King of the Children*)

The wildly antithetical backgrounds of Gutta and Korczak could not have foretold their powerful synergy. Korczak, born Henryk Goldszmit, grew up in an ultra-assimilated home steeped in Polish language and culture. He did not even know that he was Jewish until the age of five, when a janitor's son barred him from using a cross as a grave-marker for his pet canary. This boy declared that the bird—like its grieving owner—was Jewish, and therefore undeserving of a cross and ineligible for heaven.

While the Eisenzweig family was steeped in Chassidic learning and the rhythms of religious life, young Korczak flung himself into the political and cultural maelstrom of Polish society. He was initially a staunch supporter of the Polish head of state Jozef Pilsudski. But after Marshal Pilsudski's death in 1935 (and in the wake of the Friendship Treaty between Germany and Poland of 1934), the status of Polish Jewry deteriorated significantly, and many Pilsudski followers felt that their only hope of competing with the far right was to adopt a policy of venomous anti-Semitism, thus Korczak was ejected from their ranks.

Anti-Jewish legislation placed restrictions on all Jewish economic, social and cultural life in Poland, and physical attacks were commonplace. Jews who did not passively allow themselves to be plundered had heavy fines imposed by Polish courts for the "crime" of self-defense. After Germany withdrew citizenship from its Jews, thousands of German Jews of Polish origin were expelled by the German Government to the Polish border station of Zbaszyn.* Eighteen thousand freezing victims were quartered in pigsties and horse stables still filthy with horse dung, stuck inside a no-man's land, rejected by both countries.

The eminent Dr. Korczak visited the Jewish homeland in Palestine twice during the 1930s and came back a changed man. He had developed a love of Zion as profound as that of any Torah scholar, and was torn between his personal dream of aliyah (immigration to the Holy Land) and his commitment to the hundreds of children he tended to so lovingly. Ultimately he had but one choice, for he knew that these orphaned youngsters could not live one day without him.

Not only did Dr. Korczak change during those years, the world changed. The celebrity who was once hailed as one of Poland's most respected authors and educators was now ostracized because of his Jewish origins. His contract with Polish Radio was terminated and he

---

*   Among them was a man named Zindel Grynszpan who wrote a postcard to his son Herschel in Paris, detailing how they were suffering. The son was enraged and went to the German Embassy in Paris and shot the first official he saw, Ernst Vom Rath—triggering, or more accurately providing the pretext for, *Kristallnacht*.

was forced to resign from the Polish-Catholic orphanage that he had managed for fifteen years.

For the next three years, Korczak's Jewish orphans—like all the Jews of Poland—were cruelly taunted and separated from the mainstream. Korczak struggled fiercely to shield the helpless children not only from hunger and deprivation, but also from the virulent anti-Semitism that surrounded them. He designed and flew a flag for them, a green banner with a chestnut blossom and the Jewish star emblazoned upon it, a symbol of unquenchable hope, Jewish pride, and the moral spark that blossomed, despite everything, within every child.

AFTER GERMANY'S SURPRISE ATTACK in 1939, Polish morale plummeted, and the powers-that-be deemed it critical to put "The Old Doctor" back on the air in order to calm the populace. Korczak's soothing voice resonated of Poland's honor and the merit of valor, and advised children how to conduct themselves during dangerous times so as not to panic and suffer needless injuries. Between broadcasts, he combed the streets, aiding casualties—especially children.

When the German conquerors decreed just a few months later that all of Poland's Jews must wear a white armband bearing a blue Star of David, "The Old Doctor" refused, and in brazen contempt for the German authorities, insisted upon wearing his Polish army officer's uniform. He had attained the rank of major, having served in two of Poland's wars. "I accept only the laws of nature and God," declared Janusz Korczak, "not man-made laws."

After the orphanage was forced to relocate inside the ghetto, Dr. Korczak was arrested for attempting to block the Germans from confiscating a truckload of potatoes that he had labored furiously to acquire for his starving orphans. The potatoes did make their way to his children inside the ghetto, but Korczak—whose trademark military garb (and absence of Jewish armband) clearly infuriated the Germans, was sent to the infamous Pawiak prison. He was locked in a pen with felons and members of the underworld, which was somewhat to his advantage as the Nazis were far "kinder" to these criminals than they were to those guilty of the much more heinous crime of being Jewish. He spent several harrowing months there before the Gestapo let him go for an exorbitant ransom.

Though physically and emotionally debilitated by his prison ordeal, Korczak soon parlayed his many connections and secured a relatively decent building inside the ghetto walls into which his orphanage could be transferred.

The new facility on 33 Chlodna Street was nothing like the well-appointed one on the outside, but compared with the prevailing conditions in the ghetto, it was a haven for the children.

With Korczak's non-Jewish staff barred from entering the ghetto, an advertisement for aides appeared in a ghetto newspaper. Twenty-four-year-old Gutta Eisenzweig, desperate for a way to contribute, was among the first to respond.

Gutta's interview with Dr. Korczak proved to be one of the most fascinating discussions of her life. She had already been exposed to religious Jewry's finest rabbinic minds and Poland's leading university professors, which honed her appreciation for one of the most distinguished pedagogues of the age.

Korczak was a brilliant physician with a profound understanding of child psychology and educational methodology. And it was clear that this worldly assimilated Jew believed Gutta had something to offer him as well. No one like her had ever worked on his staff before, certainly not the daughter of a Chassidic family, nor a graduate of the Bais Yaakov seminary!

As foreign as her background was to Korczak—who had no formal religious education and was hindered by his inability to speak Yiddish—he deeply valued her upbringing and considered it a supreme asset to his orphanage.

Little of Korczak's pedagogic genius was applicable to the squalid Warsaw ghetto. It is impossible to engage the mind when there is a hole in the stomach, he reasoned. Korczak spent every waking hour scavenging for food to ensure the survival of the two hundred orphans in his care, exploiting every single one of his many contacts with both non-Jews and Jews, including the collaborators he despised.

Everyone in the ghetto was crazed with hunger, yet Janusz Korczak worried only about the children whom he had placed under his wing. After Hillel Seidman helped acquire ration cards for his charges, Korczak—and he alone—was allowed to cut to the head of the food lines. Whenever he returned wearily to the children—whether laden with food or, at times, empty-handed—he was engulfed by their grateful hugs and kisses; he was their father, he was their lifeline.

With their beloved patriarch absent for hours on end, the orphans frequently looked to Gutta Eisenzweig to fill the void. She had no parenting experience, but she did possess one asset that even the eminent Dr. Korczak lacked: she understood the healing powers of faith and tradition.

Gutta's mission was not to "indoctrinate" the children, but to provide them with comforting rituals that could divert their minds from hunger and fear. Every evening she would recite the *Shema* (the prayer declaring God's oneness) for them, tell stories from the Torah and the prophets, and sing Yiddish and Hebrew hymns of comfort and hope. Korczak was often witness to this practice, as he elected to sleep with the children.

While most nights Korczak would relieve Gutta so that she could return to her family's quarters before the curfew, one night he beseeched her to stay. He shared with her his growing conviction that under the wretched circumstances of these children's lives, there was nothing more valuable in the world than the faith that Gutta instilled within them.

Korczak entreated her to teach him more about the life of the devout. And so from dusk to dawn they sat together, the renowned educator listening in rapt silence as Gutta passionately shared the insights of Sarah Schenirer and Rivka Alter and Chanke Grossfield Biegun and of the great rebbes and sages and mystics of the past.

Hours into the marathon discussion, Korczak's questions led to a startling confession. "Jewish observance was something I was denied, preventing me from choosing the correct path," he said, his voice quavering, tears coursing down his cheeks. "The only hope for these children is that they follow the direction in which you are guiding them."

Gutta had little doubt that during that unforgettable night, amidst the bitter cold and wretched filth of the ghetto, Janusz Korczak's soul had refracted some pure light, and he was transformed into a *baal teshuvah* (a penitent). Many would later comment on how Korczak's lifelong ambivalence towards religious practice appeared to subside in the ghetto, where his own fate became inextricably tied to the suffering of his people.

In the fall of 1941, Dr. Korczak took great pains to arrange High Holy Day prayer services in the orphanage. Clearly he believed that the liturgy of Rosh Hashana and Yom Kippur would fill an acute spiritual need during those dark times—and not only within his frightened orphans. Clutching a Festival prayer book with a Polish translation, Korczak remained with the children and was observed to be deep in prayer throughout the long, emotion-filled days.

Gutta Eisenzweig, too, prayed inside the ghetto walls during these High Holy Days, begging God for redemption. Although the worst was yet to come, her prayers, ultimately, would be answered.

But Janusz Korczak and his two hundred orphans faced a different destiny.

They would not live through the year.

WHAT SORT of "miracle" would, in due course, recast Gutta's fate? It was another of her providential connections: the renowned Sternbuch family of Switzerland.

Just prior to the war, Recha and Yitzchak Sternbuch transformed their St. Gallen home into a rescue headquarters, a key base for the refugees (both legal and illegal) who had managed to escape to Switzerland. Mattresses lined the floor and tables laden with food and drink filled the rooms. Every new arrival was given sustenance, clothing and respect.

In 1938, when conditions for Jews in Germany and Austria deteriorated considerably, Recha Sternbuch traveled there to distribute thousands of false visas. She spent several months in Italy trying to acquire additional visas, in order to extricate Jews from German dominion. The result was a steadily increasing number of Jewish refugees on Swiss soil who needed to be fed and housed.

At first the couple worked with the Swiss arm of the Joint Distribution Committee, but after the organization took issue with some of their methodology, Recha and family sought other avenues to help them save Jewish lives. An association with a police commander "on the take" even caused Recha Sternbuch to be arrested for violating border controls, and she was jailed for several days. After a lengthy legal battle, the charges were eventually dropped.

The Eisenzweig family's connection to the Sternbuchs pre-dated

World War II, but only by a matter of hours. Yitzchak Sternbuch's younger brother Eli, also a key figure in the family's rescue operations, came to Poland on business just before the outbreak of the war. Several of Gutta's relatives met this earnest young man and were convinced that he was "the one" for Gutta, who was away for the summer.

Eli Sternbuch was so taken by their descriptions of this accomplished young woman that he decided to travel immediately to the countryside to meet her. On his way there, frantic radio announcements instructed foreigners to depart Poland at once, as war was imminent. The two young people managed to meet for just one hour before Eli was forced to flee home to Switzerland.

There was no time for a real courtship to develop.

There was, however, just enough time for a delicious dream to take root.

By the year 1941, Gutta's pleasurable encounter with Eli Sternbuch had been eclipsed by the horrors of war. The name "Sternbuch" now meant something other—something more—than a dim fantasy of marital bliss.

For Gutta and her family, it meant their sole, slim chance of survival.

The Sternbuchs had succeeded in acquiring a number of Paraguayan passports through that country's consular office in Bern, Switzerland. The Germans apparently recognized the holders of Latin American passports as foreign citizens entitled to the rights stipulated by international law.* Eli Sternbuch arranged for a Paraguayan passport to be sent to Gutta, and promised that passports would soon be coming for her parents as well.

But in the winter of 1941, Gutta's father Yehoshua Eisenzweig traveled to the Lublin region to visit his own parents—a journey from which he never returned. Tragically, neither he nor his parents were ever heard from again.

GUTTA LEARNED that for her new passport to be valid, it would need to be stamped by the Gestapo. What in another time and place

---

* It is contended that they did so to ensure the protection of the thousands of Nazi spies entrenched throughout Latin America, agents whom they believed would be extremely useful in the final stage of the war, when Germany was to launch its planned attack against the United States.

would have amounted to a mere technicality, was now a harrowing prospect of exquisite anxiety.

Getting the stamped validation meant departing from the ghetto (which was forbidden), removing her Star of David—equally forbidden, and making her way down the notorious Aleja Szucha Street, where Gestapo headquarters was located. This was an unthinkable act for a Jew, even before the war. Whenever a Jew dared to set foot on that street, the Poles would beat him unconscious.

Miraculously, Gutta made it safely inside the lion's den. A Gestapo officer took the passport from her trembling hand, eyeing her up and down. He smiled sardonically, indicating he was well aware of what sort of "Paraguayan" she was. Nonetheless, he stamped the document and Gutta carried it back to the ghetto with her heart in her throat. The abject terror of the experience did not allow her, even for a second, to savor the brief freedom and fresh air of the outside.

This passport would ultimately save her life. But first, it would— more than once—nearly cause her death.

Eight months later—twenty-four hours before a major deportation of forty freight cars crammed with suffocating men, women and children from the Warsaw ghetto, and nine months before the Uprising— all holders of Latin American passports were instructed to report to the dreadful Pawiak prison. The purpose of interring them was ostensibly to separate them from those scheduled to be deported over the coming days. But for those crammed inside the two large, filthy holding pens, one for males and the other for females, there seemed to be little advantage conferred by their (bogus) documents.

Twice a day the Gestapo scoured the premises with massive, wolf-like dogs. Individuals were pulled from the group and never returned. Who would be summoned next? How much credence had the Germans awarded their documents? Already shaken by the appalling and frightening conditions, they felt their uncertainty rapidly morphing into terror.

Gutta and the others sat in prison, helplessly awaiting their own deaths. The gloom was overwhelming, heightened by the noises that penetrated the viewless windows above their heads. Their cells were directly above the execution site. At six o'clock every evening, men, women and children who had committed "capital" offenses (such as violations

: outside the building and shot. There was no
 the progression of desperate screams and ri-
silence and the departing sounds of German
ng out, the Pawiak prisoners shuddered and
ets had penetrated their *own* flesh.

ther in the Pawiak prison, Gutta felt the taste
: as never before. She felt trapped—even en-
no avenue of escape or of communication,
until a daring notion entered her head.

Gutta observed that Jews from the ghetto were routinely brought
into the prison as day laborers. *If only—if only!—she could make contact
with one of them, and get a message out to her mother!* But, where was
her mother? With each deportation, the ghetto was shrinking, and the
survivors were forced to relocate. Also, could Gutta really count on one
of these anonymous slaves to actually risk his or her life by smuggling a
communiqué out of the prison? And what would happen to her, if her
note fell into the wrong hands?

THE PLAN, she knew, was crazy; for it to succeed would be nothing
less than a miracle. But Gutta's nature was not to sit passively and, with
the gunshots and gut-wrenching screams ringing in her ears, await her
own execution.

In a corner of her filthy cell she found a few crumpled scraps of
paper, a pencil fragment, and an empty matchbox. She scribbled furiously, addressing her words not to her mother, but to her longtime
friend Hillel Seidman, a member of the ghetto's *Judenrat*. Everyone
would know where to find Dr. Seidman, and he would surely know her
mother's whereabouts.

Gutta stuffed the shred of paper inside the matchbox, clutching it
tightly until, from outside, she could hear the sounds of the laborers being marched back to the ghetto. She scarcely breathed as she tossed the
matchbox out of the window. Had one of the guards been looking her
way, Gutta's demise would have been certain. Had a prisoner stepped
out of line or bent down to pick up the matchbox, his or her fate would
have been the same. And even if the matchbox was miraculously re-
trieved, why would its courier undertake the insane risk of searching for
Dr. Seidman after curfew?

All night long, Gutta fixated upon what might have become of her little "message in a bottle," traveling though time and space to parts unknown. Would it bring about some poor soul's untimely death? Or had the matchbox been kicked aside by a Nazi boot, its contents a scream heard by no one?

Staggeringly, the very next morning Gutta had her answer. The impossible had occurred! The very same matchbox arched through the opening between the window bars; the brave stranger who jeopardized his or her life to deliver Gutta's message had apparently jeopardized it once more to deliver a reply.

Folded inside was a miniscule note from Hillel Seidman. He wrote that Gutta's parents' passports had just arrived, but as her father had already been deported from Lublin, he would take her father's place.

How could a contemporary of Gutta's impersonate her father? The question was answered a few weeks later, when Gutta saw her old friend again. Dire starvation, fused with the plight of the remaining Jews that weighed so heavily upon his broad shoulders, had taken its toll. Indeed, young Hillel Seidman could have posed as Gutta's grandfather.

MEANWHILE Gutta's mother, Sarah Eisenzweig, was unaware of her passport to freedom. Before Seidman could reach her, she had been snatched and forced to march to the *Umschlagplatz*, the assembly point where unsuspecting Jews—who had been promised "resettlement" in the east and an end to their misery—were being loaded aboard boxcars. Their true destination was the Treblinka extermination camp. Every day a total of 6,000 innocents were deported, with a thousand-man Jewish police force* (well aware of where this "cargo" was headed) charged with dispatching it efficiently and without delay. SS guards were interspersed throughout the columns to ensure that the wretched police did their job.

One of the Jewish policemen, a fine individual and a friend of Gutta's, recognized her mother as she trudged along. Although these policemen had worked for the Germans to save their own necks, not all had abandoned their consciences along the way. Many churned with despair over

---

* The Jewish police were appointed by the *Judenrat*. They were chiefly composed of individuals who were willing to inflict harm upon their brethren in order to save themselves. The inclusion of religious men among them was rare.

the terrible role they were forced to play. Attempting to save a prisoner from deportation was a capital crime. Yet on this occasion, the policeman seemed to have been reminded of his friend Gutta Eisenzweig, and he summoned in his heart the very same courage, selflessness and overwhelming decency, the moral spark that Gutta herself exuded.

Standing in full view of the German overseers, he brusquely separated Sarah from her column, feigning punishment for some imaginary infraction. He tossed the horror-struck woman into a doorway and bellowed about her impending beating, as the gleeful SS men, who reveled in Jews beating their own, herded along the rest of the group, ruthlessly maintaining the schedule.

The policeman's gallant charade saved her life, but it would not put her out of harm's way for very long. But then the Paraguayan passports arrived. Sarah Eisenzweig and her young "husband," Hillel Seidman, were remanded to the abominable Pawiak prison.

Pawiak was a hellhole, to be sure, but it had two saving graces. One was that it was not the Warsaw ghetto, which was becoming dreadfully quieter each day, with some 300,000 Jews having already been deported. Orders had been issued to liquidate the remainder of the ghetto and a violent uprising would soon be launched that would leave the decimated area in flames.

And second, in Pawiak, Sarah would finally be reunited with her daughter...

They reasoned that at least they would be together as they awaited the future, a complete unknown over which they had no control.

WITH THE IMPOSSIBILITY of receiving news from the ghetto, Gutta could only pray feverishly for Janusz Korczak and the two hundred children she had grown to love. Perhaps it was best that she was spared the heartbreaking and heroic end of the good doctor and his beloved charges, which has been chronicled in a number of different ways by those who watched the horror unfold.

They say it was a hot, sunny morning on the fifth or sixth of August, 1942, when the Jewish orphans lined up for what could arguably be labeled the first modern "protest march" on their way to the *Umschlagplatz*. Dr. Korczak and Stefa Wilczyńska had done everything they could to prepare them emotionally and sartorially for this moment.

Dressed in their finest clothing, the children arranged themselves in formation behind their cherished green flag and their beloved "father." Jehoshua Perle in his eyewitness story, *The Destruction of Warsaw*, recounts:

A miracle occurred. Two hundred children did not cry out. Two hundred pure souls, condemned to death, did not weep. Not one of them ran away. No one tried to hide. Like stricken swallows they clung to their teacher and mentor, to their father and brother, Janusz Korczak, that he might protect and preserve them... Janusz Korczak was marching, his body bent forward, holding the hand of a child in both hands, without a hat, a leather belt around his waist and wearing high boots. A few nurses marched behind him, wearing white aprons. They were followed by two hundred children dressed in clean and meticulously cared for clothes, who were being carried to the altar... On all sides the children were surrounded by German, Ukrainian and this time also Jewish policemen. They whipped and fired shots at them... The very stones of the street wept at the sight of this procession.

As Janusz Korczak neared the *Umschlagplatz*, the ghetto police stood at attention and saluted. According to one report, a German officer made his way toward Korczak in the commotion of the last moment and handed him a letter permitting him to return home. According to a different version when the children were already loaded onto the boxcar a Nazi officer turned to the Old Doctor and asked, "Was it you who wrote *Little Jack*?"*

"Yes."

"A fine book. I read it when I was a child. You may step out of the wagon."

"And the children?"

"The children will continue their journey. You, however, can stay behind."

"You are mistaken," Korczak replied, "not everyone is a rascal!" And he remained with his children.

There are other versions that tell how the Polish underground had presented a plan for Korczak to escape, and how another group had

---

* Dr. Korczak authored over twenty books for both adults and children.

coordinated a pass for him as a drainage system engineer. To each offer
he replied that the children would be afraid without him, and he point-
edly refused to abandon them.

The prayer that was answered was that Janusz Korczak and his children were all together, hand in hand, as they went to their deaths.

SIGMUND FREUD wrote, "At bottom, nobody believes in his own
death." This may have been an unimpeachable truth for the father of
psychoanalysis from his perch in Vienna, but not for the desperate inmates of Pawiak. For six torturous months, they had no inkling what
each day might bring. They had no contact with the outside world, rendering their morale even worse than that of the Jews still in the ghetto,
who were living in delusion, much in line with Freud. Ghetto inhabitants received letters and postcards from relatives who had been deported. Postmarked and purportedly sent from enviable locations like
Brześć, Bialystok, Pinsk, and even faraway Smolensk, the correspon-
dence from their loved ones announced that life was vastly improved
in their new surroundings, where there was work for the adults, and
school for their children.

These upbeat missives were actually written under duress in
Treblinka, and were supremely effective in nurturing the fallacy that
deportation was not synonymous with annihilation. Basic human optimism—manipulated with ruthless cunning by the Germans—enabled
the Jews to reconcile the deep inconsistencies between their fears and
their hopes.*

Because the Jews in the ghetto had no idea what lay ahead, they
nurtured memories of their world as it once was and dreamt that their
lives would one day be returned to them.

However, in Pawiak, Freud's theory would have been disproved, for,
in time, death became the one thing they *could* believe in.

Then one day, without any warning, the Germans announced that
the inmates must prepare to depart. No destination was disclosed, and
the prisoners assumed that it was finally their turn to be transported

---

* "The wish to live, the inability to believe in one's own imminent death, the
universal human faith in one's own immunity to disaster—all these factors conspired to make the Jews believe that resettlement, not death, was the fact." (Lucy
Dawidowicz, *The War Against the Jews*, page 414)

to either the *Umschlagplatz*, or to the execution site. They were duly resigned to their fate.

But they were in for the surprise of their lives.

The pitiful remnant was taken to a civilian railway depot, free of brutal overcrowding, public beatings, shouting or executions. There wasn't a boxcar to be seen.

The prisoners were dumbfounded. They could hardly remember what it felt like to live as normal human beings, to go about their lives free—even momentarily—of unrelenting terror and abuse. Incredulously, 163 former Pawiak inmates filed onto two pre-designated cars on a regularly scheduled train carrying ticketed passengers, and took their own seats.

After a full three days and nights of uneventful travel, the train pulled into Vittel, an exclusive resort town in the northeast of France that since the mid-1800s had been celebrated for its mineral spas.

From the train station, they were transported to the grounds of an elegant resort that now doubled as an interment camp. There was nothing about Vittel that resembled a Nazi prison; there were no filthy cells or firing squads, and the Jewish prisoners received accommodations alongside non-Jewish internees. A flimsy fence surrounded the perimeter of the grounds, with the prisoners free to stroll through the resort's manicured gardens.

"Would you care for a room next to your parents, Miss?" a German soldier politely inquired as he processed Gutta's entry. The man's courtesy caused her to do a double take. The place was so gorgeously picturesque, their captors suddenly so bizarrely congenial, that Sarah Eisenzweig blurted out to her daughter, "We must no longer be in this world, we have arrived in Paradise! There can be no other explanation!"

Indeed, the conditions were a little bit of heaven. The other internees on the premises were thousands of foreign nationals, primarily from the United States and Britain. A hospital on the premises was staffed by French POW physicians, and nutritious, plentiful meals were provided by the Red Cross; Jews who declined to eat the non-kosher meat that was offered could exchange the tins for kosher provisions. Astonishingly, prisoners who wished to take temporary leave of the camp were simply required to submit a request, which was almost never denied.

One must ask, then: why did the dazed ex-prisoners of Pawiak not try to escape from picturesque Vittel? The question is a simple one, but the answer is complicated. Exhausted and traumatized, finally having a decent roof over their heads and food in their bellies, they could not bear to exchange this security for the hazardous unknown. None of them spoke French, the only language in which they could make their way on the outside without arousing suspicion and risking re-arrest. Perhaps it was wishful thinking, but they were unquestionably duped by the tranquility of Vittel … duped into believing that the Final Solution would never catch up with them, there.

But of course, they were wrong. The Jews would soon discover that the road from hell to Vittel was paved with still more Nazi treachery. The Germans had transported them there—ostensibly as Latin American nationals—with the expectation of a possible prisoner exchange. But when the countries that had purportedly issued their papers refused to allow entry for their citizens, it brought into question the validity of the documents, and German civility reverted to type.

Until that point, life in Vittel was a balm to Gutta's spirit, for it was there that she and Rivka Alter (now Rappaport) revived their precious friendship. Rivka and her husband had also been interned in Pawiak, and were able to engage in genuine discourse. For the fifteen months they were together in Vittel, Gutta—who exulted in relationships above all else—deepened her bond with her brilliant and compassionate schoolmate.

BY APRIL OF 1944, the Germans suspected the legitimacy of the Latin American passports, and their holders were separated and taken to a hotel just outside of the Vittel camp. While conditions there were not awful either, it did not augur well that they were under suspicion of attempting to defraud the Germans. Frantic, veiled messages were dispatched to the courageous rescuers in Switzerland, Recha and Yitzchak Sternbuch. Switzerland, being neutral, was one of the few countries with which Vittel's internees were allowed to correspond; all letters had to be written in German, but codes were used to throw off the Gestapo censors.

The Sternbuchs were a duo of unusual daring and activism. This time, their determination was fueled by extreme desperation. The revered spiritual leader of Antwerp, Belgium, Rabbi Mordechai Rottenberg, was among the prisoners of Vittel. He and his noble wife were now the shepherds to a terrified flock.

They were also the parents of Recha Sternbuch.

The Sternbuchs explored every conceivable method in their furious efforts to persuade the Latin American countries to validate the passports that had been issued to the Jews of the Warsaw ghetto, who were now interned in Vittel. This entailed pleading before the Polish government-in-exile and the Vatican, and with Washington's War Refugee Board, to immediately issue strongly worded communiqués to the German Foreign Ministry in Berlin.

None of these august agencies deemed this rescue a priority, dashing the only hope for these last surviving Polish Jews. Recha Sternbuch was frantic, and after receiving no cooperation from the foreign governments she had petitioned, she managed to dispatch a number of Palestinian "certificates" (akin to visas) to the Vittel internees, but it was too late.

The Gestapo machine proceeded with its ruthlessly crafted agenda. Wanton murder could not be committed inside lovely Vittel as it could on the streets of Warsaw, due to the presence of witnesses from Western Europe who were more high-minded, including the foreign POWs and Norwegian nationals. The solution to this problem had long ago been perfected under the euphemism of "deportation," which sounds ominous, but nowhere near as reprehensible as "murder." The evil genius of the "deportations" was that not only were the Jews duped into thinking that they were being sent where their labor would be utilized—and they were prepared to do anything, rather than remain one more second in the ghetto—but also the non-Jewish spectators couldn't discern what was truly transpiring. Gentile youth were constantly rounded up by the Nazis for labor in Germany and Austria, and they were also transported at night by rail. Thus the Jews being sent to their deaths were always camouflaged by civilians being sent to factory employment.*

Each day, the hapless Jews of Vittel became more and more of an endangered species. The enduring beauty of their surroundings was now a cruel irony; for them, the elegant resort had become a deathtrap.

---

* Interview with Sir Martin Gilbert, April 4, 2006.

It would take nothing less than a miracle to orchestrate the elaborate international plan that might free them in time.

IN APRIL OF 1944, the day after Passover (and the one-year anniversary of the Warsaw Ghetto Uprising), the Germans informed the Jews that they were leaving Vittel. A collaborator was enlisted to lull them into believing no harm would befall them. The traitor's name was Schwartzbard and he dutifully parroted what the Nazis instructed him to say. Schwartzbard allayed the fears of his co-religionists by assuring them that he had personally visited the camp they were all going to, and it was no less civilized than Vittel.

Once again the deadly combination of brilliantly orchestrated German deception and the Jews' wishful thinking resulted in wrong-headed submission to the German dictates. In this case, the victims were neither emaciated nor in the throes of despair; they were all highly intelligent people, including Talmudic scholars and university graduates with advanced degrees.

Yet remarkably, only Sarah Eisenzweig would not be taken in by Schwartzbard's canard. She could not for a moment forget the grisly education that she had received in the Warsaw ghetto, convincing her that the Germans and their agents were never, under any circumstances, to be trusted.

"Don't listen to him. He's lying, he's lying!" Sarah screamed as the others prepared to depart for the railway platform. But the more agitated she became, the more desperate the others became to silence her. They didn't want to listen to her; they were afraid to listen to her. One man even forced his hand across her mouth.

The area around the camp was not particularly well patrolled. Yet all of the prisoners lined up passively with their meager belongings, like tourists about to leave for a weekend jaunt. Though some of them were grim-faced and whimpered softly, Schwartzbard had clearly carried the day.

Moments before departure, a fellow prisoner named Mrs. Frankel quietly placed herself alongside Sarah Eisenzweig. An employee of the hotel had promised to leave a cellar door unlocked, she whispered, suggesting that Sarah join her in hiding there.

The dreaded assembly to the train had already begun. Menacingly,

SS men closed in on the group to ensure that every one of them would be on board.

The whimpers of the prisoners turned into wails.

Every second counted.

Sarah Eisenzweig gave a barely perceptible nod to Mrs. Frankel and motioned for Gutta and Hillel Seidman to join them. Gutta was prepared to accompany her mother, but there was one final act she needed to perform before descending the steps to the cellar.

She darted from the stairwell and made her way to Rivka Rappaport. Gutta pleaded with the dearest friend of her life to come and hide with them. Rivka motioned that she had not the resolve to carry on alone without her husband, who was already at the train platform. "It's too late, Gutta," she said urgently, in a hushed tone. "But you go, go and be safe … and I will pray for you every single day for the rest of my life."

Gutta's heart sank and she felt as if she would faint. What could she do to change Rivka's mind? How could she possibly leave Rivka?

There was no time for discussion; the SS were verifying that no one was left in the hotel. Sarah Eisenzweig appeared at the top of the cellar stairs and hissed at her daughter that she must come at once. Her voice was quiet but the wild look in her eyes bordered on hysteria.

Gutta's inability to break away from her friend was risking everyone's life!

"Go!" Rivka commanded her, sternly this time. "Remember, be strong, and I will pray for you!"

Those were her final words to her friend.

The Germans would send every last Jew from Vittel—except those who happened to be patients in the hospital, and the handful who managed to escape—to Auschwitz. Upon arrival, their transport would not be subjected to the standard, grisly selection process. All of the human cargo would be shunted directly to the gas chambers, including Belgium's esteemed Rabbi and Rebbetzin Rottenberg.

Recha Sternbuch was one of thousands of Jews who would become orphaned that day.

And Gutta's own angel, Rivka Alter Rappaport, would have barely a moment for prayer before her own light was extinguished forever…

LED BY MRS. FRANKEL, Sarah and Gutta Eisenzweig and Hillel

Seidman groped through the pitch darkness for their portal of escape, the unlocked cellar door. At the same time, the Germans discovered that not all the prisoners on their list were on the platform. Several search parties were dispatched—one of them, just a few feet away.

But where was the door?

Mrs. Frankel's fingers suddenly found the opening, and the four fugitives rushed inside, turning the lock on the door behind them. Their eyes quickly adapted to the miniscule amount of light, which emanated from a slim shaft. They were able to see each other's outlines, and to discern an industrial oven straight ahead. Without a word uttered between them, they pulled open the door to the oven and inched inside, feet first. As the unit was designed exclusively for baking bread, it was wide but extremely shallow. It was clear to Gutta that squeezing their four bodies inside, in a race against time, meant literally defying the laws of space and matter.

Entombed inside the oven within the hotel's cavernous basement, the four fugitives were engulfed by silence. The bustling establishment that had teemed with life and activity was now eerily still. Silent like the liquidated ghettos.

Did any life remain, upstairs?

As Gutta lay crammed inside the oven, her face shoved up against the grates of its iron door, the ghettos and the transports, the orphans and the suffering, the hunger and the loss, all converged inside her brain.

Did life, as she knew it, remain anywhere?

Suddenly, the silence was shattered by an earsplitting clank. The oven's heavy iron door had come loose from its hinges and went crashing to the floor. In an almost superhuman feat, the prisoners of the oven managed to lift up the door and wedge it back into its proper place, but they continued to grip it with every ounce of strength, lest it dislodge again.

FROM THE TIME she was a little girl, Gutta could invariably handle every situation that came her way. She was a model of maturity, leadership and pragmatism. But for every individual, there is a breaking point. For Gutta Eisenzweig—alumna of the Warsaw ghetto, of the Pawiak prison—the breaking point came as she lay motionless inside that narrow oven.

The fear and helplessness, the final leave-taking from her beloved Rivka, the airlessness of the pitch-dark space with not a centimeter in which to move, were the final assault on her sanity.

"I can't breathe, I'm going to die!" she panted. "I must get out of here!"

Her mother, whose body was wedged alongside Gutta's, had no words left to soothe her—only some hideously pragmatic advice. "That's all right—just die silently. If you crawl out of the oven you will surely be finished, and so will the rest of us…"

Sarah's response only served to heighten her daughter's terror. What began as a low, insistent mantra, escalated into hysterical screams. "I want to go with Rabbi Rottenberg!" Gutta wailed. "I … WANT … TO … GO … WITH … RABBI … ROTTENBERG!" Sarah managed to squeeze her hand around Gutta's face and clamped her mouth shut. Though muffled, her desperate chanting continued.

And then, the most terrible sound of all: the heavy thud of Nazi boots on the cellar stairs!

Just as the door to the cellar was forced open, Gutta finally, finally fell silent. Like the others, she ceased breathing, and every nerve in her body leaped and shuddered as one of the soldiers shined a powerful flashlight into the grating. The light was as bright as a projector, forcing shut her eyes from its blinding rays.

"Hans, they're not here, those cursed Jews!" a voice called out brusquely. "Let's look elsewhere."

And still the foursome dared not emerge from their awful hiding place. Not even after the men left the cellar. Not even after a ghostly night silence descended upon the hotel. Not even after they heard the plaintive whistle of the train pulling out of Vittel on its doomed, one-way journey the following morning.

They did not emerge from their terrible prison for the next two days and two nights.

Even after they climbed out of the oven, they had no intention of leaving the cellar. They searched in vain for additional places to hide there—a nook, a cranny, a secluded corner or an even lower level. But it was over two days since they had last eaten and their hunger could be ignored no longer. Exhausted, they staggered up the cellar stairs.

Gutta's brain felt as though it would explode. Terror and hunger propelled her matchstick legs madly. She was the first to reach the hotel's once-splendid main floor. It was in shambles. Corpses—some of them suicides—were strewn through the lobbies and landings. Discarded bottles and debris were piled in every corner.

The others followed closely behind Gutta. The very first person they encountered after emerging from the stairwell was none other than the traitorous Schwartzbard. When he saw his nemesis Sarah Eisenzweig, he looked as though he had seen a ghost—a quartet of the undead, in fact—and he shrieked for his wife. He had sold his soul to deliver Vittel's unsuspecting Jews to the ovens, and he would undoubtedly be called to task for not completing the job.

The sight of Schwartzbard caused Gutta to reach a new crescendo of fear. It was not over! What more could befall them? What more?

Delirium overtook Gutta as she broke away from the rest and staggered up the steps from the lobby as quickly as her feeble feet could carry her. Sarah attempted to follow, and could only gasp at the chaos that surrounded them. Just up ahead, Gutta disappeared after clearing the landing. Sarah called out her daughter's name, but strangely, there was no reply. She was filled with foreboding as she turned the same corner...

And then Sarah Eisenzweig saw a sight more horrible than anything she had ever seen before in her life ... or would ever see again.

Gutta lay sprawled out on a landing, her body stiff, her face frozen in a terrible grimace.

There was no doubt in Sarah's mind that her daughter was dead.

It took only a moment to figure out what had happened. There was a nearly empty bottle of ammonia alongside Gutta's lifeless form. The terrified girl had spotted the container of unmarked liquid upon reaching the first flight, and in her disorientation and thirst, downed most of its contents.

The German commandant of the camp arrived on the scene and ordered—unbelievably—that Gutta be taken to the hospital—a real hospital—located on the premises. Physicians did not believe they stood a chance of reviving Gutta, as the corrosive substance had burned its way down her esophagus and through her insides. Still, they abided by their Hippocratic oath and pumped her stomach. The procedure far surpassed their expectations and Gutta's life was saved.

For the next several weeks, the doctors and nurses continued to award her superior medical treatment, looking the other way as her mother hid inside a deep closet in her hospital room, with Hillel Seidman in an adjacent one.

Poor Gutta was not especially thankful. Her body was healing, but her spirit was broken. Bitterly, she asked herself, what point was there in being nursed back to health if only to be fit to be murdered? This was the twisted logic of the Holocaust Kingdom.

Indeed, the Allies had already landed on Normandy, and Germany was losing on two fronts, with German troops retreating across France. But the Reich stubbornly refused to lose sight of its ultimate goal: the Final Solution. And so a train was earmarked exclusively for the deportation of Vittel's remaining Jews—a train that might otherwise have been useful for troop redeployment, or the delivery of ammunition, supplies and reinforcements.

This transport that would render Vittel virtually *Judenrein* was a terrible sight to behold. Its passengers were mostly those who had failed at suicide attempts at the time of the first deportation. Many were carried to the train on stretchers, and all around there was weeping and mourning.

Gutta remained in her bed, still gravely ill and much too weak to walk. Still, she was not a creature of passivity and knew that they would be coming for her as well. Gutta simply refused to be carried to her death.

With Herculean strength she leapt from her hospital bed and dove from the balcony of her room, but only managed to land on the balcony half a story below. Suffering the disgrace of an aborted escape, Gutta remained in a pile of herself, unable to move.

It took two nurses to haul her back to her bed, and a guard was posted outside her door. In addition, an elderly German officer stood over her and insisted she had nothing to fear.

So many of the mighty Reich's resources, marshaled to eliminate— after first saving—a single Jewish girl!

With the German in uniform at her bedside, Gutta's screams grew louder and more shrill. He attempted to offer her assurances and his solemn word as an officer that harm would not befall her, but nothing could comfort her. The officer exited in alarm, and Gutta continued to scream until she had no more strength to make a sound.

Once there was silence, out of the closet crept Sarah Eisenzweig, to comfort her lost, frightened daughter.

When finally Gutta was released from the hospital, there were almost no Jews left in Vittel and they were terrified to draw attention to themselves. Each night, Gutta, her mother and Hillel Seidman looked for a different place to hide and to lodge in the camp, as they were afraid to return to their room, which was guarded by a soldier. Indeed they were afraid to sleep in any room where they could be easily found, which posed a thorny challenge every single night.

They were joined by Mrs. Frankel, who had leapt from the bathroom window of the second transport from Vittel. This daring woman could not forgive herself for locking the train's bathroom door, depriving others of an escape route.

At the end of August 1944, the war suddenly arrived in Vittel as the American army launched a two-day assault on the region. Cannon fire and automatic weapons thundered day and night. By the time the last shot was fired, every German had retreated from the region.

The camp was now open and unguarded, but no one dared leave. Having survived until now, no one wished to step into the crossfire. Soldiers from General Eisenhower's army finally arrived at the camp on September 1, 1944, but were under orders not to enter for fear of contracting typhus and other diseases. Reticent to disobey army commands, they tossed chocolates and parts of their rations over the fence to the hungry prisoners.

The non-Jews of Vittel spontaneously broke into songs of victory, exulting that the war was finally over. The Jews, however, huddled together and wept. They were alive, but their families and homes—their very civilization—had been destroyed.

Altogether only seven Jews survived the Vittel camp, including the traitorous Schwartzbard and his wife. The walls of the camp were defaced with declarations of "Death to Schwartzbard," which should have rightfully been engraved upon the collaborator as a Mark of Cain.

EPILOGUE

After the war, Gutta and her mother briefly settled in Aix-les-Bains before leaving France for Switzerland. Not long after Germany's surrender, Gutta began receiving letters from the man who was responsible for saving her life—her ephemeral suitor, Eli Sternbuch. They had met only once before, five years earlier, and she truthfully no longer even remembered what he looked like. On Eli's side, however, absence had made the heart grow fonder, and in every ardent missive, he proposed and re-proposed. But Gutta was so busy with piecing her shattered life back together that she had no time to savor the dreams of every young woman. When they were finally reunited a few months after France was liberated her answer was "yes," but it took months before they could actually wed because of bureaucratic hurdles imposed by France and Switzerland.

After their marriage, Gutta and Eli together continued the refugee relief and resettlement work for which the Sternbuch family had become famous. For twenty years they lived in St. Gallen, Switzerland, where Gutta assisted her husband in managing his raincoat factory. Their gracious home routinely hosted scores of strangers in need—some staying for just a weekend, others for years!

When the Sternbuchs moved to the more cosmopolitan city of Zurich in 1968, their legendary benevolence, communal outreach and activism only grew. Festive Friday night meals with dozens of guests would stretch deep into the night.

Dr. Hillel Seidman settled in Brooklyn and continued his valuable historical work. When he would see a school bus stop on the street to pick up or unload yeshiva students, the venerable historian would freeze in reflection and tears would cascade down his cheeks. He passsed away on August 28, 1995. The infamous Schwartzbard and his wife moved to Paris, where they died a natural death.

Gutta—teacher and friend to so many young people—was blessed with six children of her own, and many grandchildren and great-grandchildren. She was cherished as a modern-day matriarch not only by her own family, but by so many others throughout the Jewish world who have been nurtured by her kindness and moral spark. She passed away on August 30, 2012.

Parental Devotion

ISSER

This is a story of deep parental devotion.
It is the story of a young boy whose life was miraculously saved, on a daily basis, by the steadfast intervention of two fiercely loving parents: his Father in Heaven—and his mother, on earth.

ON A SUN-DRENCHED SUMMER DAY, little Isser Fisher scampered happily through the countryside surrounding his family's *dacha* (summer cottage). Outwardly, it was a scene of great tranquility, of a carefree vacation at a summer home. But meanwhile Isser's regular home, and his entire world—the legendary Jewish civilization of Vilna—was on the brink of destruction.

Days earlier, on June 22, 1941, the German Air Force had launched a surprise noonday attack on Vilna that continued and intensified through the night. Since it was a Sunday, all municipal institutions were closed, adding to the chaos and confusion.

While Rabbi Moshe Dov Fisher, his wife Esther and their seven-year-old daughter Ita were cowering behind the furniture inside their Vilna apartment, four-and-a-half-year-old Isser kept dashing to the window, agog at a sky that glowed red from anti-aircraft fire.

The anxious parents decided to vacate the city immediately. They took the children via horse and buggy to their country home, about an hour away. While they felt safer from aerial assault, even there the skies echoed with the rumble of distant cannon fire. In this bucolic setting, the young rabbi and rebbetzin agonized and debated over their family's future. Both of them were proud standard bearers of the rich rabbinic heritage of pre-war Lithuania. Moshe Dov Fisher was a leading disciple of Rabbi Naftali Trop, dean of the Yeshiva of Radin, which had been founded by the world-renowned Chafetz Chaim. Rabbi Fisher was the spiritual leader of a prominent synagogue known as *Di Grois* (The Great) *Shnipishok*, located in Vilna's old Jewish enclave of Śnipiszki, which the Jews called *Shnipishok*. The rebbetzin's father, Rabbi Dobber Pianko, a respected alumnus of the Slabodka Yeshiva, was the rabbi of Mior, Byelorussia.

If Isser sensed his parents' agitation, it did not detract from his eagerness to frolic in the surrounding woods. He slipped out of the house, and trotted happily into the forest.

The excitement of the adventure quickly faded when the child realized he was lost. He began to wail for his mother, but he was so far from the house that, coupled with the incessant bombing, no one could hear him. Drifting aimlessly into a clearing, the sobbing child tripped and slammed his head on a rock. He slumped to the ground, unconscious.

The story of Isser Fisher could have ended at that moment. But a gentile maid who worked in one of the adjacent cottages witnessed the accident. She quickly carried the boy inside and attempted to revive him.

When Isser finally came to, the maid's employers tried to determine who he was. But the boy was frightened and disoriented, and remembered only his first name. The sole clue to his family's identity was that he was murmuring, "Everybody calls my Papa 'Rebbe,' but Mama calls him Moshe." On this basis, the homeowners, who were Jews, were able to return him to his frantic and grateful parents.

Soon after, as the bombings began to wane, "Reb Moshe" persuaded his wife that the family should go back to Vilna. With the heart of a true scholar, he yearned to return to the company of rabbis, his students, and his congregation.

Nothing could have prepared him for the devastation that lay ahead.

NAPOLEON had dubbed Vilna "The Jerusalem of Lithuania"* upon encountering its Great Synagogue. Over half a millennium of vibrant Jewish life and world-class scholarship was centered there. *Vilnius* (as it is called in Lithuanian) was the birthplace of the revered Vilna Gaon (The Genius of Vilna, Rabbi Eliyahu), the seat of the yeshiva of Rabbi Yisrael Salanter (founder of the *Mussar* Movement), and countless other jewels in the crown of Jewish history. On the eve of World War II, Jews were the largest ethnic and religious group in Vilna—nearly 100,000 individuals, comprising 45 percent of the city's population.

The Fisher family returned to a city they scarcely recognized, as it had been conquered by the Germans. The steady onslaught from the air had reduced many of its beautiful buildings and plazas to rubble, and there was a strong police presence in the streets. But the true eeriness was one of absence, not presence. Great numbers of Jews had already disappeared, never to be heard from again.

Still, it would take a massive and carefully executed campaign to solve "the Jewish problem" of the Jerusalem of Lithuania. Therein was written one of the most sorrowful pages in the tome of modern rabbinic history: what would be remembered as *Der Tog fun di Rabbonim* (The Day of the Rabbis).

The infamous roundup of the rabbis of Vilna began on Saturday night, the 13th of July. With terrible appropriateness, it was also an annual day of fasting and lamentation: the 17th day of the Hebrew month of Tammuz, marking the beginning of three weeks of mourning over the fall of Jerusalem and the loss of the Holy Temple.

Vilna was home to over a hundred synagogues, large and small,

---

*   An alternate tradition for the origin of this title dates back to 1623, when Lithuanian Jewry ceded from the Council of the Four Lands, which would meet regarding matters pertinent to the Jewish communities of Greater Poland, Little Poland, Galicia and Lithuania. The Lithuanian communities sought to establish their own independent council, and Vilna believed that she should be recognized as its chief community. To bolster their claim, the Vilna delegation presented a declaration signed by the city's paramount rabbis, boasting that Vilna had more than 300 residents who worked full-time as manual laborers, yet were also fully accomplished scholars in both the Babylonian and Jerusalem Talmuds. Upon hearing this, one of the council's officers exclaimed, "What a holy community—a Jerusalem of Lithuania!"

many yeshivos, and hundreds of rabbis. Distinguished among the many rabbinic scholars was an elite group of nineteen, the revered Torah leaders of the community. The Nazis kicked off their roundup by arresting all nineteen on that one night, including Rabbi Henoch Eiges, the elderly sage who authored the noted collection of halachic responsa, the *Marcheshes*.

The shocking arrests cut off Jewish Vilna at its knees. The only one of the nineteen luminaries to escape was Rabbi Yisroel Zev Gustman, who, as it happened, was the rabbi of the other synagogue in the *Shnipishok* neighborhood, the *shul* referred to as the *Kleine* (Small) *Shnipishok*.

While arresting Rabbi Gustman, the Gestapo inflicted a savage beating upon him. "Why, why?" the rabbi beseeched, staggering under the blows. The brutal officer's answer was succinct: "*Weil du rabbiner bist* (Because you are a rabbi)."

Rabbi Gustman was temporarily placed under house arrest while the Gestapo continued the roundup, but he managed to slip past the sentry and take cover in a nearby potato field. A search party was hastily organized to comb the area. As Rabbi Gustman silently recited *viduy* (the last-rite confessional prayer), one German actually stepped on the rabbi's foot, and a snarling hound dog came just as close. Yet miraculously, Rabbi Gustman was not discovered.

The search was discontinued and the superintendent of the building, a gentile woman, arranged to have a pair of scissors and a hat of the style customarily worn by Lithuanian commoners smuggled into the potato field. Rabbi Gustman gave himself as close a shave as the scissors would allow, donned the hat, and left the area perfectly disguised. As the grisly day wore on, the Gestapo continued to hunt down the rest of Vilna's rabbis, but Rabbi Gustman managed to hide, undetected, in the home of a Jewish man.*

Rebbetzin Esther Fisher pleaded with her husband not to attend the *mincha* service in his synagogue that afternoon, but the rabbi would

---

* For the rest of the war, Rabbi Gustman hid with the partisans in the forests. After surviving the war, he became rabbi of the remnant of the Vilna Jewish community. In 1949, he immigrated to the United States and established a yeshiva in the Crown Heights section of Brooklyn. In 1970 he moved the yeshiva to Jerusalem.

not be deterred from his communal responsibilities. Just as he returned home, a Gestapo vehicle pulled up in front of the family's apartment and a storm trooper verified that the man who looked the part was indeed the rabbi they were looking for. Rabbi Moshe Dov Fisher was ordered into the car.

The desperate screams of the rebbetzin only caused the storm trooper to strike her and threaten that she would join her husband in the vehicle if she continued. *Who would take care of the children?* Helplessly she locked eyes with her husband as he was pushed inside the car, and it sped off.

Now the Fisher family, too, was cut off at the knees.

In the days that followed, the violence and humiliation of "The Day of the Rabbis" devastated the synagogues and communities that were now rudderless without their beloved rabbinic leaders. Little Isser, who had romped blithely through the woods only weeks earlier, was a child no longer. He did not comprehend the abrupt disappearance of his father or the public degradation of his religion (even the adults could scarcely fathom the horrific events), but he felt them to the core.

The gentile Lithuanian populace required little arm-twisting from the Nazis to take an active and gleeful role in the ongoing reign of terror. Deputized and armed by the Germans, they burst into the *Grois Shnipishok* synagogue and forced the powerless Jews to ignite a giant bonfire using the holy Torah scrolls. This barely whetted the locals' lust for violence.

They grabbed Jews from the streets—including a mere bar mitzvah boy—forcing them to undress and jump through the flames. This torture continued all night, until the singed victims collapsed from smoke inhalation and exhaustion and were then summarily shot in the synagogue's courtyard.

Like Romans watching the infidels being pulled apart in the ancient Coliseum, a throng of spectators cheered the proceedings on. And who were these bloodthirsty spectators? The synagogue's gentile neighbors, who had lived side by side with the Jews for generations, many of them conversant in Yiddish.

In the minds of the savage crowd, there was only one drawback to the sadistic spectacle: what a shame that Rabbi Fisher could not be present to witness the agony of his flock, and be chief among the victims.

AUGUST 3, 1941. Three weeks later, on the apex of the annual communal mourning period—its final day, the sacred fast of *Tisha b'Av*—a decree was issued banning Jews from the center of Vilna. They were also restricted from treading on any paved surface and forced to walk in the gutter like animals. Three days later, the Jewish community was fined five million rubles to be delivered to the German authorities the next day. The Jews were warned that failure to remit the full amount would result in a massacre the likes of which they had never seen.

The fine was paid but the punishment was carried out nonetheless. On August 31st, two Lithuanians in civilian garb entered a Jewish home and fired shots in the direction of German soldiers standing in the square below. They then ran out of the house, shouting that it was the Jews who had opened fire.

The innocent Jewish homeowners were dragged from the house, beaten, and shot on the spot. But this frame-up had a much broader agenda, in what came to be known as "The Great Provocation." Additional laws were posted, further restricting the movement of Jews, and 3,700 of these Jewish "menaces"—primarily women and children—were seized in reprisal for the Lithuanians' shooting. All those who were arrested that day, an entire neighborhood, were executed. With the Vilna Jewish population efficiently thinned out, the Germans were now able to fit them all into two newly created ghettos, in what had once been a quiet and meager Jewish neighborhood.

On September 6th, what remained of Vilna Jewry was herded into either Ghetto I (the larger) or Ghetto II, or taken to the Lukiszki Prison, a holding pen on the way to the killing field known as Ponar. The Jews, including the Fishers, were expelled from their homes and told that they had only fifteen minutes to relocate to the ghettos. The Lithuanian municipal police felt duty-bound to hurry the confused mob along as violently as they could. Many people evacuated in that horrific transfer were never seen or heard from again.

It was an unusually hot day, and Isser Fisher, his mother and sister huddled together, sweltering among the densely packed crowd pouring into Vilna's Ghetto II. With them was Faigel, a woman in her early twenties from Zelva, Byelorussia. Faigel had been visiting Vilna when the war broke out, and became stranded there. Rabbi and Rebbetzin Fisher had taken the frightened girl into their home. Now, she clung to Esther Fisher, only a few years her senior, as if she were her own mother.

A wave of grief overcame Rebbetzin Fisher as she stood at the threshold of the ghetto, and she could proceed no further. It was a long time before she could actually take hold of herself and submit to the prison of Ghetto II. An astute woman, she grasped the German intent and figured that the odds of survival would be greater in the larger ghetto. Based on this hunch she escaped with Faigel and her children to Ghetto I just a few days before Ghetto II was liquidated.

Once in the ghettos, the Jews were in the dark as to what was happening to their co-religionists. It would have been far too incredible for fundamentally gentle, law-abiding Jews to fathom the goings on in the Ponar forest eight kilometers south of Vilna. On Yom Kippur, Rebbetzin Fisher crept inside a once-thriving synagogue that had secretly remained active within the ghetto walls. She walked directly to the ark housing the Torah scrolls, gingerly opened its doors, and cried uncontrollably, "*Who will live, and who will die? Who will be inscribed in the Book of Life?*"

Esther Fisher feared that a terrible decree had been recorded. Alone and defenseless, she felt that all she had were her prayers.

She would soon discover that her extraordinary shrewdness and determination were no less valuable assets in her formidable quest to save her children and herself. Individuals far more mighty and influential than she—and unencumbered by little children—proved neither as capable, nor blessed with as much Heavenly assistance.

Later that day, on the Jewish Day of Atonement, Yom Kippur— October 1, 1941—the Jews of the Vilna ghetto had their full, and final, awakening to true German intent.

THE GHETTO POPULATION had already been divided into two separate groups: those who had work passes, and those who did not. The coveted work passes indicated that the bearers were moderately useful to the German war machine, and their skills as masonry workers, carpenters, roofers, tailors, shoemakers, and so on, were duly exploited. Registered workers were also entitled to rations for themselves, their spouses and up to two children—and were seldom targeted for roundups.

Even the *Judenrat*, when commanded to assemble a specific number
of Jews for removal from the ghetto, would surrender those without
passes. This gut-wrenching decision, indeed their compliance in this
unconscionable act, stemmed from their legitimate fear that if they did
not supply the number demanded, the Germans themselves would remove whomever and as many as they pleased. They desperately reasoned that it was better to comply by turning in the "unproductive"
Jews in the hope that this might save many more lives. Ultimately, the
absence of a work pass meant being marked for expeditious execution.

On this fateful Yom Kippur morning, the Jewish police did not
produce enough "non-workers" to meet the Nazi quota. Because of the
Judenrat's failure to fulfill German orders, there was a stern decree that
all work passes must be validated that evening. Thus, at nightfall—
even before breaking their Yom Kippur fasts—the workers reported
en masse to the *Judenrat* office to undertake what they hoped would be
a mere formality.

Thousands of Vilna Jews learned that night—tragically, too late—
the twisted depths of German deception. All those who registered, earnestly believing that they were doing the most prudent thing to stay
alive, were loaded on trucks bound for Ponar.

The meaning of "Ponar" was still unknown to the masses that were
sent there, but the members of the *Judenrat*, who had greater access to
information, were not as naïve. The Germans did not intend to confide
the hideous reality of this killing field to them, either, but the steady
swirl of rumors could not be ignored.

One woman managed to escape from the execution site. She returned to the ghetto with two bullet wounds in her hand and horrific
tales of genocidal mass shootings, though she had no idea where she
had been. A number of ghetto inhabitants were able to identify the location due to the ants crawling on the woman's festering wound. The
type of insect was indigenous to Ponar.

The widowed rebbetzin had not been entitled to a work pass. And
so, the pitiful irony: the precarious status that had rendered her and
her children leading candidates for selection, spared them from that
German ruse on Yom Kippur.

Still, they remained prime targets for future deportation to Ponar.
Esther Fisher made sure her little ones and Faigel always stayed out

of public view and within arm's length of their *"maline"* (a bunker-like hiding place).

Virtually every day, when the alarm sounded that the Germans were coming, they dove inside the *maline*, sealing the entrance with a piece of furniture. There they would remain for hours on end, without making a sound, never sure when it was safe to emerge.

Esther had little way of knowing what had befallen the rest of European Jewry, but she concluded that the situation in Vilna was hopeless, and desperately sought a way out.

THE FROST OF LATE FALL had already gripped Vilna by the time Esther Fisher found her first sliver of hope. One day she met a yeshiva student who informed her that he had arranged a way to be smuggled out of the ghetto, via a truck driven by a bribed Nazi. For a fee, he could find room aboard for Esther Fisher, her children and Faigel. The rebbetzin bought in immediately, and was told exactly where to go the following night at 2 A.M.

The top-secret information was supposedly sold to only 70 other ghetto inhabitants, but by the time the truck pulled into the courtyard, hundreds of frantic Jews had congregated to be driven to freedom. Traffic in and out of the ghetto was closely scrutinized, so absconding with just two stowaways would have been a risky and improbable mission. But scores of passengers! The insanity of the plan only contributed to the confusion and before Esther knew it, she was on board and her children were left below. The rebbetzin was beside herself, but when the driver came behind to inspect the proceedings, he quickly hoisted the panicked children onto the truck.

Since it would be impossible to camouflage the exponentially increased number of Jews, a revised plan called for the Nazi driver to explain to the guards at the ghetto's gates that he was transporting Jews for execution—a standard mission. The driver's cooperation was generated purely by greed, and his set fee would yet grow.

When they arrived in the small Byelorussian town of Warinowa, the driver grunted, "Last stop!" Coming from a German, the words had an ominous ring. Indeed, though the truck had ground to a halt, the passengers were still not free to go, as the driver demanded an additional premium for his efforts.

He passed around a satchel and declared that anyone who did not hand over all of his or her watches and other valuables would be killed. This final extortion was at least an improvement over the German smugglers who extricated Jews from the ghetto for exorbitant sums, only to murder them as soon as payment was received.

Rebbetzin Fisher was concealing the gold watch that had belonged to her husband, of blessed memory—one of the last mementos of Reb Moshe. She could hardly breathe as she shook her head, and the satchel was thrust at the next person.

Afterwards, the driver made a quick getaway. And the fugitives soon learned that they were in no less peril in Warinowa. The Germans had discovered their defection and were in hot pursuit of all the Lithuanian Jews who had crossed the border into Byelorussia. Fortunately, every one of the truck's passengers managed to find shelter in the home of one of their co-religionists in Warinowa, a town that had not yet been ghettoized.

But a locked door was never an obstacle for the SS. Rebbetzin Fisher had to think fast. She handed her little boy over to Faigel, who had Byelorussian identity papers, and told her to pretend that Isser was her child. (Ita, who was nearly eight, looked a bit too old to be Faigel's, which could unmask the entire charade.) The Nazis were zeroing in on the escapees from Lithuania, and this was the best strategy she could come up with.

Sure enough, Faigel and Isser were permitted to remain in the Warinowa home, while Esther and Ita were duly rounded up and, with all of the other Vilna Jews, incarcerated in a movie theater that was under construction.

WHILE SPIRITS are usually dimmed by degradation and suffering, Esther Fisher's intuitive and decisive nature was being honed to razor-sharpness. Her gut feeling was that all those who were assembled in that building would be murdered. If she did not act immediately, there would be no second chance.

Her daughter was a tiny girl who had learned well how to go unnoticed. The air would hardly stir if she slipped out an exit door. Rebbetzin Fisher commanded Ita to tiptoe behind the Nazi guard ... and escape the premises. Her chances were better with Isser and Faigel, in the near-by house where they had been previously apprehended.

The girl had her brother's gumption and her mother's steely resolve. In a flash, Ita disappeared out the back exit.

The rebbetzin knew an adult could never flee in similar fashion. Her fingers closed around the watch that was buried deep inside her pocket, and she edged her way toward the guard. His eyes narrowed, and she met his suspicious look unflinchingly. Standing so close that she could feel his breath upon her, she unveiled the treasure in her hand.

"This will be yours if you march me out of this building with your gun at my back," she whispered tersely, leaving nothing to his imagination. "I will put my hands up, and neither of us will do anything to arouse suspicion. By killing me, you gain nothing—but by letting me go, you'll have a gold watch."

Then, without giving the guard a moment to consider her proposition, Esther Fisher raised her arms over her head and began marching toward the exit. The German followed, exactly as he had been instructed. Outside, they looked around furtively, and the watch changed hands.

Isser and Faigel were exactly where she had left them, and Ita was safely there as well. The children rushed into her arms with yelps of joy.

Although a terrible fright was behind them, untold danger still loomed ahead. Looking into the trusting eyes of her little boy, Esther Fisher knew that a new plan was required. *They had to get out of this region, where the Nazi machine was operating with ruthless efficiency. Could anywhere else be worse?*

Her mind darted, she grasped feverishly for an answer. And then it came to her.

Radin.

It was the site of the renowned yeshiva where her husband had learned for years. No doubt some of the townspeople would remember him kindly. And Radin had been the home of the most saintly scholar of the century: Rabbi Yisrael Meir HaCohen, better known as the Chafetz Chaim, who had died several years earlier at the exalted age of 95. Esther's fervent hope was that this sage's merits would improve the lot of the town. The trip would be arduous, and dangerous. But there was no better plan.

They departed on an exceptionally raw morning, and the rebbetz-in suddenly realized that the street was oddly and blessedly devoid of German presence. Perhaps they were all inside the construction site, tormenting the remainder of the prisoners. Esther quickly tore the yellow star from their clothing and positioned her shivering tribe at the roadside in search of a ride. A peasant driving a horse-drawn sled came into view, and Esther waved her arms and called out to him. Was he traveling in the direction of Radin? Yes! And he took them almost the whole way there.

When they arrived they found lodging with a widow named Dobbe. The poverty in Radin, even by the standards of those wrenching times, was exceptional. This could be ascertained by the nickname given to their landlady: "Dobbe *de Gvirte* (The Rich One)." She had earned this moniker because relatives in America had always—until the town was ghettoized—sent her ten dollars before the Passover and Sukkos holidays. This biannual stipend rendered her the wealthiest Jew in town!

Despite the poverty, the overall situation in Radin was better than what the Fishers had endured in Lithuania. The fact that "only" a number of Jews were regularly taken from the Radin ghetto to be executed was an improvement over the daily mass roundups that were taking place in Vilna.

A "better" life for any Jew under German dominion was clearly a relative term.

On one occasion, a citizen of Radin named Berel Lipkunski was accused by a non-Jewish informant (with whom he had a pre-war dispute) of being a Communist. Germans took this uninvestigated charge as truth, and for the crime, Lipkunski was hanged and his wife and four children were shot, execution-style. But one of the bullets missed its mark, and the youngest boy was not killed. A group of courageous Jews smuggled him out of the burial area and slowly nursed him back to health.

Later that day the Germans, always obsessed with proper documentation, returned to the burial site for identity papers they had neglected to remove the from the victims' pockets at the time of the killings. (Whenever possible, Jews would take pains to ensure that anyone who was murdered for being a Jew was buried (according to religious law) in the very clothing that they were wearing.)

Terror seized the residents of the ghetto. Once the Germans opened the grave and discovered that one "corpse" was missing, how many others would be slaughtered to make up for it?

But this time, all they did was retrieve the identity cards after hurriedly exhuming the bodies. Notwithstanding their characteristic precision, the Germans had come face to face with so many Jewish corpses that the absence of one went unnoticed, and unpunished. This time.

This was one example of the "better life" that the Jews of Radin enjoyed. In Vilna, hundreds would have been gunned down on the spot in retaliation for one boy who dared to live.

THE ALL-CONSUMING PRIORITY in the ghetto (aside from avoiding being murdered) was to combat starvation. Scrounging morsels of food was a full-time job. And yet matters of the spirit also prevailed. Parents taught religious precepts to their children, individuals struggled to follow the teachings of the Torah, and religious services were conducted despite the threat of death. A quorum of Jews even risked their lives by absconding from the ghetto so that they could pray at the grave of the saintly Chafetz Chaim.

Those who deny that the Jews resisted their Nazi oppressors have no awareness of what took place inside the ghetto of Radin. The insurrection was not with knives or Molotov cocktails, but it was no less heroic. Although the circumstances fostered dehumanization, kindness and decency were institutionalized. In an atmosphere that cultivated looking out only for one's self, superhuman efforts were made to care for those who suffered the most.

Rebbetzin Fisher joined the other righteous women of the Radin ghetto who operated the equivalent of a soup kitchen to provide for the helpless. Her great asset to the collective was that she spoke Polish in addition to Yiddish, and was therefore able to negotiate with non-Jews for food. She regularly risked her life by speaking though the ghetto wall to those on the outside, or quietly bartering for food at the gate.

The children, too, had their own form of insurrection. They stubbornly observed every Jewish holiday, commemorating and observing Jewish rites despite the lethal consequences. In this way, little Isser Fisher and the other youngsters who were crowded within the confines of Dobbe *der Gvirta*'s home were all freedom fighters. They fought, too, to hold on to some semblance of the childhood that was ripped from them.

They played with dolls made of rags and created elaborate fantasy games—for in their world real dolls, toy trucks, balls and block towers did not exist. Yet their make-believe games were not like that of other children: they were about burying the dead, smuggling food, and making sure their "babies" didn't cry lest they be taken away and murdered.

For Isser and the other children, it was the only world they knew.

AS INSUFFERABLE as the winter was, it had its advantages. There was ample water thanks to the snow, and (as the elders painfully understood) the cold made it the safest season; with the thaw of the spring, it would be possible once more to dig mass graves.

On Friday, May 8, 1942, the prognosis for Radin Jewry looked very grim. A large contingent of German soldiers, along with Lithuanians, Latvians and Poles in police uniforms, surrounded the ghetto. A trickle of Jews had managed to escape prior to this date, but there was no longer any way out. The Nazis, as usual, had attempted to launch rumors about a transfer to better conditions. But in this ghetto there were too many "veterans" from locales that were already *Judenrein*, for their lies to be believed.

On Saturday, May 9th, two additional truckloads of German soldiers took up positions. If this didn't signal imminent liquidation, the next arrivals surely did: peasant farmers from throughout the region pulled up in their wagons, poised like vultures to loot the premises the instant the Jews were led to their deaths.

Each Jewish family undertook its own somber preparations for the inevitable future, mostly focusing on the spiritual. But Esther would not be reconciled to the fate the Germans had in mind, despite the overwhelming sense of despair that had seized the rest of the ghetto's inhabitants.

Together with her children and Faigel, she fled the home of Dobbe *de Gvirte* and entered a house that was directly across the street. There, the frantic mother encountered the ultimate resignation; it was quiet and terrible.

Congregated inside were approximately a dozen of Radin's elderly, helpless and frail, waiting to be taken to their death.

As the patriarchs and matriarchs of this proud town, they had lived there through the golden age of the Chafetz Chaim, and many were his disciples. These were deeply pious men and women, who had never uttered an evil word or a false statement in their lives. The glory of living alongside the generation's most illustrious saint and scholar had been virtually incinerated by many months of soul-destroying ghetto life. Assembled before the Fishers was the ash.

Isser could not stop staring at these silver-haired ancients. Hunched and frail, sallow and pale, they looked as though they already had one foot in the World to Come. Their eyes would haunt him forever: sunken, watchful, red-rimmed and clouded. Those eyes had seen the pinnacle of Jewish life, and beheld the abyss.

"Go save yourself. You are still a young woman!" one man called out in a somber voice to Esther Fisher, and a wizened old crone offered her some honey.

Suddenly, the rebbetzin noticed a pull-down ladder in the upper corner of the room, and she discerned that there was an attic filled with desperate people. One of them she recognized as Moshe Sonenson, a fellow lodger in the home of Dobbe *der Gvirta*.

"Moishe!" she called out. "Let down the ladder so we, too, can come up!" The attic was already packed with people, including Moshe's family. He refused. The rebbetzin had no choice but to declare in a dead-serious voice, "If you do not let the ladder down immediately, I will inform the Germans that you are up there!"

The ladder was let down.

The dimly lit space was so crowded that Isser and Ita had to crouch in its entrance. Cardboard boxes were piled in front of them to obscure them all from view. The people hiding up there, however, had their own vantage point. From the attic window they could see a bit of the once-quaint town of Radin, even as far as the cemetery. They could also make out the gallows that were being erected by the Germans in preparation for the liquidation of the ghetto.

Among those crammed inside that hiding place were Sonenson's wife, two of their sons, and their five-year-old daughter, who later became the noted Holocaust historian, Yaffa Eliach. The Sonenson family hailed from the neighboring shtetl of Eishyshok (or Ejszyszki). Of Eishyshok's 4,000 Jews, only 29 would survive the war. Thousands had already been murdered by the *Einsatzgruppen* (German killing squads) and Lithuanian collaborators in a two-day killing spree in September of 1941. Due to that horrific event, the Sonensons were no strangers to hiding—or to unspeakable tragedy.

Isser and Ita Fisher did not comprehend what they were witnessing through the attic window, or the events surrounding it; nor did Yaffa Sonenson. But years later, Dr. Eliach's painstaking research enabled her to record it for posterity. Apparently, the Germans selected 100 healthy Jewish men who were handed shovels and told they were being taken to the cemetery to prepare graves. The purpose of this digging was not lost on these terrified men, who were led by a stalwart blacksmith named Meir Stoler.

The wily, determined Stoler was a survivor of the Eishyshok massacre, and was not about to dig his—or any other Jew's—grave in Radin. En route to the cemetery, he instructed his comrades to revolt. There was a point along the route where the bushes were high and the forest was near; at that juncture, they would use their shovels to attack their armed guards, and make a run for it. The men knew Stoler was right. There was nothing left to lose.

Leading the procession were two mounted Gestapo officers in full dress—tailored by the very men being led out to the cemetery! At the designated spot, Stoler quickly grabbed a handful of sand and stones from the road and tossed it into the eyes of the horses. The riders were thrown into the air, and the gravediggers used their shovels to assault the other police guards. In the melee, 25 managed to escape, including Meir Stoler. The rest were not as fortunate. After recouping from the surprise attack, the Germans went after the men with full firepower. All the rest—75 men—were slaughtered then and there.

A second group of 100 gravediggers was selected. This time, the diggers would be properly "prepared" for their assignment. They were ordered to strip to the waist, and were severely beaten with truncheons by the Gestapo, along with the Lithuanian, Latvian, Byelorussian and Polish reinforcements. Some of the men died from the beating; those who collapsed alive were shot. Those who managed to remain standing were marched to the cemetery under the guard of 100 policemen and an army unit.

At that same time, the roundup commenced in the ghetto of Radin.

Using loudspeakers, the Gestapo ordered all the Jews immediately out of their homes. German policemen invaded every residence to make sure that no one remained behind. The sick, the old, and the very young—and all of those who were not quick enough in obeying the German order—were shot on the spot.

As the tragic remnant left the ghetto, some of the men wore their *tefillin*, some wore their *talleisim*, and others were clad in their snow-white burial shrouds. The rabbi of Radin, Rabbi Hillel—the son-in-law of the Chafetz Chaim's second wife, was wearing all three.

The police entered the house where the Fishers and the Sonensons hid. They immediately cleared out all the elderly people who had been sitting in the main room. Just then the Sonenson baby began to cry and everyone in the attic froze. It was one baby and over a dozen adults. A coat was thrown over the baby and pressed down. Silence reigned.

The German soldiers departed the house and the coat was removed from the suffocated baby. Everyone, including the children, saw what had happened but they could not speak. They could barely cry. The ghastly scene that had taken place in other bunkers, other attics, and wherever Jews were hiding had been repeated once again. And then a barrage of shots rang out from the cemetery.

The view of the mass murder was fortunately not in a clear line of sight from the attic, so the petrified inhabitants were spared seeing how the Germans forced the victims to undress and then sort their clothing and shoes into neat piles before standing at the very edge of the pit so that their bullet-riddled bodies—whether they were already dead, or still had the breath of life—would topple in, perfectly layered. When the pit filled up, the final remaining victims were forced to sit on top of the huge mound of corpses, as a prelude for their execution.

Adjacent to the mass grave, as Yaffa Eliach records, was a well-stocked buffet of refreshments, vodka and other appropriate beverages for the murderers.

Back in the attic, the torment was unbearable. Every gunshot seemed to pierce their hearts, and there was no end—simply no end—to the shooting. When the barrage finally came to a halt, the attic survivors momentarily thought that they had gone deaf. Even after the gunfire had long ceased, they were still too terrified to emerge from hiding.

The Germans were aware that there were still some Jews in hiding and they developed yet another satanic ruse to smoke them out into the open.

The gravediggers and some of their families had been spared from the liquidation. Certainly it was not a humanitarian gesture. It was all part of an unfathomably sadistic plan; one can only speculate whether lack of space in the mass grave, or the possibility of using these survivors as bait to draw out the remaining Jews, was their intention. Whatever the reason, none of those "spared" believed that the danger was over.

Back inside the ghetto, announcements were made in Yiddish over a loudspeaker: the murders that had just taken place at the cemetery were all a mistake! A full day's worth of executions annihilating an entire town—a mistake? But the lunacy was just beginning.

"Everyone should come out of hiding," the announcer boomed, "there is nothing to fear." All those who could prove that they had been gravediggers (by revealing a back covered with gashes and welts, the aftermath of the truncheon beatings) would be granted amnesty. This gesture, the announcer continued, was to "make up for" the unfortunate "mistaken" murders at the cemetery. The entire scenario staggeringly defied reason. Anyone whose back was not mauled would be executed.

In order to make themselves eligible for pardon, those who had been in hiding—male and female, young and old—began frantically inflicting painful injuries upon each other's backs, wounds that hurt the victimizer as much as the victim. It didn't matter if their age or gender meant they were implausible gravediggers; in this incomprehensible scenario, all normative logic was abandoned. The Germans watched on as the desperate Jews spun dizzily under their senseless commands. The final step in the process required every last person remaining in the ghetto—gravedigger or not—to register with the *Judenrat*. They were assured that their petitions for life would be reviewed.

NO ARGUMENT on earth could persuade Rebbetzin Fisher to inflict wounds upon her family or herself, and she was convinced that giving her family's names to the *Judenrat* would ultimately place them in the hands of the Germans. In refusing to comply with orders, she placed herself, her children and Faigel in the supremely precarious position of being "illegals." Even their fellow Jews began to avoid their presence, lest they incur punishment by association.

This period launched a new chapter in the profound loneliness and isolation of Isser Fisher and his sister. Their ghetto playmates of yore—those few who still lived—fled when they came near, especially after dark when the chances of German scrutiny were the greatest. When the family sought shelter, they experienced the humiliation of being turned away even from Jewish homes.

As a result, in order to place a roof over their heads, they resorted to a very dangerous scheme: they entered a house located outside of the ghetto and crawled into its basement. The houses in such regions had very deep basements that were used to store perishables (in the absence of refrigeration) to prevent spoilage. This cool shaft became the Fishers' nocturnal home.

During the day there was less fear mingling with the people, and Esther continued her post at the communal kitchen. One of her steady customers in the kitchen was a lonely man from a distant town, who could only converse in Yiddish and had great difficulty fending for himself. Esther took pity upon this poor soul and made sure he received one piece of bread and a scant plate of soup daily. This was his entire nourishment, and he became very dependent upon her ministrations.

And so it pained her to inform him, one day, that she would soon be unable to serve him in the soup kitchen. Esther Fisher confided in the man that she was about to gather her children and young Faigel and flee the Radin ghetto.

The supremely pragmatic rebbetzin was convinced that Radin was a deathtrap —whether she and her children were legal or illegal. The rebbetzin believed that in order for any escape plan to be successful, it was essential that she have some familiarity with the locale. This was the strategy that had brought her to Radin, and it was the impetus in her seeking to return to Vilna.

It would be impossible for a woman alone with two small children and a young lady to clandestinely travel such a distance. She therefore recruited a partner to lead the expedition, and to help carry Isser when the little boy could walk no further. The leader was a newly married man named Shevach.

On the morning of their planned escape, Esther and her children climbed over the ghetto wall and hurried toward the meeting place that had been prearranged with Shevach and some other escapees who would be joining them. En route they heard an ear-splitting commotion of sirens and alarms. Even the fire department was involved! The German security branches were on high alert, clearly in response to some terrible threat.

Suddenly a gentile woman ran out into the road and shouted after the Fishers: "The Germans are looking for a mother with two children so you had better get away from here right away!"

So this was the great emergency: A frail woman plotting to save the lives of her two small children!

The woman on the street was too frightened to allow them inside her home, but she did give them temporary shelter in her pigpen.

With stinging disappointment, Rebbetzin Fisher realized who had informed the authorities of their impending escape: the very man upon whom she had showered so much compassion and had fed every day, the very one who was so "beholden" to her. With Esther's departure he would lose his lifeline—with no one left to turn to, he turned to the Germans; he offered this tip with the hope that they might give him some bit of reward. Who can fathom the depths of such desperation?

Esther Fisher, thigh-deep in mud and pig manure, feared that this was the end. She anguished over her decision to flee. If one of her own comrades in the ghetto had betrayed her, what were her chances of not being informed on, on the outside?

She could not have known what she and her family had avoided by departing Radin.

It would fall to Yaffa Eliach to record the story in her scholarly eyewitness report, *There Once Was A World*:

> Everyone whose name was registered with the *Judenrat* was required to strip to the waist and lie facedown on the cobblestones for three days as Nazi soldiers stomped in their heavy boots, back and forth, across their victims' bruised and bloodied backs. In the end, the officers emptied their revolvers into those with lash-marked backs and those without, those who had registered and those who had not.
>
> They were drunk on vodka and Jewish blood.

CLEARLY, fleeing the ghetto was a wise decision. And although Esther was right that their odds of survival were not good, a tragic twist of fate ensured their escape. A different woman in the accompaniment of two children was spotted and murdered—calling off the Gestapo, the SS, the *Einsatzgruppen* and the local militia from hunting the Fisher family. The Fishers and Faigel were now free (relatively) to embark upon their journey with Shevach.

The group departed only that evening, as they were restricted to nighttime travel. Isser found the endless walking extremely taxing and looked forward to vehicular traffic. Each time the headlights of a car were spotted, everyone dove into the ravine adjacent to the road where they would not be spotted by the approaching car. These were treasured moments for Isser, allowing him to rest his weary little body.

Shevach, for all of his decency and determination, possessed an extremely poor sense of direction and was unfamiliar with the route. The group soon realized, to their immense frustration, that every morning after trekking an entire night, they were practically at the same place they had departed the previous evening!

At this rate they would never make it to Vilna. At this rate they would never make it anywhere!

The moon was full at that point in June, giving them enough illumination to see through the woods and down the road. They gasped as they saw the moonlit outline of another group advancing ahead of them along the road. They quickly realized that this other group must also be Jews in search of a safe haven.

By the time Shevach's group was able to catch up to the other party, it was almost morning and everybody had to run into the forest for cover. The other group was led by a man referred to as Yossel *der ba'al aggolleh* (the wagon driver) from Eishyshok. In contrast to the hapless Shevach, Yossel knew every path and landmark between Eishyshok, Radin and Vilna.

He informed them that the wooded area in which they were hiding belonged to a townsman named Jan Adamowicz, a notorious alcoholic. Partisans steered clear of this drunken landowner, whose behavior was frequently erratic, but Yossel theorized that Adamowicz's continuous inebriation could work to their advantage, and decided to take the risk of approaching his house and asking to purchase some rations. A sober individual would have slammed the door in his face, or had him arrested.

Yossel's gamble was successful. He returned laden with enough food for all to partake. This was the first time Isser remembered eating since they had embarked on their journey one week earlier. Even more remarkable, it was already a year since the outbreak of the war in that area, yet the starving wanderers refused to partake of any food that wasn't kosher! Such behavior was emblematic of this family's—and so many other devout Jews'—faithful religious adherence.

The two groups of travelers remained on Adamowicz's property until nightfall, waiting to resume their treks: Shevach and company to Vilna, Yossel and his followers deeper into the forest. As dusk settled, Yossel *der ba'al aggolleh* approached the rebbetzin and bluntly posed a question that froze her in her tracks: "Do you really believe you have a shred of hope of reaching Vilna with two little children in tow?"

Esther Fisher stared back at the wagon driver incredulously. What did this man think her options were? To flog her children's backs—to allow them to be murdered in Radin?

Seeing her agitation, Yossel quickly explained himself. "You would be much better off if you could get this landowner Adamowicz to hide you here, rather than trying to get back into Vilna! The war can't last too much longer. And I think that this fellow will make a deal ... for the right price."

Esther saw that the wagon driver was as astute about human nature as he was at the reins, and agreed to have him negotiate with Adamowicz on her behalf. By keeping a few valuables and some currency always on her person, Esther Fisher had been violating yet another ironclad rule laid down by the Germans: Jews were forbidden to own money or valuables. She had concluded, however, that being without means was even more dangerous than breaking German law. And now, another one of her risky policies was about to pay off.

The Fishers' only hope of survival was to become utterly invisible. For all his personal shortcomings, Adamowicz came up with a stunningly clever plan. The landowner uprooted a tree deep inside his acreage, and bored a hole underneath it that widened in a bell-shape. The tree could be wedged back into the narrow shaft, sealing part of the top of the hole and making it appear, to the unsuspecting eye, like any other tree in the forest.

The widened circle that surrounded the shaft—a muddy hole in the ground—was the new dwelling-place of Esther, Isser, Ita and Faigel.

As dark and dank as it was in their coffin-like surroundings, they were much better off than their erstwhile travel companions. Shevach's contingent had to cross over a tiny bridge, but they were all gunned down in the middle and never made it to other side.

Yossel's group also came to a tragic end, but it came after a full year of wandering in the Vilna region—and not at the hands of the Germans. The pitiful Jewish itinerants, struggling day by day to simply survive until the area was liberated from the Germans, were asleep in the woods when a hoard of Lithuanian freedom fighters, themselves battling the Nazis, stumbled upon them and lobbed grenades in their direction. They all died instantly in the explosion, except for one: Yossel the wagon driver. He had left the group briefly to warm himself by the fire at the time of the attack. He ran deeper and deeper into the forest, and escaped—barely—with his life.

All these lost souls, their bones piled and scattered throughout the fields of Europe! Who would ever remember their names?

The Fishers were better off "buried" alive in a hole in the ground, where they could still have hope for another day...

AS HANDSOMELY as Rebbetzin Fisher had paid for her family's makeshift dungeon, hard-drinking Jan Adamowicz and his wife were skittish about having Jews hidden anywhere on their property when visitors came to call. On those occasions, the landowner demanded they vacate the premises. He placed them temporarily with people whose silence could be bought for the meager sums that the rebbetzin had left.

As hellish as their subterranean shelter was, being at the mercy of a revolving cast of money-hungry strangers was an even worse hell. One wintry day they had been sent to an attic crawlspace to hide, and a noisy group gathered outside the house, pointing accusatory fingers. The eagle-eyed neighbors had noticed that the ice and the snow on one section of the roof had melted, indicating that "something" was generating heat underneath. *Surely no animal would crawl onto a freezing roof when there were more spacious and better-insulated shelters. Aha! There must be Jews up there!* The Fishers barely made it out alive.

On another occasion they were concealed inside someone's home when several local officials made an impromptu entrance. Certain that these men had come after the Jews, the homeowner hastily shoved them through a hole under the floorboards. Through the planks, the fugitives could clearly see the search party, who miraculously did not see them. The men had actually come looking for animals that were not registered—but this would have been a moot point had they discovered the Fisher party.

Worst of all was the time that the unexpected arrival of a visitor forced Ita to crawl inside a hot pot-bellied stove, and pull the door shut behind her. Although she was extricated before she was seriously burned, the girl was horrifically traumatized.

Eventually, even Jan Adamowicz reluctantly concurred: the hole in the forest floor was the only safe place for the Fishers to hide. Not coincidentally, Esther Fisher hadn't a *grosch* left to pay for lodging anywhere else.

And there they remained, in that dark, fetid burial-place, for an unbelievable 26 months.

Isser and Ita could barely remember the days when they would skip through the woods around the family *dacha*, picking flowers, giggling in the grass, curtailed only by their parents' voices calling them home for supper. Now this was their life. There was no room to stand and no room to lie down, just enough maneuverability to crouch into a tight, seated position. The sanitation facilities consisted of a metal bowl whose contents could rarely be disposed of by the subterranean prisoners, contributing to the stench and overall filth.

They were surrounded and fed on by creatures of the dark who laid equal claim to the underground habitat—worms, beetles, centipedes, fire ants, cockroaches and other insects by the millions—and this was on the fortunate "dry" days. Every rainstorm brought with it a plague of frogs, salamanders and newts—but the rain itself was the most harrowing part. The pit would fill up with so much water they feared they would drown. Muddy, frigid water swamped them up to their necks, and they would use their bowl to bail out at a frenetic pace.

Then there was the fog. Eerie, translucent smoke would billow into their underground chamber, enveloping them in a damp, cool web that added yet another layer of terror to the nightmare.

Their daily food intake consisted of a single egg divided among the four of them. This was brought to them by Jan Adamowicz under the cover of darkness—on the nights that he did not forget or pass out from drinking. One time he tossed down five apples, eliciting joy that defied description—it was their heartiest repast in years.

Farmers like Adamowicz were expected to be self-sufficient, and had he attempted to purchase supplemental food in town, it could have raised suspicion that he was hiding something; something far worse than any contraband: Jews!

Adamowicz reasoned that he should derive some personal benefit from the hole he had dug for the Fishers, in addition to the exorbitant rent, so he began to cure and store his clandestine supply of meat in their underground "bunker." Food—especially meat—was at a premium at this point of the war, and thievery and impounding were routine. It was essential to conceal whatever provisions one possessed.

Thus, Adamowicz would regularly lower a barrel of salted meat into the already-crowded pit, to protect his provisions from marauders. To make sure that the starving Fishers weren't slicing off even a morsel, he made tiny incisions into the meat to "mark" its parameters. They managed, however, to reproduce his markings, and were able to shave off bits of protein without the owner being the wiser.

Chewing the salty meat made them extremely thirsty, and they begged Adamowicz to bring them additional water. He could not comprehend why they now required so much water. They convinced him that it was needed not for their diet, but for female sanitary purposes of which he had no understanding, and he grudgingly obliged.

Whatever Adamowicz provided to the Fishers was seasoned with blow-by-blow reports of Jews who had been discovered, and the awful fates that had befallen them and their benefactors. "Your days are numbered," he constantly warned. "There is only so long that I am willing to protect you!" Adamowicz's children regularly taunted that they would turn in—or murder—the stowaways.

DESPERATELY WEAK from hunger, their limbs atrophying from lack of movement, what else could the Fishers do, but remain burrowed in their underground prison—at the mercy of their tormentors, who were also, paradoxically, their benefactors. And where else on earth could they find refuge, even if they would possess the strength of body and mind to travel there?

Every day they were threatened, and every day they had to beg for their lives. After Esther's secret cache of funds ran out, the hostility became even more virulent. Adamowicz did not evict them and continued to feed them the most minimal amount to keep them alive, but with a ghastly motive: he was convinced that there were no other surviving Jews on the whole European continent, and that some cash-swollen world Jewish tribunal would pay him handsomely after the war for having saved a *rabinowa* (rebbetzin).

IN THE MEANTIME, however, the Adamowiczs decided they would get what slave labor they could from the freeloaders. On nights they were sure that the coast was clear—and their failsafe was the family dog, who would bark ferociously whenever anyone approached the property—they would summon Esther and Faigel from the pit, leaving the frightened children alone in its pitch-dark depths.

On one occasion, they had the two women peeling potatoes all night long. The peels were not discarded, but used for fertilizer. The following day, a policeman dropped in for a routine check and took note of the pile of potato skins. "This was the work of clever Jews!" the dim-witted patrolman declared. When "real" Poles peel potatoes, they cut off little pieces of skin, with bits of the actual potato—but the peels in Adamowicz's house were long curls.

Adamowicz, a glib liar if nothing else, concocted a convincing yarn to save his own skin. As a by-product, it also saved the Fishers.

Faigel, an able seamstress, was commandeered into sewing a frock for one of the Adamowicz girls. The town folk did not believe the girl's mother had the skill to sew such a garment, and again the family was suspected of harboring Jews. Faigel then made another dress and instructed the mother how to do the final stitching, in order to convince the accusers.

Time after time, ignorant, illiterate, alcohol-addled peasants were convinced that they possessed powers of genius when it came to accurately identifying a Jew. Their overall analytic abilities were, of course, minimal due to their complete absence of education and worldliness. But no one could dispute their superior natural talent in one singular endeavor, passed down through the generations: they knew how to hunt and murder Jews. Whether by examining melted snow, a potato peel or a hand-made dress; they could always "smell" a Jew!

Here and there, there were infinitesimally few individuals like Jan Adamowicz who, beneath his deeply flawed exterior and questionable character, possessed a shred of conscience. And there were even rarer individuals—precious few, but they did exist—who harbored Jews for no profit whatsoever, sharing their meager food, endangering their own lives and their families, because of convictions spawned by their God or by their conscience. And later, when praised for their heroism or questioned about it, they would respond with a modest shrug of the shoulders: *What was exceptional about what we did? It was just the right thing—the human thing—to do.*

Many who were rescued displayed a heroism of a different nature. Esther was insistent that her family continue to "live" within their grave. Hence she carried on with the lessons that she had conducted in un-imaginable conditions in the Radin ghetto, now in even more unimag-inable conditions under the forest. The rebbetzin taught her children arithmetic, lessons of the Bible and the rudiments of religion. With no other activity to fill the empty hours (years!), she regaled the youngsters with true tales of their spiritual heroes and how they had triumphed over their tribulations.

From stories of the Jewish past, Esther Fisher gave her children, and Faigel, tools for the horrific present, and for a future that—should they, by some miracle, survive—looked almost as bleak. If they were caught, she reminded them, they must not fail to say the prayer *Shema Yisrael* attesting to the unity of the Almighty, prior to being shot.

And the future? After the war ended, were they to emerge alive from their hole in the earth, they would be the only Jews left alive in all of Europe. This, their steadfast matriarch exhorted them, would confer upon them an awesome responsibility. Just as Noah had to begin anew after the flood with no one but his family, they too would have to per-severe in a world bereft of Jews, and rife with those that had brought about their destruction.

Living under the ground also filled the children with memories and anxious thoughts of their dead father. Esther spoke gently and sooth-ingly about the late Rabbi Fisher, reassuring them that his loving spirit soared high above, and regularly leading them in halting recitations of the *kaddish* memorial prayer in his memory.

Frequently, they spoke of the supernatural. Their everyday existence was in a world that others visit only in nightmares. Naturally the children were full of questions about how this all could be happening and what could be the purpose.

Esther answered her children as best she could, sharing the lore that she had learned as a child.

They, like their drunken benefactor, never entertained the notion that other Jews might still be alive. Just as Isser and Ita had once fantasized about unicorns and great winged birds and other mythical creatures of childhood, they now believed that they had become as rare as the magical unicorn. They fully believed that after the war they would be paraded before a rapt public, in circuses and exhibit halls across the continent—an exotic and utterly unique commodity. The last of the vanished species of Jew.

THE BYELORUSSIAN WINTERS were indescribably harsh, and in Jan Adamowicz's now-barren woods, snow was packed high and hard on the ground and the temperature plunged well below zero. During this weather it was extremely dangerous to approach the family in hiding, for any such excursion would leave telltale footprints. The Germans would surely pick up on any tracks.

During one such season the fugitives remained underground for several days without a morsel of bread or drop of water. The misery of their hunger and agony of the cold suddenly paled when they heard footsteps right above them. At such close proximity no one would have any trouble, even in the middle of the night, discovering that the forest bed was not natural.

In sheer terror they waited for the explosion of a rifle, or for orders in German. But they heard something else entirely. One of Adamowicz's kind-hearted daughters had been unable to sleep, knowing that the Jews were starving. She brought them a loaf of bread and a pot of water. There was a blizzard outside and no sane person would have ventured out. But Antasa Adamowicz snuck out without shoes lest she leave a mark, and then begged the family to never say a word about this to her brothers or sister.

Living underground and unable to bathe, the Fishers were easy prey for millions of blood-thirsty lice. They were afraid to reveal their situation to Adamowicz, for fear that he would drive the infected victims off his property. But one time their pain was so intense that they could not control their crying.

When they explained their distress, Adamowicz suggested a salve that he could buy in Eishyshok, 14 kilometers away. They were afraid that, in a drunken stupor, who knew what details he would reveal as to his reason for requiring the salve.

But somehow he kept his secret, and the remedy brought the foursome much-needed relief. The next day, the landowner dug a new pit and filled it with fresh straw. Before descending into the new bunker, the Fishers and Faigel took a sponge bath to remove the salve, with all of the Adamowiczes standing guard lest anyone catch on to what was happening inside the stable.

Once the winter became intense, Adamowicz brought the family inside his barn; otherwise, they would have frozen to death. The relief of rising out of their underground bunker into a world that contained light and air—though the old barn was by no means warm—was beyond description. Inside the bushels of hay that were tightly woven and piled high Adamowicz created a cavity that was perfectly camouflaged, and there the Fishers passed the frigid days and nights.

One night they could hear partisan activity several feet from where they were hiding, and the fighters were speaking in Yiddish. *So there were still other Jews living, after all!* The thrill of hearing them speaking their mother tongue, and fighting against the Germans, lifted the family's spirits to the heavens. Still, their fear of revealing their hiding place was so overwhelming that they did not call out or utter a sound.

Hiding in the barn, however, meant a greater risk of being discovered by the Germans or any one among their long list of collaborators. When it came to the war against the Jews, virtually every citizen in the area was conscripted or had eagerly enrolled in the campaign. Adamowicz, especially, having been suspected on several occasions of harboring Jews, was constantly having his property invaded and thoroughly searched. The biggest point he had in his favor, ironically, was that his two sons were enlisted in the Polish underground army, the *Armia Krajowa* (AK).

Although the declared purpose of this fighting force was the defeat of Germany and the resumption of Polish rule in its own territory, another key priority of its troops was the annihilation of the Jews.

The AK was not content to leave this work to their German enemy, and whenever they located Jews, they did their utmost to outdo Nazi atrocities.

"*Polska bez Zydow* (Poland without Jews)" was their credo, and they upheld it fanatically.

It was therefore highly unlikely that the proud patriarch of two AK soldiers would provide any aid to Jews. For this reason, Adamowicz's close calls all ended in his favor ... so far.

AT NO TIME during the war was the fighting in that region as fierce and bloody as it was during the final stretch. No small measure of the combat took place on Adamowicz's property, literally on top of the burrow to which the Fishers had returned at winter's end. After they had managed to cheat fate for so many years, it now seemed inevitable that they would be casualties of the war in its final hours!

When the Germans had finally and completely retreated, Yossel *der ba'al aggolleh* returned to Adamowicz to learn how the Fishers had met their deaths. "I'll show you!" the property owner drunkenly declared.

Yossel had no wish to view rotting corpses; he had seen more than enough abominations since the Germans had invaded. He already felt horrendous guilt over counseling the widowed rebbetzin and her family to stay behind with this butcher.

As much as Yossel tried to get out of it, however, the heavily inebriated Adamowicz insisted on taking him into the woods, as though the fallen Jews were some sort of macabre trophy.

They arrived at the hiding place, and Adamowicz began to hoist the tree out of the ground. Even with the wave of nausea that overcame him, Yossel felt a twinge of gratitude; at least the Fishers had merited a burial of sorts. *How many martyrs did not even have that?*

Suddenly, Yossel *der ba'al aggolleh* gasped and shuddered as if he had seen a ghost. In fact, he saw ... four. The rebbetzin, her children and Faigel were still alive, swallowed by the earth. They were too frightened to emerge; the ferocious fighting had already been punctuated by several lulls that had then later re-erupted into deadly battle. And so they did not realize that the war in that region was actually over and that they were free to rise up out of their dungeon. Life on earth—though not without hardship—was about to begin anew.

EPILOGUE

At Yossel's recommendation, the Fishers made their way to Eishyshok. There they learned that although the war was indeed over, the War Against the Jews persisted. The townspeople, dressed in clothing and surrounded by objects they had pillaged from Jewish homes, were spurred on by the AK. Residents were incensed that their former neighbors dared to return. Like so many throughout Europe, furious that history's most systematic genocide had not been completed, they railed bitterly: *Why didn't Hitler finish the job?* They vowed to remedy this on their own.

With *"Polska bez Zydow!"* still their rallying cry, they launched a vicious pogrom against the wearied survivors who had reassembled in Eishyshok. Among their casualties were Yaffa Eliach's mother and one of her brothers. Through nights riddled with the echoes of bullets and grenades, the majority of the returned Jews managed to hide themselves inside pigsties, latrines, or piles of manure.

The Fishers fled Eishyshok to Vilna, and found a reality even sadder than they had imagined. "The Jerusalem of Lithuania" contained no vestige of actual Jewish life—only agonizing reminders of its annihilation. The family then traveled to Lodz, Poland, via cattle car; from there, the Israeli underground aided them in traveling to Czechoslovakia.

The next stop in their escape from Europe's blood-soaked earth was the former concentration camp Trafai, near Grasz, Austria. Then in 1946 they met up with some Jewish Brigade soldiers who were working to smuggle Jews into Palestine. They joined them in their trek over the Alps into Italy.

The Fishers' grueling European journey was finally over when they boarded a ship to the United States, but their travails were not. Because their transit visas had already expired, U.S. immigration officials denied them entry. They were expelled to Cuba for a full year before they were finally allowed on American soil.

Finally in America, Isser Fisher met formal education for the first time in his life, leading to rabbinic ordination from the Yeshiva Rabbeinu Chaim Berlin, a BA from Brooklyn College in mathematics, and an MA in economics from the City University of New York.

Today he teaches computer systems analysis in both the Borough of Manhattan Community College and Touro College. He is also the rabbi of the Avenue O Jewish Center in Bensonhurst, Brooklyn. Rabbi Fisher and his wife Ada Bernstein Fisher have nine children and numerous grandchildren.

Ita married a rabbi. They have five children and many grandchildren, and she passed away in 2014. Faigel married Moishe Yurkanski, a man whose first wife and children were among those murdered in Eishyshok. They had two children, and two grandchildren.

Rebbetzin Esther Fisher settled in Brooklyn, and married Reb Dovid Schneider in 1965. She died in 1983.

...dents from Gutta's evening Bais Yaakov class, 1934.

...a with her students in the Bais Yaakov outpost in impoverished Stopnitz, Poland.

Friends from Sara Schenirer's seminary in Krakow. Gutta is in the center with the white buttons.

With her closest friend, Rivka (Alter) Rappaport.

The Eli and Gutta Sternbuch Family. Lugano, Switzerland, Passover, 1993.

Heroic Isser Children

Mr. and Mrs. Jan Adamowicz, circa 1949.

r and Ita in the Italian Alps
ing an excursion by the children
he Cremona DP Camp, 1946.

Esther, Isser and Ita, Cuba. 1947.

Isser in Santiago de Cuba, 1947,
where the Fishers lived before being
allowed into the United States.

the sheva brachos (week of celebration following the wedding) of Moshe Dov and Esther Fisher (seated first second on the left) in Mior, Byelorussia. The Rabbi of the town, Rabbi Dov Ber Pianko (with the white beard), adfather of Isser (father of Esther), is on the right of the groom. To the right of Rabbi Pianko is the *Rosh Yeshiva* an) of the Radin Yeshiva, Rabbi Boruch Levinson, the son-in-law of Rabbi Naftoli Tropp, 1932.

Ita, Esther, Isser during Passover in DP Camp #82, Cremona, Italy, 1946.

Faigel who hid together with the Fisher children.
Monsey, NY, 1992.

On the occasion of the marriage of the Fisher's youngest child, Elazar. Brooklyn, December 28, 2009. Isser (cle: shaven) is to the right of the groom.

Heroic Dolly Children

ly with her mother Rachel, Mexico City, circa 1949.

Dolly's mother, Rachel, and her maternal grandmother (with a wig of then), Lithuania.

ly's grandmother with her daughter (Dolly's mother, hel Hirsch) and a niece.

Dolly's parents, Rachel and Aryeh Hirsch.

Dolly's marriage to Eduardo Bestandig in Mexico City, January 1960.

Dolly

Illustrious ancestor of Dolly's family, Rabbi Samson Raphael Hirsch.

Dolly, Eduardo and their children, Mexico City, 1979.

Heroic Shlomo Zalman Children

Teichman Family. Back row: (L-R) Shlomo Zalman's brother, Shalom Nachman, Shlomo Zalman, sister Rizsa Leah. Middle Row: (center) brother Kalman. Bottom Row: Cousins. Munkacs, circa 1940.

vhile in uniform for the army, London, 1952.

Shlomo Zalman, after libertaion and recuperation, Satmar, Romania, 1945.

Sol in New York, 1947.

Shalom Nachman (Steve) and Shlomo Zalman (Sol), New York, 1946.

Ruth and Sol Teichman and their children (L-R) Dubby (named after Berish Teichman), Ahuva and Alan on the occasion of Alan's wedding, July 20, 1986.

Picture which appeared in the Mesivta Torah Vodaath ban[q] journal. Fourth from the right is Shlomo Zalman and third f the right is his brother, Shalom Nachman. Brooklyn, NY, 1947

On the occasion of the wedding of Sol and Ruth's granddaughter, Daphna, 2008. Back row: (L-R) Shulie and Ah Wollman, Shmulie Wollman, Sol, Dubby Teichman, Dovid and Daphna Levine, Deena, Yitzie and Moishe Woln Alan Teichman. Front row: (L-R) Leora, Ariella, Jaclyn, Ruth, Evan and Dorit Teichman.

Nonexistence

Dolly

This is a story of nonexistence. It is the tale of a tiny child who lived through three ghettos, one prison compound, a concentration camp and an extermination center. Her birth was a miracle ... her survival, an even greater one. But to those determined to create a world that was inexorably Judenrein, *little Dolly Hirsch never even existed.*

To them, the child was nothing. Invisible. Disposable. But to her people, she was a link in the golden chain of Jewish learning and high culture that had characterized pre-World War II Europe. She was from the family of the brilliant rabbinic scholar, Samson Raphael Hirsch, renowned leader of Germany's neo-Orthodox movement. Her father, Aryeh Hirsch, was his grandnephew.

On her mother's side, Dolly was an eleventh-generation *Vilner*. This was a rare distinction, even in a city that, on the eve of the Second World War, had a swelling Jewish population of almost 100,000 souls. Vilna was known as the "Jerusalem of Lithuania" (even though it briefly became part of Poland after World War I), boasting 105 synagogues and prayer-houses, and six daily Jewish newspapers. One of Dolly's illustrious forebears could claim personal dealings with the most famous Jew ever to grace the city's study halls, the Vilna Gaon, having helped the legendary scholar to publish his works.

Dolly's maternal grandfather, Moshe Braude-Horowitz, had nearly broken the chain, for it was not until he attained the ripe age of 72 that a match was arranged for him—with a 22-year-old named Ilana Rivka. Despite his advanced years, he sired many children prior to his death.

One of Moshe and Ilana Rivka's daughters, Rachel, was found to be a child of extraordinary musical gifts. Fortunately her parents could afford the best piano instruction that money could buy, and a new world opened wide.

Rachel Braude-Horowitz was soon recognized as a child prodigy. In just a few years she had exhausted every possibility of piano instruction available to Jews in Vilna, so she traveled abroad to acquire a higher level of training. At 18, she returned from Paris and delivered a bravura performance that earned her the most coveted award for a concert pianist in all of Europe: the Chopin Prize.

In 1938, at a concert in Vilna, Rachel met Aryeh Hirsch. The Hirsch family had left Germany for Vilna three years earlier, after the Nuremberg Laws (September, 1935) put an end to Aryeh's university studies in physics. A harmonious chord was struck between them, and they were married in 1939. But the backdrop to their wedding was a cacophony of doom. It was the year that the Germans invaded Poland, and the beginning of the end for the Jews of Vilna … even those whose family trees were rooted eleven generations deep.

DOLLY HIRSCH was born to Rachel and Aryeh in 1941. This in itself was a historical anomaly, the first of the child's miracles … for by the fall of 1941, Vilna's Jewish population had already been herded into ghettos. Jews of every stripe—the secular and the devout, the uneducated and the lettered, the tinsmiths and the scientists, the cobblers and the surgeons—all lived and worked and starved together. Typically, the pregnant women among them either miscarried or were executed by the Germans for the crime of perpetuating the Jewish race.

But Rachel Hirsch determinedly held fast to the new life growing inside her.

If ever there was a family ill-suited for such squalor, it was the genteel Aryeh Hirsch, his acclaimed wife, and her feeble mother. Ilana Rivka Braude-Horowitz was only 43 years old, but under such terrible living conditions she quickly became too emaciated and weak to be part of the ghetto's labor force. Because she could not work, she was denied a ration card, and thus deprived of even the pitiful provisions that were available to others. To avoid that same fate and avert total starvation, Rachel continued to work—even on the very day that she gave birth to Dolly.

Dolly entered the world in a tiny apartment designed for a small family — yet there were 25 people living there, in horrendously crowded and unsanitary conditions. All of them were present for the late-night arrival. Also in attendance, providentially, was one of Vilna's finest obstetricians. He, too, was trapped inside the ghetto.

Because of the dangers involved, there was no celebration marking the baby's arrival. Ilana Rivka watched the birth of her granddaughter with an almost unbearable mix of emotions. Despite her own frail condition, she summoned every ounce of strength to help care for this baby and to play a key role in her survival.

Ilana Rivka subsisted on the morsels her daughter and son-in-law provided her from their miniscule rations. The newborn fared even worse. There was no formula or milk substitute, and Rachel was starving and incapable of breastfeeding. Dolly's sole nourishment consisted of minute quantities of ersatz tea that her grandmother fed her.

By the logic of the ghetto, as neither grandmother nor granddaughter were members of the labor force, they simply did not exist ... a motif that would characterize Dolly Hirsch's unfolding saga of survival.

The Germans designed the ghetto to be an ever-deteriorating, toxic environment for the Jews, in which infection and deadly diseases such as typhus and tuberculosis would run rampant. Still, they never relied exclusively on starvation, contagion, and exposure to the elements to fulfill what would yet be designated as the Final Solution.

In the Vilna ghetto, if the conditions did not prove fatal, there were additional routes to the same terrible end. Failure to immediately remove one's cap in the presence of a German officer, for example, or a momentary hesitation in following an order, could precipitate a beating so severe that death was virtually assured. And collective punishment was a hallmark of Nazi methodology; one Jew's failure to act expeditiously might result in a hundred Jews being summarily shot.

And of course, one could always be punished simply for the crime of being a Jew.

Continuous transports would carry the "perpetrators" to the Ponar forest on the outskirts of Vilna: the old, the young, the infirm—anyone who could fill the daily quota. There the Germans proudly demonstrated their expert marksmanship, routinely murdering three victims with a single bullet. This practice was also a favorite of the Lithuanians, who clearly relished these mass shootings and readily provided assistance—whether it was requested or not.

ONE GROUP, however, was granted a temporary reprieve from the relentless slaughter. The Germans maintained meticulous records of their prisoners, and when it served their aims, there was a vast labor pool they could exploit. At this point of the war, the Germans were in desperate need of engineers. They knew precisely where to turn: one hundred experts trained in radio communications were requisitioned from the Vilna ghetto alone.

Aryeh Hirsch, who had worked as an engineer in the budding motion picture industry, was one of them.

Though the engineers' stock had suddenly risen, months of ghetto life had opened their eyes to an ugly truth. The fate of those they left behind would become more hopeless than ever. Inevitably, as soon as the engineers were transferred from the ghetto, their families would be annihilated.

The bold engineers, sensing the Germans' hunger for their expertise, declared that they would not leave without their loved ones. Their assessment was correct, and their request, remarkably, was granted.

The Hirsches were among the hundred families herded onto flat railcars built to transport livestock. Aryeh Hirsch, a once-robust young man now shrunken to only 40 kilos, despaired deeply over his inability to protect his family. But as he carried his baby daughter onto the transport, he was comforted that he had managed to do something to bolster her chances of survival.

For an entire week, the engineers and their families endured a seemingly endless ride to Byelorussia, arriving at a sprawling prison compound where conditions were even worse than those in the Vilna ghetto. Although disease had not yet reached the catastrophic levels prevalent in the ghettos, the extreme cold and scarcity of food defied human endurance. Winter temperatures rarely climbed above −30°F, and the Jews had neither the clothing nor the provisions to protect themselves from the unbearably harsh conditions.

One day, soon after their arrival, baby Dolly seemed to barely breathe. Rachel watched helplessly as her daughter's brief life began to ebb away. She searched frantically for answers, for hope, for strength. Perhaps there was some sustenance, deep inside the frozen earth?

With the extraordinary courage exemplified by so many Jewish mothers during those times, Rachel Hirsch decided then and there that she would risk her life to feed her child.

In the secrecy of the night, Rachel stole away to the most isolated and dimly lit section of the fenced-in compound. The prison and its surrounding grounds were so vast that they were patrolled by cavalry instead of foot sentries. This was advantageous to any prisoners who succeeded in getting to the outer limits of the camp, because the horses could not approach too close to the electrified wires that surrounded it.

Rachel dropped to the ground, and slithered her body, inch by inch, under the barbed wire fence, desperately digging her fingernails into the frozen earth. Her heart galloped in the race against time. Deeper and deeper she clawed into the unyielding soil, until her grasp closed around a buried treasure: the roots of a few vegetables.

The same lithe, delicate hands that during peacetime had never even been exposed to so much as sudsy dishwater, hands that had garnered thunderous applause in the most celebrated concert halls of Europe, were now sliced by the barbed wire and cracked and numb from digging. But Rachel dug with the strength of a farmhand, as if—no, because—her family's lives depended upon it.

During this very first foray, she was observed by a guard on horseback, who immediately shot to kill. Rachel deliberately slumped flat upon the earth and held her breath. Never before had she tasted death so distinctly; its bile pierced her tongue.

She continued to lie motionless while the sentry circled around her. Satisfied that she was dead, he finally trotted away. Rachel exhaled an explosive breath and ran her hands up and down her body, amazed that she was intact.

This frightfully close encounter with her own demise did not stop

Rachel from sneaking off as often as she could to the sparsely vegetated patch of ground. On another fateful night she was again spotted, and the guard did not hesitate to empty his pistol. That time, too, his aim was mercifully poor.

IN THE AUTUMN OF 1943, the tide of the war turned and Germany was no longer on the offensive. The Russians were gaining momentum, forcing the Germans to dismantle outposts like the one in Byelorussia. Suddenly, Aryeh Hirsch and his fellow engineers were no longer assets to the Third Reich.

The Hirschs, like all other Jews left in Byelorussia, would be dispatched on a one-way journey. Time was running out on the Final Solution and the extermination was only halfway completed. If they hadn't before, all roads now led directly to the death camps.

Rachel and Aryeh Hirsch were only 27 years old, with a tiny daughter and a frail mother in tow, when they were herded onto the boxcar. At their first stop, they found themselves back at the Vilna ghetto, which was in the throes of its final liquidation. For reasons unknown to them, the Hirsch family was transferred from Vilna to the Kovno ghetto, and then on to Minsk.

Every aspect of ghetto life that the Hirsches had previously experienced paled next to the appalling conditions of the Minsk ghetto. The level of starvation was beyond human comprehension. They spent six months there, subsisting on little more than crowded, stale air. From Minsk, the family was transported to the Polish town of Posdah. They were jailed for several months before departing, in October of 1944, for what was intended to be their final destination.

The family was loaded into yet another windowless cattle car. Before being locked inside, the Hirsches—like every other family—were given two slices of stale brown bread and two cups of a rancid-tasting facsimile of Polish coffee, to last them four days and four nights.

The heat and the odor inside the cattle car were overwhelming. It was impossible to move, to turn one's head or even to scratch. Each car contained two cans of water and two buckets for elimination—a grisly joke, for it was impossible for almost anyone in the car to reach them. The decibel level was enough to permanently destroy whatever remained of one's sanity: in every inch of the car—above and below, to the right and to the left—people retched and moaned, screamed in pain and fear, or breathed their final gasps.

BUT IN ONE CORNER, inaudible over the dreadful wailing, an altogether different sound prevailed. Crushed together, Rachel Hirsch and her mother clutched the baby and quietly sang to her, humming intricate melodies to shield her from the hideous dissonance. Though their voices were sweet, their hearts were engulfed in blackness. Rachel and Ilana Rivka had little doubt that they were approaching the end of the line.

Every morning, the train stopped so that the dead could be removed, an operation that the "passengers" themselves were forced to perform. At these stops a few ingenious youths managed to escape, pretending that they were dead in order to be thrown from the boxcar.

Only slightly more than half would arrive in Auschwitz alive.

As the train screeched to a halt at its final destination, the Hirsches knew that the togetherness that had thus far sustained them was over. The separation of families was one of the key initiation rites in Auschwitz.

It was done immediately upon arrival. At the "selection" line, children were often ripped from their parents, and husbands and wives were forced apart. Aryeh was brusquely herded away with the other men from the transport; there was not even time for a goodbye.

Every individual was forced to pass before an SS official and ordered "to the left" or "to the right." Although Dolly was nearly three, she was still barely bigger than an infant due to years of ongoing starvation. A child so small was easy to miss, but the Germans were ruthless about investigating any signs of concealment.

Hoping against hope, Rachel hid the tiny girl under her threadbare dress. From the day she was born, Dolly had managed to be practically invisible—an elusive shadow, a ghost, a puff of smoke. Most children clamor to be noticed and thrive on attention. But for Dolly Hirsch, to be invisible—eerily quiet, motionless, small—had been the miracle of her survival.

Ilana Rivka stood in front of her daughter and granddaughter in the line. From her vantage point she was able to witness and comprehend exactly what this selection process was all about. She understood that her time had come and surreptitiously smuggled the last of her earthly possessions—a few original pages of the Vilna Gaon's commentaries on *Bereishis*, and four diamonds in a little pouch—into the hands of her daughter. Her final act in this world was one of giving.

Ilana Rivka was ordered to the left, and Rachel, to the right. Rachel was scarcely able to breathe as terror and despair overtook her. Her mother had been wrenched from her, and now she struggled to conceal her baby under her dress. Along with the other women in her row, she was ordered to march a short distance to an area in which they were commanded to disrobe.

All of the dread until this moment converged in a crescendo, and fear, like the quick hot touch of the devil, shot through her. Rachel was sure that she would faint from the sheer terror. She could no longer protect Dolly.

Yet, the strange miracle of The Invisible Child persisted.

Disrobing. Shaving. Delousing. Through every excruciating phase of the intake process, Dolly was fully exposed for all to see. And yet, and yet, somehow she remained with her mother. Was it so unfathomable that a baby could have survived to this juncture, that the mind could not assimilate the empirical evidence?

Dolly went unnoticed.

Rachel chose a larger-sized striped uniform so that she would be able to conceal her daughter underneath. And when Dolly finally began to whimper, her muffled cries were drowned out by the screams of prisoners who were having numbers tattooed onto their flesh.

AUSCHWITZ-BIRKENAU was a city of death, and Dolly had arrived at one of its peak seasons. Every extermination camp was working at unprecedented capacity by that point in the war, and in Birkenau alone, more than 10,000 Jews were incinerated a day. The Germans were losing the war, but they were determined not to lose the all-important War Against the Jews.

Even this mother of all extermination camps was unable to cope with the number of transports that arrived each day. The backlog in Birkenau's gas chambers, which were now operating around the clock, was unprecedented, and the camp's overseers converged upon the steady stream of new arrivals in order to process them as efficiently as possible.

No longer were the inmates marched from Auschwitz I (the first stop in the extermination camp, referred to as the Old Jewish Ramp) to the New Jewish Ramp in Auschwitz II (the Birkenau death facility and largest concentration camp); instead, train tracks now brought them directly to their final destination. At a maddening pace the work had to be completed, and industrial murder entered a phase never before imaginable. The rush, rush, rush was catastrophic for European Jewry, but a rush can also result in oversights. For one Lilliputian child, the rush was a lifesaver.

The tiny child—who had learned to weep silently, and who was light as a feather—went unnoticed underneath her mother's garments, even in the death factory.

The vast Auschwitz main camp complex was divided into 28 cell blocks, housing approximately 20,000, primarily non-Jews; five times as many Jews lived in the adjacent Birkenau camp. Of the 400 women in Rachel's barracks, and as far as the eye could see in her camp which was teeming with women, there was not a single child; the youngest inmates were in their upper teens.

Rachel desperately searched for her mother amidst the sea of women. She called out her name and asked about her everywhere, to no avail. Finally an Auschwitz veteran told her the chilling truth. It was the answer that countless naive newcomers had received when posing the same plaintive question. "*There*," said the woman, simply, as she pointed to the acrid smoke billowing from the chimneys of the crematoria. "*There*—"

The Nazi death machine had taken her mother's life, but how could Rachel prevent it from taking her daughter's? How could she avert the inevitable? Even her cache of diamonds proved to be a useless commodity. Her fellow prisoners were interested only in what was edible, and the masters had no need to negotiate, for eventually, they would possess everything. "Everything," she swore, "but not my daughter!"

Rachel's all-consuming mission was to find a hiding place for Dolly—a place where her daughter might live ... or die. In the darkest part of her psyche, Rachel felt there would be a modicum of consolation if only Dolly could die a "natural" death—overtaken by the delirium of fever, lapsing into unconsciousness from starvation or exposure—instead of being murdered by their sadistic captors. However, the Nazi death machine at this stage had no provisions for natural death. Such an eventuality required more time and space than the final phases of the Final Solution could afford.

There were times and places in the Holocaust Kingdom, in which Jewish mothers were forced to think the unthinkable. And to do the impossible.

Chained to the outside of Rachel's barracks was a two-meter-high receptacle into which every form of trash was tossed, from conventional waste to human flesh. Rachel concluded that this putrid bin in the darkest corner of the earth would become her daughter's new home. She assembled a step stool of rocks in order to place the child inside.

But before releasing Dolly into its fetid depths, as Rachel stared into her trusting eyes, some parting words were in order. Would Dolly even comprehend her message? Rachel did not know, but her thoughts tumbled out in a torrent of emotion. She needed to give voice to them as much as she ached for the child to hear them.

What does a mother say before hiding her little one in the garbage? She held Dolly and rocked her, and spoke as if to an adult. "I am not abandoning you, my precious baby, but if I do not work they will murder me … and I must live, because I want you to live," she whispered urgently. She told Dolly she loved her. That someday, she would make it up to her. That she would come to her, if God willed it, at every possible opportunity, and bring food from the few morsels that she herself would receive. And above all, that she must wait patiently for the night-time visits … and not cry or utter a single sound.

Rachel climbed unsteadily onto the rock-pile, hoisted the child into the air, and then laid her deep inside the filthy nest. It was unimaginable that any child could truly grasp the importance of such a warning. *Not a single sound!* But what Rachel said, Dolly did. Once again, submerged and silent, the little girl became completely invisible—enabling her mother to single-handedly defy the Third Reich.

Rachel could not always fulfill her pledge to Dolly, as the inmates no longer owned their own lives. She spent the bulk of each day toiling with her work detachment, and dared not even approach the trash bin except under cover of darkness; and even then, her time there was severely limited, lest she draw attention to herself. Many nights Rachel was locked inside the barracks before there was any possibility of looking in on her daughter or bringing her some scraps of food.

Yet she was desperately determined that Dolly should never fear that she had been forgotten or abandoned, as she lay there, waiting.

No evil that the Germans perpetrated—not the subhuman conditions of the camp, not the supposed bromide-laced food (to ensure the prisoners' robotic, acquiescent behavior)—could destroy Rachel's fierce maternal instinct.

And so every day at 5 AM, when her work detail was about to begin and the dawn had not yet spread its first light, Rachel would loudly whisper a code word as she passed in front of her barracks. It was the classic Jewish mother's rejoinder—all too ironic, here: "Ess, ess, mein kind! (Eat, eat, my child!)" There was no food, of course. But the child understood her mother's message, and would never forget its meaning for the rest of her life: "Be strong, my child, your mother will soon return!" And in the meantime, with daylight not far off and the SS beginning to swarm, she must not move or utter a single sound.

Rachel's daily 14-hour shift was without respite, food or drink. Its first five hours were devoted to the torturous roll calls, which involved waiting outside and standing at attention in freezing temperatures for a work assignment or for selection to the gas chamber. Her jobs included adding or removing rocks to the rail bed, sewing Wehrmacht uniforms, stitching boots, and cleanup duties, including clearing the roads around Auschwitz and Birkenau. No matter the nature of the work, it was always done with bare hands, even when tools were essential.

Only when she returned late at night from the grueling labor was she given a shallow bowl of rancid soup and two slices of stale black bread. This ration was calculated to be almost enough to keep a person who cared to live, strong enough to work.

And it was only then that Rachel would creep outside to briefly remove Dolly from her hiding place, and mother and daughter divided the few crumbs that were never intended to be shared. There were even some nights that the two would spend the short night together inside the barracks, with Dolly being returned to the garbage before the first light of day.

No actuary in the world would have given a credible chance of little Dolly Hirsch's survival in Auschwitz. Yet without shelter or stimulation, nourishment or nurture, and in sub-zero weather, she survived the four months that she was there.

THE RUSSIAN ADVANCE in the winter of 1944 meant that Auschwitz would have to be vacated—though its mission would not be abandoned. The hustle and shifting of the evacuation afforded a brief reunion for the Hirsch family: Aryeh, a worker in the men's section of the camp, was still alive! Such "reunions" were but a few gut-wrenching moments for loved ones to huddle together before being pried apart once again. But even these encounters were a balm to those who ached for the presence of a loved one, for a small taste of life as it once was.

For some of the inmates, the evacuation journey was a death march. Anyone who dared stop to rest or attempt to relieve oneself along the way was shot immediately.

Rachel and Dolly were put in a group that was loaded onto a boxcar train to Bergen-Belsen. Dolly once again was wedged between her mother's legs and remained concealed the entire way.

Rachel's mind raced as to how she might be able to hide her daughter in the new camp. To her astonishment, Bergen-Belsen's barracks were also equipped with two-meter-high garbage cans that were tethered out front.

Dolly was returned to what was by now a familiar environment, and would spend the next four months in one of the receptacles. Familiarity, of course, in no way diminished the constant peril. Just one week before liberation, someone hurled a large, sharp rock into the trash bin, deeply splitting Dolly's lip and palate.

Dolly bled copiously; she was unable to close her mouth, and swallowing became virtually impossible. She weighed only six kilos, and in addition to her facial wound, her body was wracked with many of the diseases that were rampant in the camp—tuberculosis, typhus, dysentery, lice and blistering rashes. With every passing hour, her life was ebbing away.

The Germans estimated that British liberation forces would arrive on the 16th of April, and they were busy making preparations, including a farewell "banquet" for all the prisoners. The British, however, arrived one day earlier, spoiling the German plans. The Nazis only had time to serve the poisoned food they had prepared to some of Bergen-Belsen's inmates, but they made sure to leave their mark by murdering 13,000 more prisoners on their way out.

The beaten and starved prisoners were liberated on April 15, 1945, and their first act of emancipation was to roam freely through the camp, asking anyone and everyone if they had information about their relatives. A friend of Rachel's told her that Aryeh was still alive, and right there in Bergen-Belsen!

Rachel could think of nothing but reuniting with her husband. Everything—the unremitting horror of the past years, the struggle to keep Dolly safe, the promise of liberation—all was eclipsed by the prospect of being with Aryeh again. Rachel stood at the gate and waited. She waited and watched countless male skeletons emerge and slowly file past. The hours ticked by and turned into days.

During this period someone must have remembered Dolly and brought her some food … but it was not her mother. Dazed and disconsolate, Rachel would not abandon her post, as her anticipation soured into the deepest despair. Finally, a man relayed the news that Aryeh was among those murdered on the day of the Nazi departure.

In that one unendurable moment, Rachel lost her will to live. Her determination to survive, like that of so many others, had been fueled by the hope of seeing her loved ones again. Now she wished to join Aryeh—and the sooner, the better.

AS THOUGHTS of suicide beckoned, Rachel—with a horrified start—remembered Dolly.

She had not even brought her anything to eat! Despite her weakened state she ran, crazed, to the barracks. But the garbage had been emptied and her daughter was nowhere to be found. Rachel became hysterical as one emotion tumbled after another.

Ironically, although the camp was now governed by the sympathetic Allies, she was unable to turn to them for help; Rachel spoke seven languages, but English was not among them.

Madly gesticulating, she sputtered in half a dozen languages that she needed to find her baby. The Allied soldiers basically understood her anguished plea, but they did not grasp its urgency. Many mothers screamed for their babies and children—tiny innocents long gone to the ovens. These bereft, delirious women had completely blocked out the reality that their offspring were lost forevermore. With no young children to be found anywhere in the camp, the soldiers naturally believed that Rachel, too, was suffering from such a tragic delusion, and they tried to soothe her, as they did the others, with food and drink and gentle tones.

But this mother could not be comforted. Her desperate wails escalated to a fever pitch. The same troops that had mounted the assaults on the beaches of Juno and Gold, launched Operation Dragoon, maintained the Red Ball highways, attacked South Beveland, forced the Rhine and fiercely fought their way through the Ruhr Pocket, could not placate Rachel Hirsch.

Fortunately, reinforcements had just converged upon the site, and among them were a number of Jewish soldiers, including a contingent from Palestine's Jewish Brigade. Chaplain Avraham Greenbaum was summoned to deal with the sobbing woman. He was a responsible chaplain, a trained officer, but he had no idea how challenging this assignment would be.

Rachel screamed to the rabbi that her daughter had been inside the trash bin, but it was now empty. Chaplain Greenbaum now had the awful task of informing this poor, hysterical woman that her child had died with all the rest. His pastoral apprenticeship had not included training in offering solace in situations like this; because there had never been a situation like this. He felt as though he stood in the epicenter of Dante's Inferno. Bergen-Belsen was the first concentration camp that the liberating armies had entered, and their minds could not fathom what they were seeing.

He searched for the right words, but there were none. Finally Rabbi Greenbaum decided to be honest and direct, concluding that ambiguity would only foster false hopes. In slow, deliberate Yiddish, the chaplain said solemnly, "I believe that you had a daughter, dear lady, but that was months ago."

"NO!" Rachel shrieked. "I am not talking about months ago, weeks ago, or days ago. I am telling you, she is still alive!"

Chaplain Greenbaum looked deeply into Rachel's eyes. Although logic told him that the child must be dead, he could not ignore the intensity of this mother's conviction—he was looking at a woman who had moved hell and earth to save her beloved child. The army chaplain was overwhelmed by the incredible desperation he saw on her face, and awarded credence to her tale. He asked all the pertinent questions and then hurriedly issued orders to his subordinates. Then Rachel and the chaplain set off to the camp's newly designated sanitation area.

Bergen-Belsen was by design a cesspool of contagion and disease. The decomposing corpses, upwards of 13,000 of them, were the main focus of the grisly cleanup. The massive trash bins attached to each barracks were filled with body parts and other detritus that made them a haven for rats and a breeding ground for infection. The Allies were desperate to contain the situation, and just as Rachel and Chaplain Greenbaum arrived on the scene, the soldiers were preparing to scoop everything into a deep, mass grave.

The chaplain ordered the cleanup immediately halted. And there, amidst the tangle of every conceivable form of garbage, human and otherwise, they found Dolly Hirsch. Discarded and bleeding, skeletal and barely alive, she was a miracle risen from the ashes.

British physicians were summoned to the scene, and their prognosis was altogether grim—even more so after examining the child than when they first laid eyes upon her. The little girl had a ruptured palate, heart anomalies, tuberculosis, typhus, dysentery, and as many as seven other serious ailments. She was given virtually no chance of survival.

Rachel was unfazed by their diagnosis; she believed there was a "doctor" in Heaven who knew better. She had come too far to give up on Dolly now.

THE WAR WAS OVER, but the journey and its grinding hardships continued. Rachel learned from three orphaned gypsy girls who were among the few child survivors, that the King of Sweden was offering medical services for concentration-camp survivors who were minors, provided they had an adult guardian. Rachel agreed to fulfill this role for the three girls, while taking advantage of the offer for Dolly.

The camp authorities agreed to arrange for Rachel Hirsch and her four "daughters" to travel to Sweden. Their first stop there was a quarantine station, after which they were taken to a children's hospital in Göteborg, a port city on the Swedish west coast.

Rachel herself, also in acute need of medical attention, was taken to a different facility for treatment. Children and adults were required to be in different facilities under different jurisdictions, and the Swedes allowed for no exceptions.

After three months of recuperation, Rachel was released. It was now time to locate Dolly, from whom she had been separated.

Finding the little girl turned out to be a Herculean task. No one had a clue as to where Dolly might be. An awful sense of *déjà vu* overwhelmed Rachel. The nefarious Germans had done everything they could to separate her from her precious daughter, and now well-meaning Swedish bureaucrats were doing the same thing. She intruded upon and inspected every medical facility in the area, one by one. The first eleven hospitals turned up nothing. But in the twelfth lay a small, wide-eyed child, dwarfed among the sheets and blankets. It was Dolly.

Rachel's joy knew no bounds as she embraced her child, all that remained of her shattered family. As for Dolly, the isolation and loneliness that had governed her life—the long days spent by herself in the ghettos, in the concentration camps, in the garbage bins, and in the pediatric ward—had finally come to an end.

Although Dolly's life was no longer in immediate danger, she still required several more operations, including major surgery on her palate—none of which the hospital was willing to perform gratis, having provided the initial treatments free of charge. They also refused to allow Rachel, who was homeless, to stay in Dolly's hospital room—as critical as this would clearly be to Dolly's recovery.

Then a hospital administrator proposed the idea of Rachel working as a janitor on the ward, in exchange for permission to lodge in Dolly's room. It was strictly a barter arrangement with no salary. Rachel accepted the job, grateful to be reunited with her daughter, but she agonized over how she would pay the massive medical bills and how she would support the two of them after Dolly was released.

Mother and daughter had come so far—only to have to worry about the basics of food and shelter! Rachel's spirits plummeted until she seized upon the dim memory of the artistic endeavor that had sustained her in another life. Rachel had not a penny to her name; she was unfamiliar with the language and the locale; and she owned only the dress on her back (which she had sewn from some discarded curtains) and a pair of mismatched shoes.

But Rachel Hirsch knew that she could still play the piano and bring tears to the eyes of an audience.

A performance was arranged in Stockholm and Rachel was provided with an advance that would cover the cost of a dress for herself and one for her daughter. The performance led to a regular engagement, and after her bows in the concert hall (followed by thunderous applause and shouts of "Encore!"), Rachel would return to cleaning toilets and washing the floors of the wards. The concerts gave her a modest income, which continued until the day she was struck by a car on her way home from a performance, and was hospitalized for three months. Rachel never fully recovered, and the accident brought an end to both her musical and custodial careers.

For the first time, Rachel turned to others for help. She wrote an impassioned letter to the Chief Rabbi of the World Jewish Congress in Berne, Switzerland, describing her plight. The rabbi was able to make the appropriate contacts and some key members of Stockholm's Jewish community coordinated and paid for Dolly's surgery.

EPILOGUE

After Dolly's medical problems were finally behind her, Rachel's dream was for the two of them to immigrate to Palestine, where they could live among other Jews and feel at home. But as Rachel awaited the necessary papers, an uncle in Mexico discovered the whereabouts of the tiny remnant of the Hirsch family. He was overjoyed to find Rachel and her daughter alive. He feared that Palestine was too unstable and primitive a place for two individuals in frail health, and insisted that they join him in Mexico.

The uncle mailed them two tickets for passage aboard a luxury liner, and some spending money that bought a second set of clothing for mother and daughter. When their ship arrived in New York harbor, he was waiting for them on the dock; he then arranged for their transportation to Mexico by train.

Dolly was eight years old when she arrived in bustling Mexico City. There, for the first time, she played with dolls and toys, heard music and ate pastries. Rachel died not long after their arrival, and the little girl was raised lovingly by her uncles. It was they who eventually shared with Dolly her entire story, which Rachel had revealed to them in unsparing, graphic detail.

Dolly Hirsch was invisible no more.

Dolly studied philosophy at the university and married a Mexican Jew originally from Germany, Eliezer Bestandig-Drucker, a chemical engineer. As a result of her ordeal during the war, she was unable to bear children, and the couple adopted two children during the 1960s. Dolly worked for many years, until her retirement, as a Hebrew teacher in Mexico City's Bais Yaakov school. To this day she is a frequent speaker in schools, before youth groups and in synagogues about her experiences during the Holocaust.

She was only a tiny child when it all happened. But today, over seventy years later and a grandmother of two, Dolly can still recall the chill of lying exposed in Bergen-Belsen, in the waste amid thousands of corpses. She remembers the frosty-white, ghostly mists floating aimlessly, the billowing ashes, the fetid wind. The bone-chilling cold of that bloodstained earth, she says, has never left her body.

Honor Thy Father

ESTHER

This is a story of "Honor Thy Father"—in a time and place where even the most fundamental traditions were suspended. And the subject is a child of a most tender age, an age at which such a concept would seem to be unfathomable. But Esther Springer was no ordinary child, and these, of course, were no ordinary times.

With lightning speed, the German invasion of Poland in September of 1939 became a chilling portent of what lay ahead for European Jewry. The juggernaut swept across the country not missing a corner—except for a tiny, remote hamlet named Wieliczka. Not meriting even a dot on a local map, Wieliczka was known only for its salt mines, and was accessible only via horse-and-buggy.

Because of its minute dimensions, Wieliczka was at first not in the German cross-hairs—or even on their radar screen. For this reason, it became a haven for many Jews fleeing the neighboring city of Krakow, including Leah and Duvsha Springer and their children, five-year-old Esther and her infant brother, Yisrael.

Jewish families like the Springers, who came to Wieliczka frantically seeking some semblance of normalcy, were in the most illustrious company.

Their sainted spiritual leader, Rabbi Aharon Rokeach of Belz, was in a tiny village nearby. This towering sage conferred upon the anonymous town the stature of his illustrious Chassidic dynasty, and offered wise counsel during these wrenching times.

Little Esther Springer was far too young to comprehend the human drama that swirled around her in Wieliczka, nor the rich history of Belzer Chassidus, nor the rising gusts of war that roared in the distance. And yet, and yet ... Esther was a child of unusual sensitivity and intelligence. She felt acutely the insecurity that surrounded her, and the unspoken fears of her elders.

Esther despised life in this sleepy, desolate village. Living in unfamiliar surroundings, with almost no friends or stimulation for her restless intellect, she was bored with watching the dreary, repetitive flow of the salt-wagons. Moreover, she was consumed by intense anxiety for her parents' well-being, and a pervasive sense of doom that she could not explain.

And so in August of 1942, a year-and-a-half after the family had fled Krakow, when the little girl was offered a three-day "vacation" to return to Krakow to visit with her Aunt Perel, she jumped at the opportunity.

She did not understand what had prompted this trip. The truth would only have heightened Esther's worst, unspoken fears.

Her father had received word that the Germans were finally closing in on their secret little corner of the world.

Duvsha Springer, while not the most emotive fellow, was a fiercely devoted patriarch and by nature a man of action. He reacted swiftly, just in time to preempt his children's deportations, by moving Esther to the city, and allocating a large portion of his still-significant resources to hire a non-Jew to shelter baby Yisrael.

Esther's nonchalant departure would haunt her the rest of her life. She had no way of knowing that when she waved an enthusiastic farewell to her mother from atop the horse-and-buggy, it would be their final goodbye.

Who could blame the child? "Just three days" were not terribly many to be away from mother and father. Her very early memories of Krakow were of a grand, pulsating city, and her dim recollections of "Chochie" Perel were of a relative of unmatched grace and kindness. In fact, her tiny heart beat faster with pleasure and anticipation!

Esther Springer, looking tiny and alone alongside the driver of the wagon, left home without a backward glance.

PEREL welcomed her niece into her busy household and showered her with unbridled affection, but even this outpouring of devotion could not explain why a three-day jaunt was stretching into weeks. How does one explain to a bright, inquisitive five-year-old that she cannot return to her parents? At first Perel tried to somehow link the delay in her departure to Krakow's wartime curfew. But this lame excuse, and a host of others, soon rang hollow.

The little girl sobbed most of the day. A less kindhearted individual than Perel would have found such behavior impossible to bear.

Perel was known far and wide for her generosity. Though hard times had settled over her own family since the beginning of the war, she invariably invited hungry guests to share her table. This was a lesson learned from her father, who was said to have hosted at least thirty indigent Jews at every Sabbath dinner.

The woman's goodness knew no bounds. One day, little Esther accidentally shattered her aunt's costly crystal bowl. Even under normal circumstances, the destruction of a valuable heirloom would be greeted with fury. But in these times, a crystal bowl was worth much more than its weight in gold. The Jewish residents of Krakow were already cordoned off inside a ghetto. It had been ages since the family had had any real income, and possessions were taxed and confiscated daily. The only hope of survival was through bartering on the black market. And on the black market, this bowl was worth its weight in food.

The other members of Perel's household cast angry eyes upon Esther. Perel, however, embraced the terrified child and inspected every inch of her body to make sure that she was not injured.

BY THE MIDDLE OF 1941, Duvsha Springer's hyper-vigilance in whisking his daughter out of Wieliczka was tragically vindicated. Wieliczka's Jewish community would share the calamitous fate of so many others throughout Europe: at the hands of the Germans, it would be systematically and mercilessly erased.

As the Germans cut their swath through the town, some of its residents were executed on the spot. Others, like Duvsha and Leah Springer, were transported to the Belzec extermination camp. Baby Yisrael was left behind in Wieliczka, in the care of the gentile family that Duvsha had paid.

Belzec was a death factory. The new arrivals were routinely shunted almost immediately to the gas chamber.

And so Leah Springer—huddled amongst the other women, the children, the elderly, the infirm, the robust and the youthful—disappeared into the abyss of the camp, never to be seen again.

A small number of the men who made it to Belzec that day in one piece, Duvsha among them, were "spared" immediate execution. They would have to wait until after a full day's hard labor.

This select group of men was immediately ordered to march to a wooded area, a procession marked by standard SS brutality. The whipping, kicking and cursing were applauded by scores of Polish spectators who gathered along the brush-covered path to jeer the condemned column. How many of Europe's "good citizens" exulted endlessly in the perverse pleasure provided by Germany's Final Solution!

With every wretched step, Duvsha Springer had but one thought: escape. He had no method of concealment, nor a single prop to aid him; and he fully understood that the slightest misjudgment in timing, resulting in his being spotted by a German or a Pole, would mean instant death. To counterbalance all these negatives, he had only his intelligence, a very fleeting window of opportunity, and a picture planted in his mind that ruled his very being.

Yisrael.

His baby and Leah's, an innocent, shining soul, thrust upon peasants who cared only for the remuneration their tiny boarder would bring. He knew that Esther was safely ensconced with family; the most recent communication from Perel was that the little girl had been moved from the Krakow ghetto, which was on the verge of liquidation, to Bochnia (a town 35 kilometers southeast of Krakow), where she was living with Leah Springer's brother and his family.

As Esther had always possessed resourcefulness beyond her years, Duvsha was convinced that she would do well. But Yisrael—did the baby believe he was abandoned forever? And was the family actually even caring for him, or had they simply given him over to a fate as terrible as that of his parents?

In every such doomed procession, in every city and town in the Holocaust Kingdom, thousands of other frantic parents harbored the identical, primal fear that consumed Duvsha Springer. *Please, God of Israel, how can I protect my precious children, and be reunited with them?*

The drama replayed itself countless times throughout the war: a mother or father, against all odds and counter to logic, risking life and limb for the welfare of a child whose odds of having even survived to that point were pitifully small.

The pros and cons of escape battled relentlessly in Duvsha's tortured psyche. Those who attempted flight were promptly and publicly executed, threatening as well the secret plots of the others. Clearly, death would reduce the chances of successfully rescuing one's child to zero. Yet, on the other hand …

Duvsha made his calculation, positioned himself, and leapt. Clean-shaven,* he was able to blend in with the Polish spectators, first fading into the crowd and then racing for dear life.

For the next two and a half days and nights Duvsha literally ran home to Wieliczka. Bereft of any sustenance and allowing himself not a moment's rest, he hurtled on as invisibly as he could to determine his baby's plight.

Leah Springer—protective, nurturing, a tower of strength for her family—was gone. She had breathed her last breath in Belzec. The children no longer had a mother, and he no longer had a wife. His heart was broken, but there was no time to grieve. There was only time to act, as she would have.

He was now mother and father both.

It was nighttime when Duvsha knocked on the peasant couple's door. The moment he saw their startled faces, he knew that his worst fears were realized.

The baby was gone.

Duvsha demanded to know his son's whereabouts. No one in these times—especially vulgarians who had extorted a fortune to harbor a child—felt they owed a Jew any explanation or monetary refund for their miserable failure to uphold their end of the deal. Still, Duvsha's wild-eyed presence finally elicited a response. "The Germans proclaimed

---

*   The rabbis and the Chassidic Rebbes encouraged their devout followers to shave to avoid the humiliations and beatings that the Germans routinely meted out when they encountered a bearded Jew.

that whoever shelters a Jew will be killed," they announced coldly. "We had no choice but to abandon him."

They told Duvsha to check with the local Gestapo, before slamming the door in his face.

Even by the standards of ignorant peasants, their proposal was preposterous. But Duvsha Springer would stop at nothing to locate his missing child.

Because he had been a metals dealer whose work was considered vital for the war effort, Duvsha had an official authorization paper permitting him to enter and exit the ghetto at will. He exploited this in order to position himself on the very street of the Gestapo headquarters, in the hopes of gleaning any bit of information. The vicinity of the headquarters was the lion's den; any closer would place him directly inside its voracious jaws.

Remarkably, he loitered there for several days and was not confronted until he was spotted by a Jew who had sold his soul collaborating with the Germans, someone Duvsha had known in earlier days. "Springer, what on earth are you doing here?" the man demanded. "Are you totally out of your mind?"

Duvsha had no illusions. He had been asked a logical question, but had no logical answer. How does one explain to a hardened man in German employ that no Jewish parent can give up on a child, that such emotions supersede all self-preservation? "My heart doesn't allow me to leave," Duvsha replied helplessly. "I must find my boy!"

"I can assure you the Gestapo does not operate a 'lost-and-found' for Jewish children!" the man responded brusquely.

"I was told they know my son's whereabouts," Duvsha countered. "Unless I know for sure that he is no longer alive, I cannot abandon my search."

"Unheard of," snorted the fellow. "Impossible."

And then the man hesitated. His blank, soul-less eyes flickered, revealing a momentary glimmer of light. He lowered his voice to an urgent whisper: "Right near here is the hospital for patients with typhus and TB—it's filled to overflowing. I heard that there's a little boy there who has captured everybody's heart. Now get yourself out of here, Springer, and don't come back if you expect to see tomorrow."

Finally, a lead!

As Duvsha raced to the hospital, he knew full well that getting Yisrael out would involve kidnapping him from a heavily guarded institution. But first, had his prayers been answered? Was his Yisrael actually there?

Yes, Duvsha learned from several of the Jewish nurses, there was an adorable toddler with dark, dancing eyes, who had enchanted one of the Gestapo men. The officer had, uncharacteristically, turned a blind eye to the child's likely origins and allowed him to be admitted, pre-empting transport to an extermination camp.

The baby *was* Yisrael Springer!

Duvsha looked at his son and had to fight back his tears. Despite weeks of separation, and trauma that he was much too young to verbalize, Yisrael still possessed the same winsome smile and chocolate-brown gaze that sparkled with life. At the nurses' insistence, Duvsha proved himself to be the father, by describing the baby's distinguishing birthmark.

He scooped up the boy and held him as though he would never let him go. Yisrael tightly gripped Duvsha's neck, his little body relaxing in the warmth of their embrace. This was more than a heartfelt reunion of parent and child. In his arms, Duvsha clutched his own past, a never-to-be-recaptured tableau of a loving, happy family—a young husband and wife, blessed with a precious daughter and son. And he also poignantly clutched his only chance at tomorrow.

In a world that had collapsed around him, it was the children who kept Duvsha going.

But now, how was he to smuggle the boy out of a Gestapo-run hospital? Mercifully, the Jewish nurses were as courageous and daring as their German masters were evil. Quietly, one of them came to the rescue, injecting Yisrael with a sedative.

As the baby sagged in his arms, Duvsha gingerly placed him inside a sack that he slung over his shoulder. Together they departed to a future that was uncertain, at best. But they were, at least, together.

It was past curfew and Duvsha was traversing an area that was *verboten* to Jews. Divine protection had clearly enveloped and sustained him during the tumultuous days just past. But when he suddenly found himself face to face with a gun-toting German in the darkened street, Duvsha feared his good fortune had come to an end.

A Jew out at night with a suspicious package slung over his shoulder would have plenty of explaining to do—if he even got a chance to open his mouth. Struggling to maintain his composure, Duvsha shakily pulled out his travel permit. The officer scrutinized the document and, assuming that a few scraps of metal must be inside the metal dealer's sack, did not bother to inspect it. Grudgingly, he allowed Duvsha to continue.

Continue—but to where? Where is a man's "home," when he has no more home?

Duvsha's mind raced. Home was with his little girl. And so he set off on a long trek by foot for the Bochnia ghetto, in order to reunite what was left of his family.

DUVSHA SPRINGER was correct when he characterized his five-year-old Esther as being wise beyond her years. But sadly, he was wrong to assume this meant she was faring well in Bochnia. In fact, she was utterly bereft.

For reasons not entirely clear, Esther's uncle was permitted to live in a house outside of Bochnia's ghetto. And so the little girl was spared, at least to some degree, the horrific conditions of daily life within its confines: subhuman overcrowding, starvation, rampant disease, lack of sanitation or medical facilities. Just as significantly, survival inside the ghetto was predicated upon one's ability to work—and there were no exceptions. Children like Esther—all those under the age of twelve—were not included in the slave-labor force and thus were deemed instantly "expendable." The Germans were not about to waste a morsel of food upon a Jew who did not toil for the Reich.

Esther did not comprehend, of course, all the ugliness that surrounded her; even adult minds could not fully absorb it, never mind explain it. But being a sensitive soul, she felt everything keenly and her loneliness was grinding and profound. She had left the home of a pious, deeply religious aunt for that of a family with dissimilar values.

The sights and sounds and smells of the neighboring ghetto were an assault on the quiet child's spirit, leaving her with a constant, pervasive sense of doom.

Never had she felt so lost in Wieliczka, or even in Krakow. In Bochnia, despair was her prison. At the heart of it were the questions she knew better than to ask: *Where is my mother? Where is my father? Where is my baby brother? And when, when can I go home?*

When an exhausted Duvsha Springer, toting Yisrael (now squirming and considerably livelier), finally arrived at the home of his brother-in-law, his heart leapt at the sight of little Esther. She cried out and ran to his open arms with unfettered joy.

Soon he would understand, however, that his daughter, though still small in stature and tender in years, was, in fact, no longer a child. Her innocence had been destroyed ... like that of every other Jewish child in Europe.

But for that indescribably sweet moment of reunion, Duvsha and Esther instinctively pretended that all was right with the world.

Esther asked nothing about her mother, and Duvsha did not tell.

IT WOULD TAKE DAYS for the silence to be broken on the subject of Leah Springer, who had long ago entered the gates of Heaven with the other martyrs of Israel. And even then the full truth was not spoken.

On the tragic day she learned her mother was gone for good, Esther was walking near the Bochnia ghetto when she heard a by-now-familiar sound coming from inside—a loud BANG, and then a "thud." As a child raised near the forests of Wieliczka, she had initially assumed that these were the jarring sounds made by planks of lumber as they fell to the ground. But on this occasion, Esther was able to see the crash of the "tree" with her own eyes. She watched in horror as a weeping man marched with his hands in the air, and from behind, a German officer lifted his rifle and pulled the trigger.

Instantly she recognized the sounds—the terrible bang, the eerie thud. This was no inanimate log crashing down. Then she watched in horror as the assailant trampled over the corpse with impunity. Did she realize that a bountiful forest, family trees with many branches, had already been felled? And that her mother was among them?

Esther raced back to her uncle's house. Her father was not there, but the moment he returned, before even a greeting was exchanged, she blurted out, "Where is Mamusha?"

Duvsha was overcome with helplessness. "Mamusha...," he paused and then stammered and could come up with nothing more resourceful than, "Mamusha has gone to buy flowers."

The answer was preposterous, indeed absurd. A starving, penniless woman in filthy tatters, trapped in a disease-infested prison—leaving, to purchase flowers?

But a child who is no longer a child, a child who saw and heard the things that Esther Springer had, understood the truth that rang out inside her father's lie. She comprehended that her mother was dead, that she had returned to the earth and the flowers. And she understood more than that: she must never speak of it again. She must cause no more pain to her deeply bereaved and agitated father.

In her bed at night she wept incessantly yet silently, and during the day she bled quietly inside. She did not shed a single tear in her father's presence.

In fact, he would never see her cry, not even once, for the rest of his days on earth.

In the tear-stained chapters of how fathers and sons, mothers and daughters, were slaughtered to sanctify the Almighty's Name, few entries have been written about a child who swallowed her uncontrollable sorrow so as not to anguish her father. Does this not deserve a separate page, or at least a footnote, in the martyrology of the Jewish people?

After this extraordinary sacrifice—the total suppression of her own overwhelming grief—there was no longer any way to pretend that Esther was a child. She had become, overnight, a parent to her own father. Without Esther's quiet strength and consolation, and her tender care of her baby brother, Duvsha would have been lost. She enabled her father to focus on the grinding work of survival—lest they all be lost. She was his rock.

And from where did his daughter draw such strength and wisdom? Part of it was Esther's pure, shining faith in God and His teachings. True, her short life, its course forever altered by war, was an education in bottomless brutality and evil at the hands of the Nazis. But before the war, she had been given a devoutly religious upbringing, an education in *mitzvoth*, at the hands of her loving parents. For Esther, shielding a suffering parent from grief clearly fell within the commandment to "Honor Thy Father."

And there was more. Esther believed, with that same perfect faith, that she had an angel: her mother. The intensely spiritual, intuitive child felt sheltered beneath the protective wings of Leah Springer, receiving metaphysical solace and guidance every step of the way. As Leah had once stood steadfastly beside her husband in good times and bad, Esther now enabled Duvsha Springer to have a clear mind in order to focus on the family's critical needs.

HE UNDERSTOOD INSTINCTIVELY that every move he made on their behalf had life-or-death implications. Duvsha had an uncanny nose to detect the enemy's next move; traveling regularly between Bochnia and Krakow, he scrupulously examined his environment to steer clear of sudden *Aktions* and deportations, and usually managed to stay half a step ahead of mortal danger.

He also saw the writing on the wall. Duvsha somberly concluded that the destruction of Bochnian Jewry was imminent. He desperately searched and contrived for any ray of hope and, ironically, inside the Bochnia ghetto, he found it. There, as in all ghettos, artisans, surgeons, laborers, white-collar workers, engineers, mechanics, businessmen, housewives—Jews of every stripe—were crowded into quarters never designed to hold even a fraction of the swarming populace. But there, deep inside the ghetto of Bochnia, was also the latest hiding place of the Belzer Rebbe, Rabbi Aharon Rokeach, who had been relocated from Wisnicz. He spent his days and nights learning Torah and engaged in holy devotions, despite the wretchedness of the surroundings, and had become a tower of strength and a beacon of light in the midst of all the darkness.

Duvsha was about to activate a rescue plan and his first move, he was convinced, would be his most important: securing for his children the Divine protection that they would desperately need. Even in this time of utter chaos, there was no question where Duvsha Springer would go to fulfill this quest. He brought Esther and Yisrael to the Rebbe, his Rebbe, for a blessing—though he never explained to them who they had visited.

Esther forever regretted that she was unaware that she was in such close proximity to the Rebbe while in Bochnia. Her father felt that it was perilous for a child to be armed with such information, as the Rebbe's location had to be a carefully guarded secret.

For Duvsha Springer, raised in the court of the Belzer Rebbe, it was heartbreaking to bid farewell to his spiritual mentor. He did not know if he would ever see the Rebbe again; indeed, he had no idea what the next day would bring. All he knew was that now that his wife was gone, these two precious children were all he had left, and it was paramount to him that the Rebbe bless them that they survive the war.

Springer was asking for a lot. The Rebbe, whose broad shoulders bore the burden of guiding and comforting the tattered remnant of his flock, had no illusions about the future. He handled the situation with the grace one would expect of a prince who had inherited the kingly crown. The Rebbe was a man of few words, but his every action resonated his greatness.

He gave each child a *groshen* (a Polish penny) for safekeeping, and to Duvsha, he lent a *kittel*. Lent—not "gave." The unmistakable message was that an honest man is honor-bound to return what he has borrowed. As Duvsha Springer clutched the Rebbe's *kittel* to his heart, he understood that this obligation was intended to guarantee his survival throughout the war.*

---

*   The Rebbe would also soon be leaving Bochnia, completing yet another leg of a flight to freedom that had been (and would continue to be) fraught with danger and marked by miracles.

Beginning years earlier in the tiny Galician town of Belz, he had maintained his Chassidic court despite the constant danger. The Rebbe had followed events closely and when word came, on the solemn Jewish holiday of *Hoshana Rabba*, that the Germans would be invading Belz the next day, he made preparations and issued instructions.

He decreed that the traditional *hakafos* take place that night as usual. The Rebbe instructed that wagons be loaded with everyone's possessions so that immediately afterwards they could take flight across the border to the Russian-occupied zone of Poland.

The Germans were incensed that the intrepid spiritual leader of Belz (known as the "Wonder Rebbe") and his followers had escaped from their clutches. They attempted to vent their fury upon the Belzer synagogue—but this, too, inexplicably failed. SS troops, unable to burn down a synagogue—how could this be? This daily ritual had become a hallmark of the German invasion.

With mounting rage, the Gestapo turned to the handful of unfortunate Jews who had remained deep in hiding inside Belz, ordering them at gunpoint—in an acrid bath of their own sweat and tears—to pull apart their precious *shul*, brick by brick.

The legendary founder of the dynasty, Rabbi Shalom of Belz (known as the *Sar Shalom*) had personally directed the construction of the magnificent structure, dedicated in 1843 and with a seating capacity of 5,000. Built like a fortress with

Duvsha's next move was to come up with an earthly plan to ensure his family's survival. Toward this end, he located a non-Jewish woman who agreed to shelter Yisrael, provided that—in addition to paying for the baby's care—Duvsha underwrite the cost of food for her entire household. The massive expense would require Duvsha to marshal all of his remaining resources. And would this woman and her family be as untrustworthy as the last greedy peasants to whom he had entrusted his child's care?

Reluctantly, he returned to Wieliczka to unearth the valuables that he had hidden, including his wife's precious ring. But Duvsha was loath to squander everything on a survival plan that did not cover his entire family.

---

walls three feet thick, it reflected the *Sar Shalom's* explicit will that the soaring structure be constructed strictly by the hands of Jewish artisans and laborers, who carried out the project with the ultimate devotion and sacrifice. And so it had been part of their beloved Rebbe's plan—indeed, the Divine Plan—that it could only be disassembled by Jews...

After fleeing Belz, the Rebbe reached Bochnia, from whence he would flee to the Russian-controlled town of Sokal. The constant surveillance placed on the Rebbe by the Russians incapacitated his ability to converse with his Chassidim. Anything he said could be twisted into seditious behavior, and NKVD spies were everywhere.

The Belzer Rebbe wandered from town to town after Sokal, welcomed nowhere until he arrived in Przemylany. There he was afforded a modicum of comfort until the German invasion of Russia. Przemylany fell immediately and the Germans wasted no time setting about their priorities. Dozens of Jews including the Rebbe's oldest son, Moshe (himself a brilliant and revered sage), were herded into the main synagogue and the door was sealed. In one great blaze, the living and the written Torah scrolls ascended Heavenward.

The Belzer Rebbe remained in hiding while feverish activity was launched to spirit him out of the region. Much money changed hands, and a Polish nobleman who was an official for the Germans was bribed to take the Rebbe, his brother Mordechai (the Bilgoraj Rav), and two attendants to a safer location.

The Pole insisted that the passengers remove their beards and *payos* (among other precautions) in order to disguise their identities before boarding his car. After the five drove off in the middle of the night, they encountered miracle after miracle. Every step of the way, the German border police, Gestapo officers, and other militia they came upon were either drunk, asleep, or otherwise engaged—enabling the vehicle to travel from point to point, undetected.

They drove through the night until the driver dozed off, resulting in the car plunging off the road into a ditch, totaling the car and injuring the passengers. They did manage to extricate themselves from the wreck, and not a minute too

There was, he had heard, an alternative.

In a significant quirk of history, the Germans recognized those possessing Latin American passports—even Jews—as foreign citizens entitled to certain minimal rights and privileges. Their ulterior motive, it was believed, was to ensure the safety of thousands of German spies and operatives entrenched in Latin America.

Only later, in the spring of 1944, when it became obvious to the Germans that they had nothing to gain by abiding by international law, were the Jewish holders of these documents earmarked for extermination like all other Jews. But until then, they received preferential treatment, and could cling to the belief that they would survive.

And so Duvsha Springer moved mountains to secure Argentinian

---

soon. As they limped their way away from the accident, the engine caught fire and exploded.

It was 3 AM, way past curfew, and they had no documentation permitting them to be out on the road. The fivesome made their way to an inn outside Tarnow.

Somehow, word reached the Tarnow ghetto that the Rebbe had been injured in an accident. A doctor smuggled himself out of the ghetto to dress the wounds of the Belzer Rebbe and the others.

At this time, Eliezar Landau, whose sole motivation was to save the lives of his brethren, assumed the leadership of a clothing factory in the Bochnia ghetto. Landau figured that as long as Jews were providing a valuable service, they would be kept alive—at least temporarily. The Belzer Rebbe was protected under Landau's watchful eye as he bribed whoever was necessary to smuggle the Rebbe in and out of Bochnia whenever an *aktion* was planned or the conditions otherwise proved too dangerous to remain there.

Yet this was but a temporary solution, as Bochnia would undoubtedly be liquidated like all the ghettos before it. A Hungarian army officer was hired for the astronomical figure of roughly $20,000 to take the Rebbe and his brother, posing as Hungarian generals, back to Budapest. The masquerade worked without a hitch all the way to Hungary. Other contingencies were eventually implemented to transport the Rebbe and his small entourage from what eventually became German-occupied Hungary to the Land of Israel.

The saga of the Belzer Rebbe must be regarded as inextricably bound to the personal journey of little Esther Springer. The gleaming *groshen* that Esther and her brother and numerous other Jewish children kept hidden inside their shoes, coins bequeathed to them by their sainted Rebbes, were enduring symbols of hope—the only talismans these children possessed.

Recognized and hunted by the Gestapo at every turn, Rebbes like the revered leader of the Belzer dynasty struggled against the enemy not only for their own survival, but because the children's spiritual and physical lives depended upon them.

papers for his children and himself. The family's new last name would be Brenning.

It was their only chance.

THE VERY DAY after the "Brennings" received their new documents, they were shipped to Bergen-Belsen and placed in a barracks especially assigned to those of non-European citizenship. Esther became the only female* crowded among eighty men, ranging from the renowned Bluzever Rebbe to hardened criminals.

The possessors of Latin American passports in Bergen-Belsen were subjected to the same overall conditions as their less-fortunate brethren, with one significant difference: they were not forced—indeed, not even *permitted*—to work. This so-called benefit was a double-edged sword.

These prisoners, like all the others, were suffering from acute starvation. Yet being sealed in their barracks all day long, they had no work detail to divert them from their agonizing hunger. In the close quarters of the "stateless," tempers constantly flared, and many resorted to the predatory rage of animals locked in their cages.

The "stateless" were only permitted out of their barracks for a regulated visit to the latrine and for the morning and evening roll calls. Though one might imagine that any excuse to exit a crowded, airless prison would be welcomed, the Germans characteristically saw to it that no Jews ever had any relief from their suffering. The latrine barracks consisted of one long, putrid ditch with a walkway on either side, and the daily roll calls were harrowing and debilitating beyond imagination.

In the *Appellplatz*, the site of the roll calls, the masters of sadism transformed a simple procedure into acute torture. Whether in blistering heat or bone-numbing cold, the prisoners were forced to stand ramrod-straight at attention for hours on end, enduring endless rounds of meaningless counting and re-counting, with even the slightest deviation from their row being punished by immediate execution; and as the shots rang out, the counting would begin all over again.

---

* There was a stateless barracks for females, but as Esther did not have a mother, she remained with her father.

EVEN WITHIN the horrific, logic-defying world of Bergen-Belsen, Esther and Yisrael Springer's existence defied all human comprehension. Tucked away among eighty desperate, starving, overcrowded adult males, were a six-year-old girl and her two-year-old brother. There was only one other child, and not a single teenager.

Inside this barracks, the dangers that the "Brenning" children faced from inmates that had been hardened by their experience and from Germans whose perverse sense was intrigued by the presence of a young female and a little boy among so many men, were numerous and complex.

To the prisoners themselves—Jewish fathers pushed way beyond their emotional equilibrium, mourning their own dead and missing children—the incomprehensible presence of these two youngsters was an unbearable affront, and the two bore the brunt of enormous hostility. Far from being taken under anyone's wing, Esther and Yisrael were treated as pariahs. The men seethed over having to share even a morsel of their meager allotment of rations with two puny creatures who they believed were doomed anyway. With the exception of the compassionate Bluzever Rebbe, who was also trapped among the miserable inhabitants of this barracks, no one uttered a kind word in the children's direction. No one even looked at them.

Duvsha was gravely concerned that even the slightest vexation on the part of his energetic son—childish tears or laughter, careening through the barracks, even an all-too-common toileting "accident"—would ignite the hair-trigger tempers of his brooding comrades, and of course the German inspectors. And so he issued a stern edict to his children that parents in normal circumstances would consider unthinkable—and impossible. The command was explicit: the two of them were never to get out of bed. Never to step on the floor, never to join the company of others, never to peek out the door—never to get out of bed!

"Bed," of course, did not refer to a cozy childhood retreat of downy comforters and cuddle-toys; it was a splintery, narrow berth among the three-tiered wooden shelves where all of the prisoners were warehoused, topped by a threadbare, lice-infested blanket—a prison within a prison.

Once again, a huge responsibility fell upon the tiny shoulders of Esther Springer. Keeping a two-year-old corralled in one spot all day long, day after day, is an unbelievable feat—even when the child is placid by nature, which Yisrael was not. Equally incredible was the fact that the caregiver charged with providing a nonstop repertoire of stories and songs and sedentary amusements, was herself only six. Esther could have much more easily involved her brother in a game of hide-and-seek, or some other outlet for his restless, pent-up energy. But this would have violated her father's instructions.

And for Esther, whose world had now been further reduced to a small rectangle in a far corner of a filthy barracks, the word of her father was akin to the word of God.

Esther had little respite from the exhausting care of her sibling. At night she would verify that Yisrael had fallen asleep by lightly running her fingers across his eyelids. Only then was she permitted by her father to leave the bed and approach him and the other men where they congregated.

She was allowed to remain there quietly for about 20 minutes before Duvsha inevitably declared, "It's late now, hurry on to bed!" This brief interlude was what Esther looked forward to all day long. Her only other diversion was watching her father don his precious tefillin each morning—another clandestine privilege of the "stateless" barracks.

THE MEN caged inside this barracks had only one avenue for retaining a shred of their sanity: each other. Under subhuman conditions, with death lurking around every corner, even the most taciturn prisoner would spend every waking hour in heated discussion with his fellow inmates, engaging his mind so he did not go mad. Huddled together along one of the walls of the barracks, they debated and discussed and described—what, exactly, Esther Springer did not know, from her perch on the slab at the far end of the room. She only knew that her father was a key participant in these symposia, and that it was her duty to keep Yisrael away—none of them would have appreciated a toddler underfoot.

And there was more that Esther did not know. The simmering ire of his fellow inmates was not the only reason—in fact, not even the main reason—that Duvsha had decreed his children must remain sequestered in a remote corner of the barracks. His overriding fear was actually the deadly scourge of infection, as typhus and a host of other diseases ran rampant in Bergen-Belsen.

There, as in all other camps, once an infection was contracted, there were no antidotes. Every illness was likely terminal, with no palliatives to reduce fever or pain. To Duvsha's thinking, the best way to avoid exposure to disease was to keep the children permanently "quarantined."

And indeed, the father's obsessive vigilance paid off: for the duration of their incarceration—despite the most appalling conditions—not one of the "Brennings" ever took sick.

If only all of Duvsha Springer's fatherly instincts had been as keenly developed. If only he had thought to explain to his puzzled daughter why he was pushing her and her brother away. She was only a child, yes, but she was expected to behave as an adult; surely she would have understood a rudimentary explanation of disease-prevention, but he never attempted to enlighten her! Day and night, Esther's mind exploded with questions—about their "stateless" designation, this wretched barracks, why was she the only girl, so many other mysteries! But clearly Duvsha welcomed no discussion ... just as when he had tersely informed his daughter that her long-absent mother had gone "to buy flowers."

Esther's rare attempt to broach their nightmarish circumstances only elicited her father's pent-up fury. One day she innocently inquired of him if they would ever again be known as "Springer." "Don't you ever, ever, dare ask that again!" replied Duvsha, barely suppressing his rage behind clenched teeth.

He was right to fear that their existence would become even more perilous if their true identities were revealed—that unquestionably, they would no longer remain in the "privileged" stateless section of the camp and would be split apart. But he was wrong (as were his fellow inmates) to believe that his children did not have the slightest grasp of what was going on all around them.

On more than one occasion the children observed inmates stashing stolen items right before their eyes, as they looked over their shoulders every second to see if any "person" was watching. The fact was that the children absorbed everything, and had matured with sickening speed.

Unanswered questions and silence only compounded Esther's bottomless grief and isolation. But the tablet of law told her what she must do: honor her father, so that her own days on earth might be lengthened.

Caring for children had always been a rather foreign concept to Duvsha Springer. Thanks to his devoted Leah, the task was never shared, freeing him to conduct his business affairs far away from home.

This knowledge lived in Esther's memory, and she could not hate her father for it; she only felt deeply sorry for him, and did exactly as she was told. She had been bequeathed her mother's patient and nurturing nature, and she heaped upon Yisrael all the love and attention that she herself was craving.

This she did—a six-year-old tending to a starving two-year-old in the confines of a narrow splintery plank—for the entire time they remained imprisoned in Bergen-Belsen: two and a half years.

A consequence of this situation was that Yisrael became utterly— even pathologically—dependent upon his sister, and would become frantic if she strayed from his line of sight, even for a moment.

This raised a thorny problem every six weeks when the prisoners of this barracks were led to showers. Esther was diverted to a detachment of about one hundred females, with whom she would wash. These desperately ill, bald, skeletal, beaten women were almost indistinguishable from males, having lost virtually all feminine characteristics, both physical and emotional.

Here, too, the lonely child was an object of fierce jealousy and scorn. The loss of their own children, plus months of grievous maltreatment and deprivation, had destroyed whatever maternal tenderness these Jewish matriarchs once possessed. The sight of a traumatized little girl aroused nothing in them. Like cattle, they had been herded; and like cattle, they now responded only to whips, to shouting, and to the lure of food and water. To walk naked among them was such a macabre rite that Esther derived little satisfaction from cleansing her body.

Besides which, each time she returned from the showers, she found her brother hysterical.

And she herself could hardly shake the unspoken terrible fear that would grip her throughout the entire ordeal: that afterwards, she might not be returned to her father.

If that ever happened, she agonized, *what would he and Yisrael do without her?*

DUVSHA SPRINGER'S nimble mind had enabled most of his family to circumvent the killing grounds of Belzec and the deadly *Aktions* of Wieliczka, Bochnia and Krakow, and it had not shut down in the confines of Bergen-Belsen. Duvsha understood that their Argentinian passports were but a temporary stopgap as the Final Solution loomed.

His plan was to ascribe some value to himself that the Third Reich might deem strategic. But what worth could he have, with Jews deemed as barely equal to vermin?

Some of his fellow prisoners, in desperate attempts to save themselves, had resorted to collaboration—performing the dirtiest work imaginable for the Germans. The very idea was an anathema to Duvsha; and besides, even the most trusted accomplices who had, under duress, assisted in the elimination of their own brethren, were ultimately executed by the Germans for knowing too much.

Duvsha's logic was that if powerful individuals on the outside were to become aware of his family's plight, it would become more of a liability for the Germans to do away with them. Questions would be posed, and answers would be required.

But how, from the bowels of a concentration camp, could a former metals dealer from Krakow capture international attention? With his characteristic ingenuity, Duvsha hatched a bold plan.

Its utter implausibility never crossed his mind.

He strategized that the best way to achieve recognition would be through an international agency. His scheme was to become the recipient of a series of packages from the Red Cross in Switzerland. The idea was as expensive as it was ambitious: each package would cost 50 U.S. dollars, with no guarantee of delivery. But if it accomplished its purpose, it was well worth the price.

Duvsha had a contact in Switzerland who could make all the arrangements; the seemingly insoluble issue was getting word to the man! And then opportunity arose—and Duvsha Springer, as was his nature, grabbed it swiftly with both hands.

The opportunity came in the form of the notorious Kastner train,*

---

*   The Kastner train refers to a trainload of Jews who escaped from Nazi-controlled Hungary in 1944. The train was named after Rudolf Kastner, the leader of the Zionist movement in Hungary. In April 1944, for reasons that are still disputed, German officials under the direction of Adolf Eichmann, acting on behalf of his superior, Heinrich Himmler, offered to free Hungarian Jews in exchange for

which departed from Bergen-Belsen in December of 1944 with 1,686 Jews on board, including the renowned Satmar Rebbe. Destination: Switzerland.

The motives behind this controversial transport, and who would, and would not, be included, were (and would remain) the source of fierce historical and moral debate. In any event, Duvsha entrusted his crucial mission to the famed rabbi.

The Swiss connection did as he was instructed, and arranged to have the "Brennings" sent several Red Cross packages. At least some of their contents did reach the family, and were a much-needed source of sustenance. Was Duvsha's status indeed enhanced as a result of receiving these packages? The answer would remain a mystery forever.

AT THE DAWN OF 1945, even the sequestered Jews of Bergen-Belsen could tell that the war was going poorly for the Germans. Aerial battles raged overhead, and the already overcrowded camp swelled to more than 300 percent of its previous population. Thousands of prisoners arrived daily with the German troops retreating from the east.

To make room for the new internees, the "stateless" refugees were taken from their barracks and boarded onto a cattle train for a destination that they sensed was their final one. After years of hanging by a thread in their miserable pen—with liberation just around the corner—this was truly the lowest moment for Duvsha and his children.

The train was en route to Magdeburg, Germany—literally minutes away from the killing field where they were all to be shot—when their miracle came. Air-raid sirens wailed as a vicious dogfight erupted in the sky above. Terror-stricken, the Germans abandoned the rails and their captives.

Shortly afterwards, the U.S. Army's 30th Infantry Division liberated the prisoners aboard the previously doomed train, and brought them to the nearby village of Hillersleben.

The frightened townspeople had been driven away or fled on their own, leaving their homes vacant for those who had been their sworn

---

10,000 trucks from the Western powers to be used for the retreat from the Soviet Union on the eastern front. In a goodwill gesture to demonstrate that they would keep their part of the deal, 1,686 Jews were diverted from Auschwitz to Bergen-Belsen and eventually to Switzerland. The trucks never materialized.

enemies. For Esther and Yisrael Springer, the comforts of a normal dwelling defied description after the horrors they had endured. Duvsha wisely forbade his children from eating, while others with less foresight died as a consequence of consuming quantities of food that put extra strain on their weakened hearts.

Duvsha right away availed himself of the opportunity to properly wash his body and relished every moment of this privilege that had been denied to him for five full years. Esther climbed onto a bed that was not a ragged wooden shelf, but a comfortable mattress adorned with clean, white linen. As soon as she lay down, she felt a deeply calming, soothing sensation as if she were gently sinking into a cloud. It was a feeling she would never forget.

Two orphaned Jewish girls, both teenagers, moved into this house with the Springers, and the very first thing they did there was to play with some dolls that were abandoned in the home. Esther could hardly believe her eyes. Two young women, practically grownups, playing ... with dolls? What she did not comprehend was that these girls were picking up their childhood where it had been left off. It was a stage that Esther had not even reached before war and displacement had shattered her life.

INDEED, WHILE ALL of the survivors launched a new chapter of their lives after liberation, for the youngest among them—children like Esther and Yisrael—it was, in many ways, a first chapter. And it was not always a joyful one, despite the fact that the Nazi terror was behind them. Life was still uncertain and volatile—indeed, often agonizing— for those searching frantically for family members they believed were still alive, and for those who returned "home" but were not allowed to enter their own houses and were taunted by former neighbors, "Too bad Hitler didn't finish the job!" And then there were those who yearned to go to Palestine but were blockaded by the British. And those who could not forget the horror in the eyes of their liberators, who could not look at them without wincing or retching at their diseased, skeletal bodies. They had arrived at this new juncture of their lives, bearing the heaviest of burdens.

Yet ultimately for Esther, this would become the most glorious period of her life. While her father focused on rebuilding himself after the trauma of the war, Esther and Yisrael were admitted to a *kinder-heim* (orphanage) with approximately 150 other children in Antwerp, Belgium, co-sponsored by the Joint Distribution Community and by the city's resuscitated Jewish community. The director of this institution was the righteous and benevolent Yona Tiefenbrunner, who took these deeply traumatized Jewish orphans from all walks of life under his wing and into his heart. He devoted every waking moment to providing them with a nurturing home and an education that could help them heal and rebuild. He was not merely a "father figure" to these children; he was their father and their mother.

Every moment of the day was carefully planned so that these fertile minds, which had long been denied access to any form of education, could be enriched—enabling the children to leave behind at least some of their trauma and move forward into full lives. As if he were a psychological master with a limitless budget, Tiefenbrunner and his dedicated staff employed every pedagogic trick to engage and rehabilitate youngsters like Esther and Yisrael, infusing their shattered lives with meaning and hope.

Spiritual education was an integral part of their lessons, as were outdoor activities and cultural entertainments. Tiefenbrunner even saw to it that at gift-giving time—birthdays and holidays—each child received precisely what he or she dreamed of. It had been so long since they had dared to dream!

The *kinderheim* accomplished the impossible: it prevented children who had lost one or both parents from drowning in their grief. Furthermore, at the *kinderheim*, Yisrael was slowly able to wean himself away from his total dependency upon Esther, so they could both have the space to develop normally.

Above all, under Tiefenbrunner's tutelage, children who had been denied any semblance of childhood could make up for all they had missed, through the simple but essential pleasures of friendship, play and learning.

EPILOGUE

Duvsha Springer remained in Belgium with his family—which grew to include a new wife and another child, a boy—until 1951. They then immigrated to Borough Park, New York, but not before he had fulfilled his promise to return the borrowed *kittel* to the Belzer Rebbe. Duvsha died in 1982.

Esther threw herself into advanced studies at Bais Yaakov School for Girls in Borough Park. She never forgot how her life had been transformed by dedicated teachers—first in the *kinderheim*, and then in Bais Yaakov—and devoted her life to "giving back." For over fifty years she has been a senior instructor in religious education and the history of the Holocaust in Belz institutions in Brooklyn. Married in 1957, Esther is the proud mother, grandmother and great-grandmother of many Belzer Chassidim.

"Baby" Yisrael, says his sister, grew into a man of seriousness and depth. He and his wife have eight children, all of them scholars. He works as a jeweler.

The Belzer Rebbe, Rabbi Aharon Rokeach, made his way to Eretz Yisrael (the Land of Israel) after losing his entire family—including wife, children, grandchildren and in-laws and their families—to the Germans. He became an acknowledged leader of Torah Jewry there, laying the groundwork for the rebirth of Belzer Chassidus through the establishment of schools and *yeshivos* in Tel Aviv, Bnei Brak and Jerusalem. He died in 1957, and tens of thousands of admirers followed his casket to his burial site in Jerusalem.

The Belzer Rebbe had declared that anyone who survived the war had a special angel watching over them. Regarding the remarkable saga of Esther and Yisrael Springer's survival, he once commented, "*Malachim, mamash!* (True, genuine angels!)"

Brother and sister both still have the precious coin given to them by the Rebbe, and access it in difficult times. Who their guardian angel was, they have no doubt: it was the devoted mother they scarcely knew, Leah Springer, who taught them the Commandments, and who has carried them on her wings to this very day.

Sheer Will

Shlomo Zalman

This is a story of sheer will. Against all odds, even against all logic, Shlomo Zalman Teichman—a boy against the Nazi war machine—was determined to remain alive, and to safeguard the life of his younger brother. To achieve the impossible, he mustered superhuman powers.

Every child needs a hero, and Shlomo Zalman Teichman did not need to look far for the one who would illuminate, for him, the Righteous Path. His grandfather, Berish Teichman, was a legendary member of the Jewish community of Munkacs, Czechoslovakia, a man whose name is still revered by scores of families whose ancestors had benefited from his largesse.

There were, in fact, thousands who were aided by Shlomo Zalman's benevolent *zayde*. But in the scourge of the Holocaust Kingdom, precious few Munkacsers would live to tell the tale.

Every Friday night without fail, at the conclusion of synagogue services, the boy would watch his grandfather fulfill to the highest degree the *mitzvah* of *Hachnosas Orchim*—the sacred Jewish obligation to welcome the stranger and to share one's blessings. Among the hundreds of Sabbath worshippers in Munkacs' celebrated *Belzer Klois* were many poor travelers with no prior arrangements for food or lodging. Berish, the largest grain distributor in all of Europe and a consummate organizer, would line up his sons and sons-in-law and assign guests to each of them. Then he would turn to his neighbors and fellow congregants and loudly inquire who else wished to participate in the *mitzvah* of hospitality. Thanks to Berish, even the shyest traveler would find a gracious host.

But the lion's share of visitors, Berish Teichman kept for himself. He was a widower twice over, yet his Sabbath table was always full. It was not uncommon for as many as eighty people to accompany him home from the synagogue, where a generous feast awaited them—much of it prepared by his own hands, with the assistance of his domestic staff.

Young Shlomo Zalman was an inquisitive and observant child. "Love your neighbor as yourself," he had learned from the *rebbes* in his *cheder*. And as the boy watched the chain of humanity wend its way through the lamp-lit streets of Munkacs to his grandfather's home, he instinctively understood that he was watching the Torah and its commandments spring to life.

Shlomo Zalman also knew that his patriarch's zeal for performing *mitzvos* was not relegated only to the Sabbath. Every weekday afternoon, Berish Teichman placed his kitchen and spacious dining area at the disposal of Munkacs' celebrated yeshiva. The Munkacser Yeshiva attracted scholars from far and wide, and it was not uncommon for 170 of them to enjoy lunch *chez* Teichman.

And the poor, too, never needed to seek out Berish Teichman; it was he who sought them out. Destitute Jews who lived in and around Munkacs dined almost nightly at his table and were treated like royalty. His inviolate policy was that he would not allow meat to enter his mouth unless he was sharing his repast with at least nine other men. This way he could recite the Grace after Meals with a quorum of ten. In fact, Berish would not eat at all unless he could share the meal with at least two others, so that the introductory prayer requiring a minimum of three could be chanted.

Some of his grandfather's *mitzvos* only became known to the boy by word of mouth. It was widely told that when Berish Teichman traveled by train—and the nature of his business had him trekking by rail virtually every week—he would not eat unless he could locate another Jew who would partake with him. Inevitably he would make his way through each car and every cabin to see who could use a square meal.

Berish Teichman knew what it was to struggle for bread. During World War I, he lost his entire fortune and became a broken man. It was the Belzer Rebbe who consoled him and restored his spirits; he also blessed Berish that he would become rich again, and suggested that he leave the wine trade and go into grain commodities.

From 1918 to 1920, the Belzer Rebbe lived part-time with the Teichman family in Munkacs, hiding from the Polish authorities in the aftermath of the war. Times were uncertain and the Belzer *beis midrash* had been destroyed, so it was best to keep a low profile. During this period, the Teichmans left the court of the famous Rebbe of Munkacs, the *Minchas Elozar* (Rabbi Chaim Elozar Shapiro), and became devotees of the Belzer Chassidic court.

Berish's grain business grew so large that he required a massive staff to oversee its various operations. What all the managers, supervisors and executive vice presidents had in common was that they were either Teichmans or married to Teichmans. Berish governed the ultimate family affair.

Apart from one son who was the office manager, all the partners would spend their week on the road administering their far-flung districts. Shlomo Zalman's father, Shmuel, for example, was in charge of all of Italy.

Every Saturday night, a staff meeting was conducted in the home of Shmuel Teichman. These roundtables were legion for the business acumen, camaraderie and high level of professional ethics displayed. Naturally they were closed to outsiders, but one uninvited observer always managed to attend. He did not say a word, but absorbed everything. He did not sit at the table, but huddled underneath it.

From his secret perch, young Shlomo Zalman stared at the well-polished shoes of his grandfather, who presided over each meeting with enormous dignity and insight. The boy understood nothing of running an empire (though someday, he would), nor did he comprehend the complex technical language of debt consolidation, earning forecasts, or grain production.

But week after week, he listened quietly, transfixed. He grasped that high finance was on the table and that vast quantities of produce and cash were changing hands. He also grasped that it was paramount that no one's honor ever be compromised. If any of the managers failed in an assignment, Berish did not deride them; without argumentation or insult, he would spearhead a discussion of creative solutions and offer encouragement for the future. Voices may have been raised and discussion may have grown heated, but no personal affronts were allowed. This was the way Berish ran his business and his life, and this was the way it had to be.

The boy was enthralled by this introduction to the world of big business, and waited eagerly through the week to assume his secret hiding place at his grandfather's feet. The older he got, the more he recognized what big shoes there were to fill.

INITIALLY, World War II did not affect the Jews of Munkacs as severely as it did the Jews of Poland, and subsequently all of European Jewry. Nevertheless, they had experienced a radical change for the worse, beginning in November, 1938 when the Hungarians took over the town from the Czechs.

Shmuel Teichman was inducted into the Hungarian army, but as was the case for most Jews, this did not involve any military training. The Jews were assigned to menial labor such as cleaning the bathrooms, barracks, and kitchen, and inspecting the ammunition; on the front lines, they were used for hazardous tasks like scouring the minefields. As soon as Shmuel learned that Jews without trades were being shipped to the front, he announced that he was a tailor.

Shmuel had been raised in the grain business and had never threaded a needle in his life. But recognizing the danger at hand, he acquiesced readily when a Jewish friend of his whispered, "Say to them exactly what I say, and afterwards, I'll explain to you what to do!" Overnight, he became a tailor. This pronouncement kept him out of the combat zone.

Two years into his service, when the military transport in which he was traveling neared the Russian border, Shmuel Teichman realized that his days as a needle worker were over. The Hungarians were slated to assist the German army, which meant minefield-sweeping for the Jews, or any other perilous duty that would ensure their elimination.

Shmuel weighed his limited options and made a daring jump out of the moving train, mercifully negotiating a soft landing. Swiftly and stealthily, he made his way to Budapest, where he managed to hide for the duration of the war.

With his father gone, thirteen-year-old Shlomo Zalman became the oldest male of his household. Although he had always been short for his age, he recognized that four brothers and a sister looked up to him as a leader and role model. He vowed to himself that he would not disappoint them, his worried and desperate mother, Leeba Breindel Teichman, nor his father in absentia.

He was, after all, the grandson of Berish Teichman, who had taught him to stand tall, and that nothing was impossible.

But in these dark times, even Berish's power and influence were greatly diminished. For the second time in his life, his financial empire crumbled, and in May of 1940, he passed away. The Hungarians took over the huge Teichman plant, leaving the family access only to the residential wing that was attached to the corporate headquarters.

The Teichmans were fortunate to have a roof over their heads, but they were destitute and ravaged by hunger. The food shortages were horrendous, and conventional procurement was no longer an option. Shlomo Zalman had to resort to other means to acquire the bare necessities: selling the family's meager possessions on the black market for food, or bartering with commodities that could eventually be converted into potables.

And yet, these days would soon be remembered as the "good days" of the war. The full horror of what the Nazis had in mind was still unknown in Munkacs, but the writing on the wall was already legible. Hungarian youths assaulted Jewish neighbors with fury and unprecedented passion; violent anti-Semitism was becoming the norm.

At first, young Shlomo Zalman was unfamiliar with the term "Nazis" and was unclear about their insidious role in poisoning the society that surrounded him. All he knew of the vagaries of war was what he overheard from the men in the synagogue. They were all saying that the Russians were getting closer, and Shlomo Zalman understood by their tone that this was a good thing.

Barely a month after the Germans swooped down upon Munkacs in March of 1944, even the roof over the Teichmans' heads was no more. Their residence was impounded on the second day of Passover. They were given minutes to gather up a few necessities for new accommodations—which, of course, the Germans did not provide.

The family hastily moved in with an uncle who lived nearby, but this was not for long. Ghettoization was coming to Munkacs. Soon, a tiny section of the town—whose population was seventy percent Jewish—was converted into a crowded lockup.

Shlomo Zalman's family was forced to relocate and join a different uncle, who had a one-room apartment within the ghetto. Already cramped inside those tight quarters were the uncle, his wife, and their three children. They were all soon joined by yet another uncle with his family, who piled inside the same space, hardly bigger than a closet.

In mid-May the Germans announced that ghetto life was coming to an end; it was time to advance to the next phase. Pitifully unsuspecting, the Jews did not greet this news with remorse. Life was so unbearable in the ghetto that they could not fathom anything worse, and many were guardedly optimistic about their impending transfer.

The perverse genius of the Nazis consistently enabled the worst to, unthinkably, get worse. How could the innocent Jews of that community—famous for hospitality, magnanimity and warmth, graced by saints like Berish Teichman—ever imagine what awaited them?

All of Munkacsian Jewry were shunted into two makeshift ghettos. Those from Munkacs proper were sent to a brick factory at the southern side of the city called Sajovics.* The Jews from the towns and villages that surrounded Munkacs were by and large forced into a different brick factory, called Kallush, in the northern side of the city. Conditions were appallingly crowded, the heat was unbearable, thirst was overwhelming and the suffering, indescribable. Once it was determined that the region outside the ghetto was indeed *Judenrein*, boxcars began to arrive at the squalid factories to transport the human cargo.

GENERATIONS OF TEICHMANS, from septuagenarians to the youngest babe in arms, crowded together inside Kallush, one of Munkacs' miserable ghettos. And now, generations of helpless Teichmans would depart Munkacs, where their dynasty had been revered, on a final journey together—to Auschwitz.

For Shlomo Zalman, the worst aspect of that indescribable ride was the arrival. The cacophony assaulted his ears and penetrated his soul.

---

* Where Srulek Storch and his family were interred. See p. 164.

As babies wailed and prisoners sobbed, German officers screamed and cursed, and Jewish *kapos* thundered orders at their own people.

A mysterious man—whom Shlomo Zalman never saw again—appeared and asked how old he and his brother Shalom Nachman were.

"I am sixteen-and-a-half and my brother is three years younger."

The stranger did not like the boys' answer. "You are nineteen and eighteen!" he informed them in a grave and urgent tone, and then vanished. Shlomo Zalman never knew the man's name, nor would he ever be able to recall how he looked, but that single instruction saved his life.

Immediately, the brothers Teichman were shoved into the selection line. Did they understand that this was the moment that would determine who would live—for the time being—and who would die? By and large, Dr. Mengele's interview consisted of but one question. The boys replied as they had been instructed. With that, they were spared instant entrance to the gas chamber.

But the rest of the Teichman family was not so fortunate.

Seventy close family members—including the boys' mother, three brothers, a sister, grandparents, uncles, aunts and cousins—all perished in Auschwitz. They had not even uttered a final goodbye on the platform, innocently assuming that they were temporarily being separated into work details.

Having been sent "to the right," Shlomo Zalman and Shalom Nachman were led to a huge barracks where the new arrivals were ordered to strip naked and then file past a shower that consisted of a brief splash of cold water. They were then given uniforms and taken to another barracks filled with three-tier bunks.

Life for prisoners in this particular barracks consisted of roll call followed by roll call. The ear-splitting clang of bells governed their pitiful lives, commanding "*Vorwärts marsch, zurücktreten!* (Forward march, turn around!)" In between the endless tedium of the roll calls, the prisoners were ordered to perform cleanup duties in the vicinity of the barracks.

The Germans deliberately scattered scraps of paper and debris to ensure that their prisoners would never be left idle, and to provide additional justification for inflicting brutal punishment. If those on cleanup detail missed so much as a solitary hair, skulls were summarily cracked, ribs crushed and backs whipped.

It was there that Shlomo Zalman first learned—although he would be afforded ample opportunities for review—that a Nazi equipped with a weapon would never allow for a second chance.

The mind-numbing cycle of roll call/clean-up/roll call lasted about ten days. Then, once again, Shlomo Zalman, his brother, and the other surviving occupants of their barracks were herded into boxcars. They had no idea where they were going; in fact, on a certain level, they had no idea what they were leaving.

For the duration of their stay in Auschwitz, they had been isolated from the rest of the camp and hence unaware of the gas chambers and the crematorium that operated at full throttle in its Birkenau sub-camp.

THE TEICHMAN BOYS had found a way to stay together through the various roll calls and deportations: they held hands at all times. Clutching each other as they were herded into the boxcar, Shlomo Zalman and his younger brother saw that the remaining Teichmans were also on board. The boys were comforted by the presence of familiar faces, but there was no rejoicing. They recalled a time when their grandfather Berish's illustrious clan of Munkacsers could fill a grand shul or wedding hall to the rafters. Now five uncles and nine cousins, starved almost beyond recognition, were all that remained.

They were being sent to the Gęsiówka concentration camp, at the site of the former Warsaw ghetto. The barracks there were freshly constructed, yet without a single convenience. Several prisoners were assigned to the same cramped, splintery wooden shelf that was to pass as a bed.

Before entering their new quarters, the inmates were forced to go through a delousing procedure consisting of shaving off their hair (in most cases there was not much to remove, as the majority of the boys from Munkacs were Chassidim whose only hair was side-locks), a brief gush of cold water, and then the application of a caustic chemical. This was followed by the distribution of striped uniforms, and threadbare blankets.

One aspect of daily life in Warsaw was a notable improvement over Auschwitz: at this work assignment there was actually some food to be had. The meager rations could not assuage the prisoners' hunger, but it was better than the terrible starvation that had ground away at them in Auschwitz.

If the slave-laborers surpassed their assigned work-quotas, it was conceivable that their masters might even reward them with a few additional crumbs. They were also given one cigarette daily, used by most to barter for an additional morsel of bread. The most gifted wheelers and dealers managed to trade their cigarettes for as much as an extra quarter-slice.

The work assigned was backbreaking and mind-numbing—the sort of labor even the poorest man, in normal times, would refuse to undertake for pay.

Shlomo Zalman's contingent was forced to salvage the remains of the buildings that had been damaged or razed in the Warsaw Ghetto Uprising. They were to be transported and reused as construction materials elsewhere. Only the Germans, who were obsessed with their mastery over people and property, could be concerned about each and every chunk of concrete amidst the ruined heaps.

The workers had to remove one brick at a time from the caved-in buildings and turn them back into prime construction material. This entailed detaching the cement from the bricks with a hammer and chisel, sanding and smoothing the surfaces, and scouring the scorched blocks until they were pristine. Once the bricks were restored they were loaded onto pallets and placed aboard trucks.

This labor was done under the blistering heat of the summer sun and under the muzzles of German guns. The sweltering temperatures, the deteriorated physical condition of the prisoners, the mutilated and blackened condition of the bricks—these were immaterial to the Nazi overseers. Failure to meet the quota resulted in capital punishment. Indeed, whether provoked or not, the truncheon-toting guards felt duty-bound to unleash their weapons at regular intervals.

The task of recycling the ghetto's rubble into the German economy took several grueling weeks. By that point, with the Russian army on the advance, Warsaw was no longer an optimal place for the Germans to hold their chattel.

The orders arrived to vacate, and it was time for the slaves' next assignment.

With classic German perfidy, the Nazis inquired whether the prisoners would prefer to march or to travel by truck or train. Their replies were duly recorded and everyone was ordered out.

But it was all a trick. Those who preferred to be transported had betrayed themselves as too weak to work, and they were never heard from again.

The death march from Warsaw to Germany did not include any vehicular transportation, nor was it ever intended to. There would not be a drop of food or liquid for the duration of this wretched exodus.

What ghettos and camps and the vast array of other tortures could not accomplish, was now the inevitable. This was the Final Solution.

THE FIRST LEG, covering over seventy miles, was neither a march nor a walk; it was a mad sprint supervised by SS men eager to whip and determined to shoot. The intense heat parched everyone, a situation worsened by dust kicked up by six thousand beleaguered souls. The SS rode in cars and on bikes, alternating when their own troops guarding the retreat grew tired.

In the oppressive heat, day after torturous day, the prisoners were forced to march without respite. Never, for even a second, was one permitted to lag behind. At no time was there relief from the scorching summer sun, from the thirst, the hunger or the unrelenting terror from the trigger-happy guards. A phalanx of vicious dogs pounced on anyone who lost their footing.

A single step out of the column meant the end for the straggler. By the second day, certainly the third, those who could not keep pace had toppled, and lay by the side of the road, victims of the endless barrage of bullets, the canine's foaming jaws, or terminal exhaustion. Anyone who slowed down to aid a fellow marcher was doomed to die beside him.

Marching set off at dawn and ended at midnight. Only then were the prisoners allowed to lie down—in the open, completely unprotected from the elements.

Young Shlomo Zalman Teichman's compact, teenaged body had withered to the size of a young child's. He knew that to survive he had to block out the horror that surrounded him. He willed himself to suspend all thought, all emotion but one: to persist alongside his brother—from one day, one hour, one minute into the next.

The delirium of hunger and thirst, the steady rhythm of his dragging feet, the fiery brightness of the midday sun—all coalesced to turn him into a moving, mindless machine.

And yet. And yet.

The God of his Fathers, on this road to hell, watched over him.

For as Shlomo Zalman—by the looks of his shrunken frame, and the degraded status imposed by his captors—appeared to become less than human, he was, in reality, transcending the limits of human capability.

How?

As his younger brother Shalom Nachman began to stumble, Shlomo Zalman—always the "runt" of the Teichman clan—scooped up the boy's lanky, spent body. For the duration of the death march, in an act of brotherhood and physical prowess that surpasses mortal comprehension, he carried his brother on his back. Shlomo Zalman marched for both of them. He marched for all the Teichmans of Munkacs. For his grandfather Berish and for his mother and sisters, left behind in Auschwitz. For his father ... somewhere in the world, dead or alive— who knew? Shlomo Zalman knew nothing. Only to put one leg in front of the other and to not loosen his grip on the terrified youth whose spindly arms weakly encircled his neck.

Shalom Nachman was neither a grateful nor a compliant passenger. He had lost his will to live and saw no point in prolonging the inevitable end. He wanted it all to be finished, but his brother would not allow it. Shlomo Zalman's will to live was tenacious enough for the two of them.

After several days of nonstop marching, the pitiful caravan was ordered to stop by a riverbank. The location was calculated, and its outcome, chillingly predictable. Scores of the dehydrated prisoners staggered to the water and guzzled it.

These thirst-addled souls had committed a fatal error for which they were shot on the spot. In a short while the azure river was pink with their blood—and still many of their comrades could not hold themselves back from moistening their cracked lips.

Although they were as emaciated and parched as the rest, the Teichman brothers hung back from the river. Bearing his brother in his arms, Shlomo Zalman displayed the fierce discipline, calculating intelligence and family loyalty that he had learned at the feet of Berish Teichman. Nothing would deter him from his mission.

THE BLEAKEST DAY of the Jewish calendar, *Tisha b'Av*, fell during the death march. The date was calculated by the distinguished Klausenberger Rebbe, who had started out with the group in Auschwitz. (This saintly scholar would also later be remembered for somehow concealing a set of *tefillin* on his body—and for sharing his treasure with hundreds of devout prisoners in a towering act of defiance—through Auschwitz, Warsaw and much of the death march, until they were taken away when the prisoners were forced to strip.)

On the night of *Tisha b'Av*, the heat wave finally broke under a drenching summer shower. The downpour was a godsend to the prisoners, who gratefully sucked the rainwater from their tattered clothing. Even this brief alleviation of suffering was unacceptable to their captors, who were furious at nature's intervention. They would yet exploit the rain to their cynical expedience.

The Jews were forced to sleep that night in a drenched potato field. Many of them filled their stomachs with the small spuds, were unable to digest them, and died during the night.

Six thousand prisoners had set off on the death march. After one week, only six hundred of them clung to life. At that point, they were loaded onto boxcars bound for Dachau.

On that long ride to hell, another of the Teichman uncles drew his last breath.

ARRIVAL in Dachau possessed a familiar cadence. A shower upon arrival, the issuance of a new uniform, thundering commands, merciless beatings, roll call after roll call, interspersed with orders to scrub down the camp. This routine continued for only one week. They arrived at night and departed at night—standard operating procedure, so that the local populace would not observe the human cargo. For this reason, Shlomo Zalman's memories of the transfer remain shrouded in darkness.

The surviving members of the Teichman family were once again crammed into boxcars and this time sent to a slave labor camp in

Landsberg, Germany, west of Munich. They arrived in the early hours of the morning and were immediately put to work.

Under a hail of kicks and curses, the Germans ordered the prisoners to jump from the boxcars and run to a cargo train, where they were forced to unload bags of cement weighing 25 to 50 kilos. Many of the prisoners weighed less than the sacks that they were commanded to haul to a distant site. But their captors' rifles, whips, and a host of other brutish instruments of torture ensured that the job got done.

The Teichman boys and the others in their work detail toiled the entire night, transporting the cement with their last ounce of strength. Afterwards, they were introduced to their barracks, where they again fell exhausted upon the bare wooden shelves. Despite how the slaves were driven past all norms of endurance, sleep was at an absolute premium in Landsberg. Work shifts spanned day and night, and only brief naps were grudgingly permitted.

The prisoners were assigned to build an underground factory involving tasks so dangerous that they could only be performed by an expendable workforce. Shlomo Zalman's detail had to run wheelbarrows of wet cement at a feverish pace along a narrow walkway above a ten-story plunge. They commenced work in the darkness before dawn, and finished late at night.

Once Shlomo Zalman and his brother surpassed the life expectancy in Landsberg, they were transferred to a camp in Kaufering, Germany. The Teichman brothers had already beaten the odds many times over, but they knew this did not ensure they would live through the following day.

In Kaufering, the boys were assigned to remove and replace railroad ties that had been damaged by Allied bombings. Primarily, this entailed hauling sections of rail so heavy that Landsberg's sacks of cement seemed featherweight. The track work was extremely labor-intensive, and there was never the satisfaction of completion. Invariably, as soon as the tracks were laid, the Allies would bomb them again, and the backbreaking work would begin anew.

The inmates toiled not only on the local spur, but also on vast rail lines that fanned out throughout the region. Every day, hundreds of German residents from many cities and towns witnessed the prisoners slaving away on the tracks in freezing weather, their bare feet covered only with newspaper. Yet these same individuals were stricken with amnesia the instant the Allies conquered Germany. They never saw a thing, they claimed, and were shocked and appalled to learn of such flagrant abuse of human beings!

Although in Kaufering there was no risk of plunging to one's death from a building scaffold, survival was even less likely than it had been in Landsberg. The slaves were mercilessly driven nonstop. A worker daring to look off to the side, to glance upward, to appear unfocused, would pay with a public execution. Each day, several of these "criminals"—who might be one's father, brother, neighbor—were hanged with great fanfare, their corpses left to dangle for hours as a warning to others who might consider slackening in their service to the Führer.

But all the terror and grueling work paled next to the labor assigned on the eve of Yom Kippur and during the holy day itself. The Nazis were fully aware of the solemnity of this stringent fast, and that Jews believed that this day determined "who shall live and who shall die."

Throughout the Holocaust Kingdom, the SS and their cohorts saved their most diabolical tortures for this day; it was their favorite occasion to hold selections for the crematorium. The very concept of the "Day of Judgment" appealed to their imperious sense of domination.

It was their favorite holiday.

In preparation for the holiest of days, Kaufering's prisoners were subjected to labor more torturous than any they had ever experienced. By the time they finished work on the eve of Yom Kippur, they would have sacrificed a limb for a slice of bread. But care had already been taken to ensure that the miniscule rations were provided only after sundown, when the fast had already commenced.

Shlomo Zalman Teichman and his brother Shalom Nachman were among the not-insignificant number of prisoners, composed primarily of men from devout, religious backgrounds, who refused to violate the fast and allowed nothing, not even the few crumbs that were set before them, to pass their lips. The seventeen- and fourteen-year-old were prepared to die to sanctify the sacred law of the Almighty. Ironically, this stalwart refusal to consume life-saving morsels actually fueled their determination to persevere.

Yom Kippur day was a headlong plunge into the abyss. Work was stopped, and the day devoted exclusively to unmitigated torture. The *Muselmänner*, the walking skeletons who had previously been ordered to transport steel ties and sections of track, were now forced to carry literally tons of lumber—entire trees—quickly and without respite.

FOR MONTHS, under the most deplorable conditions, the Teichman brothers continued to build the German railways. Their slave labor finally ended in April 1945, when the Germans were forced to retreat, marking the final phase of the war.

Never, of course, would the Nazis admit the real reason that they were swiftly abandoning Kaufering. Instead, they announced that it was time to move on to a new work assignment and again offered the prisoners their choice of transportation. As the shrunken survivors had been subjected to this ruse before, they knew the offer was hollow. Some feared that leaving the camp would bring a surer death, and they refused to go; others, who had not an ounce of strength left, were simply unable to depart.

Shlomo Zalman continued to live by his sharp instincts. He and Shalom Nachman decided not to stay behind. For the very first time, it was bright daylight when the brothers staggered into the departing boxcar—some adaptations had to be made for Germany's imminent defeat. Yet as before, they had no idea of their destination. All they knew was that, once again, the ride was intended to be one-way.

The barracks that had housed the prisoners of Kaufering were doused with gasoline and set on fire. Inside them, the inmates who had chosen to remain also went up in flames.

The brothers Teichman had long since surpassed the law of averages. But that same law propelled them inexorably closer to being engulfed by the Final Solution.

Nearly a thousand prisoners from three labors camps in the Landsberg and Kaufering region crowded into the chain of boxcars. The Teichman clan now numbered only six—the two brothers plus three of their cousins, and one surviving uncle. After several hours en route, the prisoners were jolted by an awful shudder, and the transport screeched to a halt. Smoke billowed through the train and screams echoed through the cars. The train's locomotive had been squarely hit by an Allied bomber.

What happened next stunned and bewildered the dazed prisoners: The Germans—their captors—fled the train en masse.

Virtually delirious from starvation, exhaustion, torture and disease, the prisoners were unaware that they had been evacuated from their labor camps because Germany was in the throes of defeat. They had been uprooted and crammed into boxcars so many times before, that they did not detect anything different about the current transfer.

At first they were confounded by the Nazis' rapid escape from the train. Who but the Germans, they wondered, would bomb a train filled with Jews? On the other hand, why would they risk destroying their own transportation system in the process?

Questions raced through the acrid air of the train. High anxiety kept them frozen in place until it suddenly occurred to them that the most dangerous place for them to be was aboard the rail cars. If a year under German domination had taught them anything, it was that trains transported people to their death. They were all veterans of numerous death centers, and their current accommodations were no different than their conveyance to the extermination camps. Fortunately, exiting was not a problem. The doors were not bolted, since armed SS men had been positioned between all the cars.

In a mass panic, the prisoners leapt off the rail cars in both directions. This was a potentially fatal error, because the track bordered a steep embankment. Many, their frail bodies unable to withstand the impact, plunged to instant death. Those who survived the jump began to run as fast as their matchstick legs could carry them. They had no idea which way to go and fanned out in all directions.

They ran, but did not get very far.

During this last gasp of the war, every living prisoner was stark evidence of the Nazis' crimes against humanity—evidence that the Germans were determined to do away with. And precious little time remained to finish the job.

Once the Germans were sure that the bombing was over, they returned with their dogs and went about collecting their chattel, who were too weak to have gone far. By unhappy coincidence, there were German army camps in the vicinity, which could serve as holding pens.

One of the Teichman cousins become separated from the others at the time of the locomotive bombing and ended up in a different lock-up from the rest of the family. He believed that all of his cousins had perished.

Four cousins and their uncle were thrown into a tin hut in another camp. They were sure that their missing cousin had perished; they also had no doubt that they themselves had reached the end of the road.

They spent the rest of the day and the entire night trapped in the shack, without a morsel of food.

Throughout the night, rumors coursed furiously through the hut. The more optimistic inmates became war strategists overnight. Piecing together what they knew of the events of the war prior to the Nazi invasion of Hungary in 1944, and what they had witnessed that day, they predicted that the Russians already stood at the gates of the camp. Some reports suggested that the Germans planned to systematically slaughter everyone in the morning; others averred that they wouldn't wait that long. Every five minutes the stories changed, and it was impossible to trace where or how the rumors got started.

The whispers, the theories, the drama, the excruciating tension of that night contrasted sharply with the eerie quiet of the next morning. The prisoners awoke to utter silence. No sound was heard, and no German was spotted. The guard towers were abandoned. No one knew what to do. Was it liberation or was it a trap?

One brave individual finally had the courage to investigate their collective fate. He gingerly crept outside the hut, while the rest, wedged tightly inside, held their breath. Several long moments passed without the inevitable explosion of gunfire. It felt like an eternity since the man had committed the unthinkable: "moving without permission."

Finally the scout called out that the coast was clear: The Germans had deserted the camp.

With a burst of energy that belied their desperate condition, the survivors streamed outside. There stood several horse-drawn wagons loaded with freshly baked bread from the local bakery. Desperately, everyone grabbed a chunk of bread, and fled the camp, fearing the imminent return of the SS guards.

The Teichman clan followed the others at first. But after they exited the camp and came upon a field of tall grass and high bushes, they reassessed their situation. They had no idea where to run and were reluctant to deplete more energy through aimless wandering. The cover provided by the foliage seemed to be adequate protection for the time being.

From the field they could hear the rumble of military trucks and tanks along a nearby highway. It was impossible for them to tell if the tanks were Russian, American or German. All they knew was that they were precariously close to a war zone, for the continuous echo of exploding mortar and shells reverberated through the air.

The Teichmans feared they would once again be tracked by dogs, but the day passed without incident. Later, under a blackened sky, they began inching their way toward a farmhouse that was faintly visible across the field.

They realized they were risking their lives by trespassing on premises that undoubtedly belonged to the enemy, but what choice did they have? They hovered on the brink of starvation. And by nightfall, they reasoned, the Germans would surely regroup, and the dogs would easily locate the ex-prisoners in the open field.

Adjacent to the farmhouse, the family spotted a barn. They prayed that it would not be inhabited, and might even contain something to eat. Thankfully, the door was unlocked, but the family members were too frightened to hunt for food. Instead, they huddled in a corner and rested their weary bodies.

Several hours later, the farmer entered his barn, turned on the light, and five Jewish hearts stopped beating.

The property owner had never witnessed such abject terror. He quickly invited the intruders inside, gave them food from his larder, the opportunity to bathe, and some clean clothes to wear. Were his motives truly altruistic, or was he simply attempting to save his skin, when the days to come would surely be a time of reckoning and settling scores by the Allies?

The Teichmans were too spent to ponder the answer. That night, they relived a sensation almost totally forgotten: they slept on mattresses, the six of them luxuriously sprawled out in three beds!

WHAT DREAMS would come that night, following years of deprivation and torture? When morning broke, Shlomo Zalman found himself in the vortex of a frightfully vivid nightmare. Barely millimeters away from his face hovered a gleaming bayonet, pointed by a soldier in battle fatigues whose skin was as black as if he had been burned in an oven. All of Shlomo Zalman's brushes with death paled next to the sudden paroxysm of fear that now gripped his heart.

Until that point he could not have imagined anything more frightening than an SS trooper with a skull-and-crossbones emblazoned on his uniform. Yet the image of this black face looming over him forced his every nerve to leap and shudder.

The soldier in the nightmare, he looks so ... real!

And when the screams of his relatives reached a crescendo around him, Shlomo Zalman realized that he *was* real.

Neither Shlomo Zalman nor any other member of his family had ever seen a black person before, and had no way of knowing that this soldier was an American. The GI was also unable to determine who they were, until he spotted the filthy, striped prison garb adjacent to the bed. The soldier quickly withdrew his rifle, and Shlomo Zalman resumed breathing.

The infantryman was joined by two of his comrades-in-arms, and they showered candies and canned goods upon Shlomo Zalman and his family. Wisely, the Teichmans did not eat too much of what was offered; had they indulged just a bit more they might well have died as so many other unsuspecting, undernourished souls did after being fed more than their heart and circulation could tolerate by their well-meaning liberators.

AFTER PARTING WITH THEIR RATIONS, the soldiers themselves departed. But first they struggled to communicate to the bewildered and exhausted Teichman family that more Americans would shortly be arriving in the village to look after them; and that the war was finally over. And so it was.

The Teichmans did not move from the farmer's home—and this was in their host's best interest. Elsewhere in the village, the Americans were arresting collaborators and suspects at a lightning clip.

Within days, Shlomo Zalman—weighing 41 pounds—was admitted to a civilian hospital under American administration. For weeks he barely clung to life, eating a severely restricted diet designed to rebuild his shriveled digestive system and weakened organs. The Jewish patients were cautioned not to eat anything but the food served by the hospital staff, and those who were unable to resist paid the ultimate price.

Shlomo Zalman had been rescued not a day too soon. After a full month of hospital care he was still unable to stand on his feet. As his weight steadily increased, strength began to slowly return to his ravaged limbs.

He was seventeen-and-a-half years old, 5'2" tall, and after six weeks of dedicated nursing care, weighed almost 60 pounds.

He had his whole life ahead of him.

EPILOGUE

After discharge from the hospital, Shlomo Zalman and Shalom Nachman traveled to Budapest in search of their father.

When they arrived, the first place they looked for him was the last place they had seen him, at the home of his friend. When this failed, they turned to the locales where Jews typically congregated, in the hope that someone might have a clue as to Shmuel Teichman's whereabouts. For several agonizing days there was no information, until one man suggested that they contact a certain shopkeeper who had been friendly with their father. "If your father is alive, he will know where to find him."

Just a few days earlier, Shmuel Teichman had been informed that the last of his beloved children, Shlomo Zalman and Shalom Nachman, were dead. His already shattered spirit plunged into a consummate darkness from which he was sure he would never emerge.

The boys entered the shop they had been directed to.

A moment later, their father walked in after them.

Lost in his grief, Shmuel took no note of the store's other patrons. But a loud shriek caused him to raise his eyes from the floor.

"*TATEEE!*" yelled Shlomo Zalman. There were no other words, at first, as father and sons broke into a passionate embrace. Finally, Shmuel, with tears pouring from his eyes, broke the silence. "*Baruch Mechayeh Hameisim!*" he intoned in a trembling voice. "Blessed be He who raises the dead…" It was the blessing recited upon being reunited with one neither seen nor heard from in more than a year. Never was this blessing recited as literally and fervently.

Generations of Teichmans—a dynasty—had been obliterated. But these two boys had been raised from the dead.

THE THREE departed for the town of Satmar, as their father had already set up a little business for himself there. From there they returned to Germany, to the large Zeilsheim DP camp in Frankfurt am Main— the very camp visited by First Lady Eleanor Roosevelt and David Ben-Gurion. While there, the Teichmans were among those who were instrumental in setting up a yeshiva in the DP camp.

In early June 1945, they noticed an item in a newspaper for displaced persons, stating that children with relatives in the United States were now eligible to apply for immigration. As the Teichman boys fell into this category, Shalom Nachman went to Frankfurt to fill out the necessary papers.

A shipload of two hundred orphans was to be sponsored by none other than the former First Lady of the United States, Eleanor Roosevelt, and the brothers Teichman were included in this group.

No sooner had they set sail that the boys were told that the captain wished to see them. Timidly, they made their way to his quarters.

The captain, gripping a telegram in his hand, said, "I have information that you lied in saying that you have no parents, for I see here that your father is alive!"

The brothers broke out in tears—sincere, mournful tears—and embraced each other. This was simply too much for them. They were finally on the boat to a new future only to have it aborted before the journey even started!

The captain mistakenly believed that the boys were crying because they had just learned that their father was alive! He summarily instructed his first mate to rip up the telegram. "I shall not punish young boys just because their father is alive!" the captain declared. "Welcome aboard."

On Saturday, July 26, 1946, the S.S. Perch docked in New York harbor. Along with the two hundred youngsters, there were several thousand soldiers aboard. Each and every passenger disembarked ... except for the Teichman boys, who refused to step off the ship, since it would be a violation of the Sabbath. No one could coax them, and Saturday night, when they finally headed down the gangplank, there were dozens of reporters and photographers to record for posterity the saga of the determined young refugees who, as their first official act on American soil, had refused to defile the Jewish Sabbath.

This extraordinary act thrust the Teichman brothers immediately into the limelight, and every yeshiva in New York (although, in fact, there were only a few at that time) attempted to woo them. Yeshiva Torah Vodaath in Brooklyn was the winner.

Three years later, Shmuel Teichman joined his sons in America. He remarried and settled in California.

Shalom Nachman (now known as "Steve") married and has three children and more than a dozen grandchildren. He works with his older brother at Teichman Enterprises, a Los Angeles-based company that manufactures store fixtures. From 1951 to 1953, Shlomo Zalman (now known as "Sol") served in the United States Army and was sent to fight in the Korean War, but ended up in Europe, where he served as an English school teacher. He married his Israeli-born wife, Ruth, in 1959. They are the parents of one daughter who lives in New York, and two sons who work side-by-side with their father and uncle.

Sol and Ruth have been blessed with nine grandchildren—four boys and five girls—and three great-grandchildren.

With quiet strength and modesty, Sol Teichman continues to preside over his close-knit family, his successful business, and a constellation of philanthropic pursuits. His childhood was cruelly cut short by war and displacement, but its lessons were not. "L'dor va'dor," from generation to generation, the largesse of Berish Teichman and the Torah values of Munkacs live on, passed along by a wide-eyed boy who sat beneath the dining-room table, eagerly drinking in the lessons of a world before it was destroyed.

Glossary

The following glossary provides a partial explanation of some of the foreign words and phrases used in this book. The spelling, tense, and explanations reflect the way the specific word is used in *Heroic Children*. Often, there are alternate spellings and meanings for the words. Foreign words and phrases which are immediately followed by a translation in the text or explanatory footnote are not included in this section. As the majority of the translated words are in Hebrew, their language of origin is not indicated.

Aliyah: lit. ascent; immigration to the Land of Israel.

baal teshuvah: penitent who has returned to religious observance.

beis midrash: a house of study used for both Torah study and prayer.

Bereishis: The first book of the Torah. Its name is derived from its first word, *bereishis*, lit., in the beginning.

Chassid, Chassidus, Chassidic, Chassidim: devout follower(s) of a REBBE.

Chazan: cantor; the leader of public prayer.

cheder: (Yid.) a religious primary school for boys.

cholent: (Yid.) traditional stew prepared on Friday afternoon and kept hot until the midday SHABBOS meal.

chuppah: marriage canopy.

groshen: (Yid.) smallest coin in Polish currency.

halachic responsa: rulings in Jewish law.

Judenrein: (Ger.) free of Jews.

Kaddish: the mourner's prayer.

kashruth: Jewish dietary law.

kittel: white cloak that is a burial shroud, donned by men on various festivals according to custom.

Kol Nidrei: Solemn prayer ushering in the Yom Kippur service.

Kristallnacht: (Ger.) night of broken glass, night between Nov. 9th and Nov. 10th, 1938, when German hoards rampaged throughout Germany wounding and murdering Jews, destroying their property and setting the synagogues ablaze.

kugel: (Yid.) a baked pudding of potatoes or noodles.

matzoh: unleavened bread required to be eaten on Passover.

Mincha: the afternoon prayer service.

mitzvah, *mitzvoth*: lit., commandments; good deeds.

Muselmann: (as defined by Primo Levi) non-men who march and labor in silence, the divine spark dead within them, already too empty really to suffer. One hesitates to call them living; one hesitates to call their death, death.

Mussar Movement: An attempt to create an ethical rebirth of moral sensitivity among eastern European Jewry.

payos: side curls that fulfill a religious requirement.

Rav: Rabbi.

Reb: (Yid.) title of honor placed before the name of a God-fearing adult male.

rebbe (teacher): a Talmud instructor.

Rebbe: (Chassidish Rebbe) a Chassidic leader.

Rebbetzin: (Yid.) the wife of a rabbi.

Seder: the order of the Passover night ceremony recalling the Exodus from Egypt and the liberation from bondage; a learning session.

Shabbos: Sabbath.

shofar: ram's horn, used as an integral part of the prayer service on Rosh Hashana.

Shehecheyanu: blessing recited primarily at festive occasions; literally means "Who has kept us alive."

shochet: (Yid.) a ritual slaughterer.

shtreimel: (Yid.) decorative fur or fur-trimmed hat worn by male Chassidim on Sabbath and festivals.

shul: (Yid.) a synagogue.

Sonderkommandos: (Ger.) lit., Special Commando; prisoners who removed the corpses from the gas chambers into the ovens.

Sukkah: temporary dwelling which is a central requirement of the holiday of SUKKOS.

Sukkos: autumn holiday held five days after Yom Kippur, during which time one dwells in a SUKKAH.

talleisim: (sing. *tallis*) four-cornered prayer shawl with fringes at each corner worn by men during morning prayers.

Tateh, Tatee: (Yid) father, Daddy.

tefillin: black leather boxes containing verses from the Torah which are bound to the arm and head of a man during morning prayers.

Tisha b'Av: the ninth day of the month of Av; the fast day commemorating the destruction of the First and Second Temples.

Umschlagplatz: (Ger.) lit., collection point or reloading place, location where the Jews were gathered from the ghetto for deportation to extermination camps.

Verboten: (Ger.) forbidden.

Viduy: confessional prayer.

Vilna Gaon: (1720–1797) the most outstanding Rabbinic authority in the last three centuries.

Vilner: (Yid.) one from Vilna.

Werhrmacht: Nazi Germany's armed forces.

yeshiva, *yeshivos*: academy of Torah study.

Yiddeneh: (Yid.) Jewish woman.

yingeleh: (Yid.) little boy.

Yom Kippur: Day of Atonement, the holiest day of the Jewish year.

zayde: (Yid.) grandfather.

Bibliography

Dawidowicz, Lucy S. *The War Against the Jews 1933-1945*. New York: Holt, Rinehart, and Winston, 1975.

Eliach, Yaffa. *There was Once a World: A 900-Year Chronicle of the Shtetl of Eishyshok*. New York: Little Brown, 1998.

Frankl, Viktor E. *Man's Search For Meaning*. Boston: Beacon Press, 2006.

Gilbert, Martin. *The Holocaust, A History of the Jews of Europe During the Second World War*. New York: Henry Holt and Company, 1985.

Hilberg, Raul. *The Destruction of the European Jews*. New Have: Yale University Press, 2003.

Lichtenstein, Ruth. *Witness to History*. New York: Project Witness, 2009.

Lifton, Betty Jean. *The King of Children: The Life and Death of Janusz Korczak*. St. Martin's Griffin edition, 1995.

Perle, Yoshue. *Khurbn Varshe (The Destruction of Warsaw)*.

Sharon, Albert M. *Walking to Valdieri*. New York: MS Finan Inc, 2003.

Acknowledgments

I am a baby-boomer. Mine may be the last generation to be intimately acquainted with Holocaust survivors. Throughout my youth it was not uncommon for me to see numbers branded on forearms. I wonder how many my children have seen And will my grandchildren see any at all?

Growing up, I was deeply affected by the sobs emanating from synagogue sanctuaries during holiday recitations of the *Yizkor* memorial service. Loud moans of inconsolable mourning burst forth along with the names of lost parents, grandparents, siblings, spouses, aunts, uncles, and, yes, children—breaking the hearts of all who were spared. (This would probably be the appropriate place for me to acknowledge my paternal grandparents, Batsheva and Baruch Teller of blessed memory, two who lost their lives among the Six Million.)

Wherever we went, in those days, there they were: the survivors with their branded forearms and thick European accents. I recall feeling chagrined, on my first day in yeshiva boarding-school, that my European-born father—himself a truly "heroic child"—had managed to lose the accent that would identify him as one. Given my personal connection, it was only natural that I developed a powerful acquisitiveness regarding the Holocaust, an interest that was heightened by the rallying cry of the day, popularized by Rabbi Meir Kahane, "Never Again!" Ultimately, I guess all of this led me to write *Heroic Children*.

Typically when preparing a book's Acknowledgments, I endeavor, nay relish, thanking not only the people who aided me with the particular volume that is going to press, but also the many other individuals and organizations that steadfastly support my work overall. On this occasion, however, given the sensitivity and solemnity of its subject matter, I will confine my thank-yous to those who had a hand in the painstaking development of this project.

Vivien Orbach-Smith—herself the daughter of an Auschwitz survivor and a refugee from Nazi Germany—edited the book with expertise and supreme sensitivity; Adina Heavenrich copy-edited with the very same qualities. Typesetter Elcya Weiss contributed far more than is implied by this job title. Jeremy Staiman instinctively understood that I sought a cover worthy of the subject matter; and Akiva Bomzer's proofreading prowess was key, as always.

The notable backstory in regard to the book's cover also bears acknowledgment. Highlighting a single individual in a photo of such delicacy, to my mind, would require permission—if not from a legal standpoint, then morally. But how could I locate a little boy photographed upon the liberation of Auschwitz in January, 1945? Was he still among the living? Even the august United States Holocaust Memorial Museum (USHMM), which holds the copyright to the photo, had no information as to his whereabouts. But just *one* online article and *one* phone call later, I was speaking with octogenarian Gabor Hirsch in Switzerland, who graciously awarded me his permission. I took the stunning ease of this highly improbable connection as a positive omen for this book.

My thanks to Reb Moshe Rappoport of Zürich for being the connector, and endless gratitude to Judge Chaya Friedman, board member of the USHMM, for kindheartedly and most generously wielding her considerable influence. Thank you, too, to Mrs. Yael Etziony for weighing in; as the saying goes, "once a staff member, always..."

Major gratitude to my very able assistant, Mrs. Shira Feldman, for the stalwart administrative help reflected in this undertaking. Profound thanks to Harvey and Gloria Kaylie for contributing initial seed money for this book. Reb Avraham Pinchos Berkowitz, whose poignant Foreword uplifts this volume, has generously assisted me again on yet another project so that *Heroic Children*—after a fourteen-year gestation—could finally see the light of day.

Finally, my wife, Aidel, surely merits grateful inclusion (as always), as this deeply-felt project has taken up a significant portion of my life.

I have been affiliated with Yad Vashem—the World Center for Holocaust Research, for thirty years and I thank Rav Moshe Shapiro for insisting (not merely suggesting) that this avenue be pursued. The resources of this world-class archive were essential for researching and composing *Heroic Children*. The first story in the book, and most deliberately so, is that of Michael Thaler. Dr. Thaler, aside from being a giant in the world of medicine, is a scholar with an encyclopedic knowledge of the Holocaust, an expert in a league of his own. He graciously read the entire manuscript, offering his erudite critique. Aaron Breitbart, Senior Researcher at the Simon Wiesenthal Center, also reviewed the manuscript. Before going to press, the esteemed historian Professor Gideon Greif, former Publications Editor and Senior Researcher at Yad Vashem, read and contemplated every word of the book to ensure that accuracy was never compromised. We all mourn the passing this year of Sir Martin Gilbert; he was very enthused about this book and the contribution that it would make, and I am saddened that I will not have the honor of presenting him with a copy.

I also thank: Linda Zulberg for directing me to Cecilia Boruchowitz; Dr. Henry Romberg for making me aware of Albert Sharon's still-unpublished memoir and for the assistance provided by his wife, Lynn (who turned out to be an old family friend); Vivian Sternbuch, for encouraging me to write about her esteemed mother-in-law, Gutta; the young men seated my table at the Kahn-Brodsky wedding, for telling me about Rabbi Isser Fisher; Sara Tussie, for facilitating my meeting with Dolly Bestandig (and so much more!); Tzippy Paneth, for alerting me to the story of Esther Biegelman—just some among the many who offered invaluable information and guidance. And if it wasn't Rabbi Abraham Cooper's idea that I meet Sol Teichman—who has been such a benevolent blessing to me and to so many others—I would still like to attribute this inspired act to Abe.

Although there is no dearth of Holocaust literature, there are virtually no books that shed light upon the harrowing lives of *children*, particularly through stories told in their own voices. Through the vivid, historically accurate accounts provided in *Heroic Children*, the reader is given a rare glimpse into the daily lives of those upon whom the darkness fell. The book's protagonists represent every stripe of Jewish victim, stemming from all over of Europe and from every religious and socioeconomic background.

My hope for *Heroic Children* is that it will become part of mainstream Holocaust curricula. *The Diary of Anne Frank* (the book most commonly used in middle- and high-school settings), while of inestimable value, is not entirely reflective of what the majority of Jewish children endured during the Holocaust: torture and starvation in camps or ghettos, frequently while separated from their parents. Anne recorded a period during which she had a roof over her head and a modicum of food, and was together with her family. Had she survived Bergen-Belsen, which she never got a chance to write about, I believe that *Heroic Children* is the book that she would have penned.

Denied the opportunity to grow up and breathe the air of freedom, the one-and-a-half million Jewish children who perished during the Holocaust did not get a chance to tell their stories to the world. I thank the Lord for the privilege of being a humble spokesman for a small remnant who *did*.

Isru Chag Hashavuos 5775
May 25, 2015
Jerusalem

Index

A

Adamowicz, Jan 249–258
Aktion 40–41, 46, 297, 306
Alter, Rivka 197, 209
    See also Rappaport, Rivka Alter
American liberation force 188
amicha 130
anti-Jewish
    —measures 160
    —legislation 206
anti-Semitism 30, 116, 194, 196,
    206–207, 315
Appell 170, 172, 179
    See also roll call
Appellplatz 170, 301
Armia Krajowa (AK) 257–259
Auschwitz-Birkenau 162, 170–171,
    185, 275–277, 279–280, 307,
    318
    Oświęcim 162

B

Bais Yaakov 196, 198–200, 208,
    286
Belgium 106
Belzec 290, 306
Belzer Rebbe 297, 313

See also Chassidic Jewry,
    Chassidim
Belz, Rabbi Shalom of 298
Ben-Gurion, David 331
Bergen-Belsen 280–282, 301,
    305–307
Biegun, Chanke Grossfield 209
    See also Grossfield, Chanke
Biegun, Rabbi Yosef 197
Big Lie xxvii, xxviii
Birkenau 276, 277, 318
    See also Auschwitz-Birkenau
Bnos 200
Bochnia 297, 306
    —ghetto 294
Bon, André 119
Borsotto, Father Antonio 141, 156
boxcars 167, 318
    See also cattle cars
British 196
Brussels 105
Brzeżany 29
    —ghetto 29, 30, 35, 39, 46,
    48–50, 55
Budapest 300
Bundist 203
bunkers 40, 237, 245
Byelorussia 272, 274

C

Cassorla, Rabbi 119, 126
Castagnede du Salat 108
cattle cars 165
Chafetz Chaim 230, 239, 241, 243, 245
Chassidic Jewry, Chassidim 196, 203
—courts 197
—masters 197
See also Belzer Rebbe; Gerrer Chassidim; Gerrer Rebbe
Chavazelet School 195–196
Chuster Rav 182, 189, 192
Coarraze 115, 116
crematoria 171
Czechoslovakia 159, 311

D

Dachau 322
Darlan, Admiral 118
Dawidowicz, Lucy 162
Day of Judgment 324
See also Yom Kippur
death march 185, 320
deception xxvi, xxvii, 161–162, 221, 236
guile xxvi, xxvii, 162, 165
fraud xxvi
innocence, Jewish 162, 165
lies, Nazis' 187
mental cruelty 171
naïveté 161
rumors 165
ruse 236
satanic ruse 246
subterfuge xxvi

upbeat missives 217
verbal camouflage xxvi
defiance 184
See also resistance
defiant acts of religious fidelity 182
See also resistance
deportation 217, 220, 297
Der Stürmer See Stürmer, Der
desperation, Jewish 165
Dim, Chazan (Cantor) 135, 138
displaced persons 332
Displaced Persons Act 156
Dolchstoss xxvii
Dvinsk 57, 58, 60, 64
—ghetto 65

E

Ebensee 185, 186, 187, 188
edicts of isolation 60
Eichmann, Adolf 161, 163, 306
Einsatzgruppen 249
Eishyshok 243, 249, 257, 259, 260
Eliach, Yaffa 243–245, 248, 259
See also Sonenson, Yaffa
extermination camps xxvii, 276

F

Final Solution xxiv, xxv, 39, 162, 219, 226, 271, 274, 278, 290, 306, 320, 325
Fonseca 108
Frankel, Mrs. 221–223, 227
Frankfurt am Main 331
Frank, Hans 202
Frankl, Viktor 174
freedom fighters 241

G

Gaon of Vilna *see* Vilna Gaon
gas chambers xxvii
Geffen, Berel 202
Gens, Jacob 78, 79
  See also Vilna ghetto
German invasion
  —of Nice 136
  —of Russia 59
  —of Soviet Union 30
Gerrer Chassidim 197, 199, 201
  —Rebbe 197
  See also Chassidic Jewry,
    Chassidim
Gestapo 51, 90, 201–202, 211–
  212, 220, 232–233, 244–245,
  249
ghetto xxvii, 34, 36–37, 41, 77–78,
  164–165, 203, 217, 234–235,
  241–243, 248, 271–272, 316
  —"life" 164
  —Symphony Orchestra 80
Ghettoization 316
  See also specific place names
Gilbert, Sir Martin 161, 220
Giordano, Usebio and Anna 141,
  143–145
Goldszmit, Henryk 205
  See also Korszak, Dr. Janusz
Granat, Shlomo 133
gray-striped uniform 170
Great Provocation, The 234
  Greenbaum, Chaplain Avraham
  282
Greenwald, Rabbi Shialah 182, 189
Grenoble 133
Grossfield, Chanke 197
  See also Biegun, Chanke
    Grossfield; Biegun, Rabbi Yosef

Grynszpan, Zindel 206
guile, German 162, 165
  See also deception
Gunskirchen 172
Gustman, Rabbi Yisroel Zev 232
gymnasia 196

H

harboring Jews 257
High Holidays 112
Himmler, Heinrich 306
Hirsch, Rabbi Samson Raphael
  266, 269
humiliation 171
Hungary 159, 300
hunger 173

I

Imrei Emmes 197
incineration pits 171
innocence, Jewish 162, 165
insurrection 241
  See also resistance
Italian Occupation 133
Italian Occupation Forces 126

J

Jewish Brigade 106, 156, 259, 282
Jewish Council 34
Jewish police force 214
Joint Distribution Committee 210
Judenrat 34–35, 42–43, 50, 78, 204,
  213, 236, 246
Judenrein 242, 316

K

Kallush 164, 316

Kamionka 45–46, 50
Kanada Kommando 166–170
kashruth 150
    See also kosher
Kastner, Rudolf 306
Kastner train 306
Kaufering 323, 325
kehillah 204
kinderheim 309
Klausenberger Rebbe 322
Kolbe, Margaret 84–87
Korczak, Dr. Janusz 205–209,
    215–217
    See also Goldszmit, Henryk
kosher 115, 156, 184, 218, 250
    See also kashruth
Kovno 60
    —ghetto 274
Krakow 197, 297, 306
Kristallnacht 206
Kruminsh, Paul 58, 65–68, 71, 73

L

Lamayou 113–115
Landau, Eliezar 300
Landsberg 323, 325
Latin American passports 211, 219,
    300–301
    See also Paraguayan passport
Latvia 59–60
Laval, Pierre 116
letters and postcards 217
liberation 281, 187
    liberators 189
lice 173
lies, Nazis' 187
    See also deception
Lithuania 59–60

Lublin 199
Lvov 29

M

Marxist ideologies 196
Mauthausen 171
Melk 172, 175, 180, 182, 184, 186
mental cruelty 171
Mexico City 286
Minchas Elozar (Rabbi Chaim
    Elozar Shapiro) 313
Minsk 274
    —ghetto 274
Munkacs 159–163, 311, 314
    —ghetto 161
Muselmann 177
    Muselmänner 325
Mussolini 136

n

naïveté 161
Nay 117
Nazi, Nazis x, xii, xv–xviii, xx, xxii–
    xxviii, 33, 35 and throughout the
    book
    Nazism xxviii
New Jewish Ramp 277
    See also Auschwitz-Birkenau
New York 332
Nice, German invasion of 136

O

Ohr Somayach 62, 65
Old Jewish Ramp 277
    See also Auschwitz-Birkenau
Operation Barbarossa 30
    See also Soviet Union

Orlean, Rabbi Yehuda Leib
197–198
Oświęcim 162
See also Auschwitz-Birkenau

P

Palestine 106, 206, 259
Paraguayan 212, 215
—passport 211–212, 215
See also Latin American passports
Paris 107
Passover 152, 163, 183
Pawiak 213, 217–219
—prison 207, 212–213, 215, 223
Pawlowich, Leon 67, 73
persons, displaced 332
Pétain, Marshal 118
Pilsudski, Marshal Josef 206
Podhoryan and Munkacs 164
pogrom 31
Poland 29, 314
—German invasion of 287
—Jews of 200
policemen, Jewish 43
Ponar 79, 234–236, 271
poverty 195–196
Pyrenees 109

R

Radin 239–242, 245, 247, 249
—ghetto 241, 247
Rappaport, Rivka Alter 219, 222
See also Alter, Rivka
Rath, Ernst Vom 206
Red Cross 218
relocation xxvi, 41
resettlement xxvi, 217

resistance 35, 173, 182, 184
defiance 184
defiant acts of religious fidelity
182
insurrection 241
revolt 244
Underground 71, 122, 126–127
uprising 212
Riga 58, 59, 60
Rokeach, Rabbi Aharon 287, 297
See also Sar Shalom
roll call 170, 172, 279, 317
See also Appell
Rome, liberation 154, 156
Roosevelt, Eleanor 331–332
Rosen, Rabbi Yosef 62
Rosh Hashana 112, 210
Rottenberg, Rabbi Mordechai and
Rebbetzin 200, 222, 224
rumors 165
See also deception
ruse 236
See also deception
Russia, German invasion of 59
Rutkauskus 80, 81

S

Sabbath tables 196
See also Shabbos
Sajovics 164, 316
Salanter, Rabbi Yisrael 231
Salvation Army 131
Sar Shalom 298
See also Rokeach, Rabbi Aharon
satanic ruse 246
See also deception
Satmar Rebbe 307
Schenirer, Sarah 196–197, 200, 209

Schwartzbard 221, 225, 227, 228
Seidman, Dr. Hillel 204, 208, 213,
  214, 222, 226–228
Shabbos 200
  Sabbath tables 196
Shapiro, Rabbi Chaim Elozar
  (*Minchas Elozar*) 313
shtetl 29
Slabodka Yeshiva 230
Sonderbehandlung 171
Sonenson, Yaffa 244
  See also Eliach, Yaffa
Soviet Union, German invasion of 30
  See also Operation Barbarossa
Spain 109
SS 33–36, 40, 49–50, 68, 72, 161,
  164–165, 168, 176, 179, 187,
  201, 222, 238, 249, 320, 326
Star of David 212
  See also yellow star
Sternbuch, Eli 211, 228
Sternbuch, Recha and Yitzchak 210,
  219, 222
St. Martin Vesubie 134
Stoler, Meir 244
Stopnitz 199, 200
Stürmer, Der 67
subterfuge xxvi
  See also deception
Sukkos 181
Switzerland 307

T

Tarnopol 55
Teichman, Berish 311, 312
Tiefenbrunner, Yona 309
Tisha b'Av 322
Torah centers 62
  —scrolls 63, 233

torture 171
transports 41
Treblinka xxvii, 217
Trois Mousquetaires, Les 118
Typhus 203

U

Umschlagplatz 214, 215, 216, 218
Underground 71, 122, 126, 127
  See also resistance
underground, Palestine's 119
University of Warsaw 193, 196, 198
upbeat missives 217
  See also deception
uprising 212

V

Vienna 82, 185
Vilna 60, 74, 230, 231, 234, 236,
  237, 240, 241, 247, 249, 250,
  259, 269, 270
  —Gaon 231, 269
  —ghetto 77–79, 235, 271, 272,
  274
Vilnius 231
  See also Vilna
Vittel 218, 219, 220, 224–227

W

War Refugee Board 220
Warsaw 193, 195, 201, 202, 204
  —ghetto 202–204, 215, 221, 223
  —Ghetto Uprising 221, 319
  —Jews 201
Wieliczka 287, 291, 306
Wilczyńska, Stefa 205, 215
Wisnicz 297

work passes 235–236
World War I 59, 195, 201

Y

yellow star 34, 61, 240
   See also Star of David
yeshiva students 196
Yom Kippur 210, 235, 324

Z

Zbaszyn 206
Zeilsheim DP camp 331
Zionism 30, 44, 203
   —youth groups 195